学习强国选登和推送课程

中国大学MOOC配套教程

译言中国 文化教程

Translating China: A Cultural Course

顾　问　杜　平　[英] Katie O'Hara

主　编　王贵华　张　姝

副主编　高　长　王稀婧

编　委　邱　艳　张兵兵　周　姝

段　丁　张金梅　张俊英

唐榕蔓　高领睿　刘雪梅

邱　阳　唐　新

上海交通大學出版社

SHANGHAI JIAO TONG UNIVERSITY PRESS

内容提要

本书以思政观念为引领，以中国文化基本知识和汉译英基本翻译方法为主要教学内容，融思政性、人文性和工具性为一体。本书精选了反映中国优秀传统文化和当代建设成就的七个文化主题，每个主题穿插讲解相应的汉译英基本方法（增补、删减、拆分、合并、调整和转换）。本书旨在帮助学生了解中国文化基本知识，学会用英文表达、言说、传播中国文化，提高用英文“讲好中国故事、传播中国好声音”的能力；与此同时，旨在培养学生对中国文化的兴趣，增强其文化自信，厚植家国情怀。本书可供大学英语低年级学生使用，也可供英语专业学生作为翻译入门级教材使用。

图书在版编目（CIP）数据

译言中国文化教程/王贵华，张姝主编．—上海：上海交通大学出版社，2021.8（2025.7重印）
ISBN 978-7-313-25050-6

Ⅰ.①译… Ⅱ.①王… ②张… Ⅲ.①中华文化-英语-翻译-教材 Ⅳ.①G122

中国版本图书馆CIP数据核字（2021）第117501号

译言中国文化教程
YIYAN ZHONGGUO WENHUA JIAOCHENG

主　　编：王贵华　张　姝
出版发行：上海交通大学出版社
地　　址：上海市番禺路951号
邮政编码：200030
电　　话：021-64071208
印　　制：常熟市文化印刷有限公司
经　　销：全国新华书店
开　　本：787mm×1092mm　1/16
印　　张：12
字　　数：227千字
版　　次：2021年8月第1版
印　　次：2025年7月第4次印刷
书　　号：ISBN 978-7-313-25050-6
定　　价：55.00元

前 言

课程思政是当前高等教育的新要求、新方向、新趋势。2016年，习近平总书记在全国高校思想政治工作会议上强调："做好高校思想政治工作，要因事而化、因时而进、因势而新……其他各门课都要守好一段渠、种好责任田，使各类课程与思想政治理论课同向同行，形成协同效应。" 教育部印发的《高等学校课程思政建设指导纲要(2020)》强调要把思想政治教育贯穿人才培养体系，全面推进高校课程思政建设，发挥好每门课程的育人作用，提高高校人才培养质量。最新《大学英语教学指南(2020)》(以下简称《指南》)指出，"大学英语教学应融入学校课程思政教学体系，使之在高等学校落实立德树人根本任务中发挥重要作用。"《指南》还特别强调"大学英语课程可培养学生对中国文化的理解和阐释能力，服务中国文化对外传播"。全国课程思政改革正如火如荼地进行。如何挖掘大学外语类课程资源、实现价值观引领对于培养具有国家认同、家国情怀和国际视野的人才极具战略意义。

本书是一本以课程思政为指导，以中国优秀文化内容为依托，以培养大学生汉译英能力为语言目标的文化翻译教程，集思政性、人文性、工具性为一体。本教程的思政目标是培养学生道路自信、理论自信、制度自信和文化自信，以润物细无声的方式引导学生树立正确的人生观、价值观和世界观，厚植学生家国情怀，提升学生讲好中国故事、传播中国好声音的能力。本教程的文化目标是帮助学生了解中国文化基本知识，树立文化自信、自尊和自强，体会文化交流的乐趣，提高其文化素养。本教程的语言工具性目标是帮助学生了解翻译基本知识，熟练运用翻译初级技巧，增强翻译能力，培养翻译兴趣，体验译事之乐，最终使学生具有翻译一般语言难度和常见文化题材的能力。此外，本教程的编写还充分体现了金课建设标准，对大学英语学生和英语专业低年级学生而言展现了一定的高阶性、创新性和挑战性。

本教程的内容主要包括两个方面，一是优秀中国文化，二是翻译基本方法和技巧。在文化内容方面，我们精选了七个文化主题：节日生肖、婚嫁丧葬、生物地理、饮食服饰、古今建筑、中国文学和戏剧杂技。在翻译方面，我们广泛阅读相关书籍并听取有关专家和教师的意见，筛选出最常用、最基本的翻译方法和技巧，并将其分为六大类，即增补、删减、拆分、合并、调整和转换，简称为"增、减、拆、合、调、转"六字翻译法。

在编排体例方面，教材共有七个单元，每单元聚焦一个文化主题和相应的翻译方法。每单元第一节为文化背景，这个部分包含导入问题、背景阅读材料、词汇和文化注释，旨在帮助学生了解文化背景知识。单元的主体部分由两至三小节构成。每小节以一个文化子话题和一个翻译方法为主要内容，包含例句讲解、双语对照、译技总结、文化表达和讨论问题五个部分。其中，前三个部分围绕一篇文化短文的英译展开；文化表达部分列举了相关主题词汇的英文表达，并以汉英对照的方式提供相关文化知识的延伸阅读，文后附有词汇表；讨论问题部分包含与文化主题和翻译方法相关的两至三个问题，旨在启发思考、鼓励讨论、提升学生思辨能力。单元最后两个小节分别为单元练习和单元测验，旨在帮助学生进行相关文化材料的翻译练习和能力评估。书的末尾还附有一套综合测试和全书参考书目。

本书是以“课程思政”为特色的大学英语文化教程，除了带有鲜明思政性外，还具有以下特色。

1. 文化与翻译有机结合

众所周知，翻译是一种跨文化实践，而把中国传统文化内容和翻译方法讲授有机结合起来的大学英语教程并不多见。本教程遵循基于内容的教学（content-based instruction）理念，以中国文化主题为主线，将翻译方法的讲解有机融入各主要章节，帮助学生在学习中华优秀文化内容的同时，提升翻译能力。

2. 精选内容

在选取教程的阅读与翻译文章时，编者竭力做到知识性、趣味性和权威性的统一。选材的主要来源包括已出版的经典教材、经典翻译作品、权威媒体、主流网站等。编者在最大程度保证材料真实性的同时，对原文和译文进行了必要的修订和编辑，以更好地服务于教学。

3. 图文并茂

本教程图文并茂，尽可能以直观的方式呈现文化内容，以概念图的方式呈现翻译技巧。

4. 与在线开放课程配套

本书可以单独使用，也可以与**中国大学MOOC平台**上的“译言中国”在线课程配套使用。本书主要内容与在线课程内容基本一致，但更换了部分背景介绍文章，增加了文化知识延伸与翻译部分，修订并增加了练习和测验。本书的主要语言为汉语，在线课程的主要语言为英文。两者相互独立，又形成互补。如果采取配套使用方式，建议学生先自学在线课程内容，然后在线下课堂学习或课后复习时使用本教程。

由于时间仓促和编写人员能力有限，书中存在的不足之处，敬请广大专家、教师和学员批评指正。

目 录

节日生肖
Festivals and Zodiac

1.1 背景介绍

Lead-in Questions

(1) Can you name the Chinese festivals you know and introduce them briefly to an English-speaking friend?

(2) What do Chinese people usually do during the Spring Festival?

Traditional Chinese Festivals

China is rich with festivals, whose dates are determined in the traditional Chinese calendar, the lunar calendar①.

The Spring Festival is the first biggest traditional Chinese festival based on the lunar calendar. Also called Chinese New Year, it has more than 4,000 years of history. As one of the traditional Chinese festivals, it is the **grandest** and the most significant one for Chinese people and many other Chinese-speaking communities. The Spring Festival is the time for bidding farewell to the old and **ushering** in the new. Also, it is a time for family reunion, which is equivalent to Christmas of the West. It symbolizes the **advent** of spring which brings hope, new beginning and **vitality** to the world. In accordance with folk customs, two weeks before the Spring Festival the whole country will already be **permeated** in a festive atmosphere. People often celebrate this festival from the 23rd day of the12th month② to the 15th day of the first month according to the lunar calendar. Among these days, the Spring

Festival Eve and the Lunar New Year's Day, the first day of the lunar year, are the peak times.

The Mid-Autumn Festival is the second grandest festival after the Spring Festival in China. It takes its name from the fact that it is always celebrated in the middle of the autumn. It falls on the 15th day of the eighth month according to the Chinese lunar calendar. It is interesting that on almost every Mid-Autumn Day, the weather is fine and a beautiful moon is bright in the sky. To the Chinese people, the full moon is a symbol of family reunion, perfection and prosperity. Family always takes **priority** in Chinese people's hearts, so the tradition of having family reunion on this day has a special **appeal** to all Chinese people. That is why the festival is also known as the "day of reunion" and plays a key role in Chinese people's lives. The festival also **represents** harvest since different kinds of fruits and crops become mature at this time.

The history of over 5,000 years has witnessed the formation of many other traditional Chinese festivals, such as Tomb-Sweeping Day③, the Dragon Boat Festival④, the Double Seventh Festival⑤, the Double Ninth Festival⑥, and the Laba Festival⑦. These colorful festivals hold a **prominent** place in Chinese **conventions**, customs and culture. They have become one of the strongest bonds enhancing cultural identity and national pride.

词汇

grand [grænd] *adj.* 极重要的；宏伟的；豪华的

usher ['ʌʃə(r)] *v.* 迎接；开辟

advent ['ædvent] *n.* 到来；出现

vitality [vaɪ'tæləti] *n.* 生命力；活力

permeate ['pɜːmieɪt] *v.* 渗透；透过

priority [praɪ'ɒrəti] *n.* 优先；优先权

appeal [ə'piːl] *n.* 吸引力；感染力；魅力

represent [ˌreprɪ'zent] *v.* 代表；描述

prominent ['prɒmɪnənt] *adj.* 突出的；显著的

convention [kən'venʃn] *n.* 习俗；惯例

① the lunar calendar 农历（古代中国人基于对月亮、太阳天象变化的自然规律观察而总结出的一种中国传统历法，长期以来用于指导农耕事务或日常生活。）

② 春节的准备工作一般从腊月二十三日（小年）就开始，主要包含扫尘、贴春联、贴门神、贴年画和办年货。

③ Tomb-Sweeping Day 清明节（中国人祭祀祖先或逝者的日子，通常在公历4月5日前后，常见的风俗活动有墓祭、插柳、踏青、荡秋千等。）

④ the Dragon Boat Festival 端午节（为每年农历五月初五，是流行于中国以及汉字文化圈诸国的传统文化节日。）

⑤ the Double Seventh Festival 七夕节（传说该节日来自牛郎与织女的故事或中国古代的乞巧节，在农历七月初七庆祝。）

⑥ the Double Ninth Festival 重阳节（农历九月初九，称为“重九”，是中国重要传统节日，民间有登高的风俗。因“九”与“久”同音，故将此与祝福老人长寿联系在一起。）

⑦ the Laba Festival 腊八节（中国农历最后一个月的第八天，民间有吃腊八粥的习俗。）

1.2 春节（增补连词、介词）

很多传统节日的雏形可追溯到秦朝时期，现在我们庆祝的主要传统节日基本成形于汉朝，这些节日一般含有好运、健康、财富、幸福、团聚等美好寓意。

在中国，我们多根据“农历”来确定传统节日的时间。

本节用一篇以春节为主题的短文为例，介绍汉译英中的增益法这一翻译技巧。增益法，也叫增译法、增词法、增补法，即"在翻译时按语义、句法和修辞的需要，增加一些词，以忠实通顺地表达原文的思想内容"（方梦之，2004：113）。汉译英时经常需要增加和补充一些名词、代词、冠词、连词和介词，有时候还会增补隐含语义和文化语义。

1.2.1 例句讲解

本节将通过翻译下面这段与春节有关的文本来展示汉译英中连词和介词这两类词语的增补方法，即增补连词和增补介词。我们将重点分析带序号的句子。

> 中国人庆祝春节已有4 000多年的历史。① 这个持续庆祝逾15天的喜庆节日是中国农历中最重要、最盛大的一个。春节前各家门口挂上写着吉利字的红纸以求好运，人们涌上市镇街头购买新衣、新鞋，挑选最好的鞭炮和特别的食材以备年夜饭。② 除夕夜，家人们聚在一起，共享除夕宴上一盘接一盘精心制作的食物。③"全鱼"代表富足，"鸡"代表好运，这两道菜保持头尾完整代表来年善始善终。接着长辈就开始派发红包，每个红包外写着祝福语，里面是"压岁"钱。从初一至元宵，人们走亲访友，互相拜年，街头充满了鲜艳的颜色、兴高采烈的游行以及噼里啪啦的鞭炮声。

① 这个持续庆祝逾15天的|喜庆节日是中国农历中最重要、|最盛大的一个。

汉语原句的前半部分分别使用了"持续庆祝15天的"和"喜庆"两个定语来修饰名

词“节日”。但是按照英文习惯，如果修饰名词的定语太长，我们通常会把这个长定语置于名词之后。因此，在翻译此处时可以把“持续庆祝15天”放到主语“节日”的后面，并且增加介词with来连接后置定语与被修饰的名词。

... with the celebrations lasting over fifteen days

在翻译本句后半部分“最重要”和“最盛大”这两个并列定语时，英语译文需要增补连词“and”来连接两个英文形容词（词组）“the most important”和“grandest”。

... the most important and grandest

通过使用增益法我们可以将整个句子翻译为：

这个Ø持续庆祝逾15天的喜庆节日是中国农历中最重要、Ø最盛大的一个。

This joyous festival, with the celebrations lasting over fifteen days, is the most important and grandest one on the Chinese lunar calendar.

（注：Ø为缺省符号，下同）

② 除夕夜，家人们聚在一起，共享除夕宴上一盘接一盘|精心制作的食物。

在翻译这个句子时，首先需要增补表示时间的介词“on”，表示在除夕的夜晚“On New Year's Eve”。针对本句主语“家人们”发出的两个动作“聚在一起”和“共享除夕宴上……食物”，翻译时需要增补连词“and”来连接两个并列的动词短语。

On New Year's Eve, family members get together and enjoy the feast ...

这里需要特别关注最后一个分句：“共享除夕宴上一盘接一盘精心制作的食物”。在这句话里，名词“食物”前有很长的定语：“除夕宴上”“一盘接一盘”和“精心制作”。首先，译者使用了enjoy the feast来表达享用除夕宴，这比较符合中国人在除夕吃一顿丰盛年夜饭的风俗。接下来，“一盘接一盘”和“精心制作”两组修饰语对除夕宴上的食物作了具体描述。在英文中，表达一盘食物要用“plate”，并增加介词“of”，即“a plate of food”，“一盘接一盘食物”便可译为“plate after plate of food”。“精心制作”可用“elaborate”一词译出，并置于“food”前面。整个表达为“plate after plate of elaborate food”。最后，增加介词“with”表具有之意，再用这个表达修饰前面的名词feast。该部分译文如下：

... feast with plate after plate of elaborate food.

通过增益法的多次使用，整句可译为：

Ø除夕夜，家人们聚在一起，Ø共享除夕宴上Ø一盘接一盘Ø精心制作的食物。

On New Year's Eve, family members get together and enjoy the feast with plate after plate of elaborate food.

类似连词和介词的增补在整段春节介绍中随处可见，例如：

③“全鱼”代表富足，Ø“鸡”代表好运，这两道菜保持头Ø尾完整代表Ø来年善始Ø善终。

A whole fish stands for abundance and a chicken for good luck. Both fish and chicken are served with head and tail symbolizing a good beginning and a happy ending for the coming year.

1.2.2 双语对照

春节/The Spring Festival	
中国人庆祝春节已有4 000多年的历史。这个Ø持续庆祝逾15天的喜庆节日是中国农历中最重要、Ø最盛大的一个。春节前各家Ø门口挂上写着吉利字的Ø红纸以求好运，人们涌上市镇街头购买新衣Ø新鞋，挑选最好的鞭炮和特别的食材以备年夜饭。Ø除夕夜，家人们聚在一起，Ø共享除夕宴上Ø一盘接一盘Ø精心制作的食物。“全鱼”代表富足，Ø“鸡”代表好运，这两道菜保持头Ø尾完整代表Ø来年善始Ø善终。接着长辈就开始派发红包，每个红包Ø外写着祝福语，Ø里面是“压岁”钱。从初一至元宵，人们走亲Ø访友Ø互相拜年，Ø街头充满了鲜艳的颜色、兴高采烈的游行以及噼里啪啦的鞭炮声。	The Chinese have been celebrating the Spring Festival since 2,000 BC. This joyous festival, with the celebrations lasting over fifteen days, is the most important and grandest one on the Chinese lunar calendar. Before the Spring Festival, auspicious Chinese characters are written on red paper and hung on every door to bring good fortune. People crowd city streets, buying new clothes and shoes. They choose the best firecrackers and special ingredients for their New Year's Eve dinner. On New Year's Eve, family members get together and enjoy the feast with plate after plate of elaborate food. A whole fish stands for abundance and a chicken for good luck. Both fish and chicken are served with head and tail symbolizing a good beginning and a happy ending for the coming year. Then the elders pass out red envelopes called *hongbao*. Each has greeting words on the outside and lucky money inside. From the first day of the lunar calendar to the Lantern Festival, people visit friends and relatives, and make New Year's greetings to each other. There are bright colors, spirited parades, and the pop of firecrackers everywhere in the streets.

1.2.3 译技总结

通过上面的中英文对比，我们能很清楚地看到英文中的很多连词和介词都是在翻译过程中根据译入语的文法需要增补进去的。

如下表所示，连词用于连接单词、短语、从句或分句，使它们之间联系紧凑、意思连贯，介词用于表示其后的名词（短语）与其他句子成分的关系。

词　类	功　能	按句法/语义分类
连　词	用于连接单词、短语、从句或分句，使它们之间的联系紧凑，意思连贯、通顺。	• 并列连词（Coordinating Conjunctions）: and, but, yet, or, nor, for, hence, therefore, not only ... but also, either ... or • 从属连词（Subordinating Conjunctions）: when, until, since, because, so, although, whereas, if, unless, as if, as soon as, so ... that
介　词	用于表示其后的名词或名词短语与其他句子成分的关系。	一般可用于表示空间关系、时间、原因、目的、手段等。

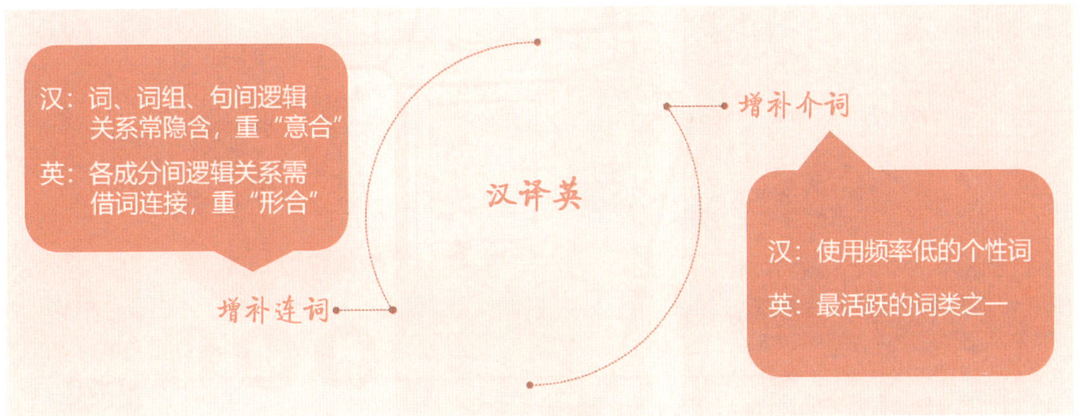

如上图所示，在介词和连词的使用上，中英文有明显区别。第一，汉语里，词、词组以及句子之间逻辑关系时常隐含，重“意合”；而英文里，各信息单元之间逻辑关系需要借助一些词语进行显性连接，重“形合”。第二，介词在英语中是使用频率非常高的词类之一，但是在汉语里使用频率相对较低。因此，在用英文讲述中国故事的时候，常需要增补一些连词和介词，以遵守译入语的文法要求。

1.2.4　文化表达

（1）文化基本知识与表达

春节是中国人乃至全世界华人共同庆祝的节日。当说到春节，我们可能会想到这几个关键词：“忙碌”（rush）、“开心”（joy）、“红色”（red）。这些词语会让我们想到一系列春节期间的传统风俗和庆典活动，其中一些已经流传成百上千年。

从腊月二十三日或二十四日起，中国人就开始为准备过年而忙碌（rush）。如一首北京童谣所唱：“小孩儿小孩儿你别馋，过了腊八就是年；腊八粥，喝几天，哩哩啦啦二十三；二十三，糖瓜粘；二十四，扫房子；二十五，冻豆腐；二十六，去买肉；二十七，宰公鸡；二十八，把面发；二十九，蒸馒头；三十晚上，熬一宿；初一初二，满街走。”

在这期间将看到被BBC称为“全球最大规模的一年一度人口迁徙（the world's

largest annual human migration）”的“春运”（Spring Festival travel rush）。从春节前15天左右开始，持续约40天，人们都尽量在除夕夜前赶回家乡与家人团聚，共度新春。

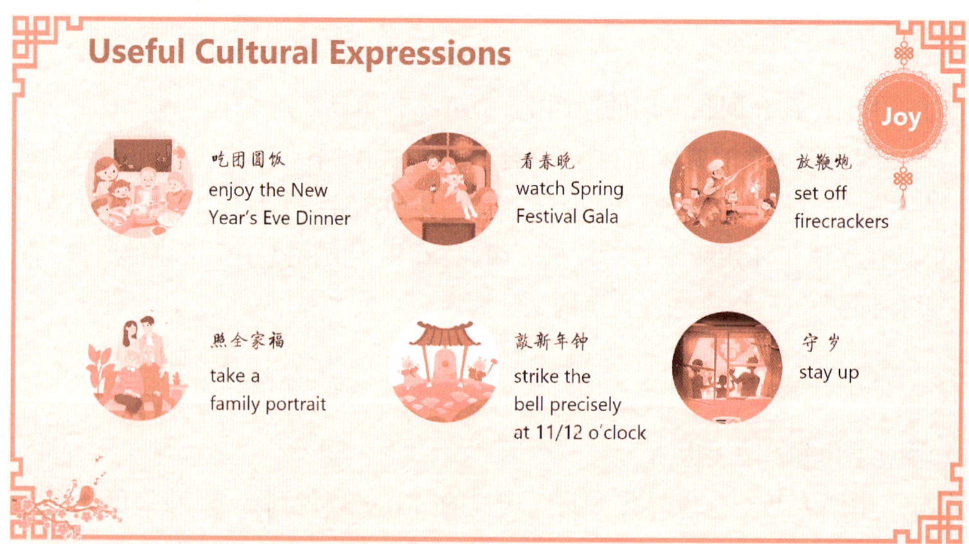

传统上，春节节日庆祝会持续16天左右，从除夕年度家宴到正月十五元宵节期间有各种令人开心愉悦（joy）的活动。亲朋好友聚在一起吃团圆饭（enjoy the New Year's Eve Dinner）、看春晚（watch Spring Festival Gala）、放鞭炮（set off firecrackers）、照全家福（take a family portrait）、敲新年钟（strike the bell precisely at 11/12 o'clock）、守岁（stay up the whole night）、拜年（pay a New Year's call）、祭祖（offer sacrifices to the deceased/ancestors）等。

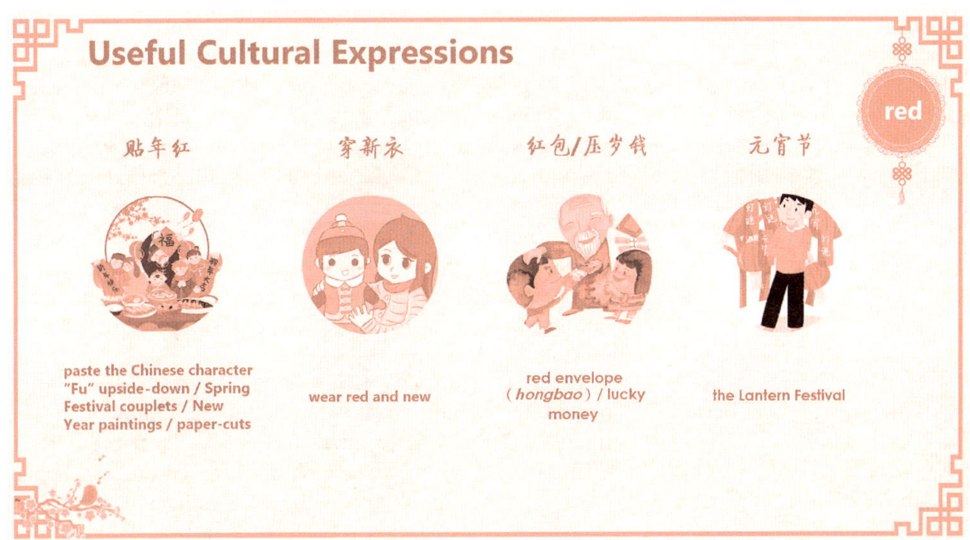

红色(red)是春节的主色,它象征着喜庆与祥和,也有驱邪避恶(to drive away evil spirits)的功能。整个春节期间,大街小巷悬挂着红灯笼(red lanterns)来欢庆节日。春节的一个传统习俗是"贴年红",即张贴各种红色饰品,如倒立的"福"字(the upside-down Chinese character *Fu* for blessing)、剪纸(paper-cuts)、春联(Spring Festival couplets)、年画(New Year paintings)等。另外,人们喜穿新戴红来渡过新年,如红色衣服(red clothes)、红色围巾(red scarfs)、红色袜子(red socks),甚至还会穿红色内裤(red pants/underwear),以增添喜庆的节日气氛,寄予对美好新生活的期盼。人们也会相互赠送红包(red envelopes),内装压岁钱(lucky money),用以表达美好的祝福。如今,网民中流行抢电子红包(snatch digital red envelopes)或抢网络红包(grab online *hongbao*)。

(2)文化知识延伸与翻译

元宵节是农历正月十五。"元"有"开端"的意思,"宵"代表"夜晚",因为这天晚上是一年中的第一个月圆之夜,所以被称为"元宵"。一般认为,元宵节始于汉代,随着佛教的传入,出现了正月十五之夜在宫廷和寺院里燃灯的习俗,后来这一习俗由宫廷传入民间。唐代元宵节观灯的习俗得到很大发展,宋代出现了灯谜,明代以后又增加了戏曲表演,使元宵节的活动更加丰富多彩。

The *Yuanxiao* Festival falls on January 15th of the lunar calendar. *Yuan* means "beginning", and *xiao* means "evening". It is called *yuanxiao* because it is the first night with a full moon of each year. It is generally recognized that the Lantern Festival began in the Han Dynasty when, after the introduction of Buddhism, the custom of lighting lanterns in palaces and temples appeared and spread to the whole society. The great development of the custom of viewing lanterns in the Tang Dynasty, the appearance of lantern riddles in the Song Dynasty and the opera performance in the Ming Dynasty make the activities of the Lantern Festival all the richer.

（续表）

在元宵节，中国各地都会举办灯会，如江苏秦淮灯会、四川自贡灯会。元宵节花灯的种类很多，北京就曾以生产宫廷使用的宫灯和纱灯著称，其中用于元宵节的“皇家花灯”由宫中能工巧匠精制而成，皇太后将其赐予文武百官，以示“与民同乐”之意。	During the Lantern Festival, lantern shows are held throughout China, such as the Qinhuai Lantern Show in Jiangsu province and the Zigong Lantern Show in Sichuan province. There are a great variety of festival lanterns during the Lantern Festival. Beijing was once known for its production of palace lanterns and **gauze** lanterns. The royal lantern used in the Lantern Festival was refined by skillful craftsmen in the palace and **granted** by the empress **dowager** to civil and military officials symbolizing the meaning of “sharing happiness with ordinary people”.
元宵节的另一个活动是猜灯谜——灯谜就是贴在或挂在彩灯上的谜语，又叫“灯虎”。因为灯谜内容常常艰深难懂，不易猜中，好像用弓箭射老虎那么难，所以猜灯谜在古代又被称作“射灯虎”。一边赏灯一边猜谜是元宵节的传统活动。由于灯谜能考验人的智慧，所以自宋代产生以来一直受到人们的喜爱。灯谜内容丰富，形式多样，既有知识性，又有趣味性和娱乐性，至今仍是节日游园会上不可缺少的活动。	Another activity is guessing lantern riddles which are posted on or hung on the lantern and also known as “lantern tigers”. Being able to guess the **elusive** lantern riddles is as difficult as shooting a tiger with a bow and arrow, hence the phrase “shooting a lantern tiger”. Enjoying watching the lanterns while guessing the riddles is a traditional activity in the Lantern Festival. Guessing riddles, which can test people's wisdom, has been popular since the Song Dynasty and remains to be **indispensable** at festival parties, for the riddles are rich in content and form, as well as informative, interesting and **entertaining**.
元宵节的节日食品是元宵。传说正月十五吃元宵的习俗也是从宋代开始的。当时人们过元宵节除了悬挂花灯、燃放烟火以外还要互赠“圆子”（即元宵），以象征在新的第一个月圆之夜合家欢聚团圆。	A representative food of the Lantern Festival is rice **glue** balls. It is said that the custom of eating rice glue balls on the lunar day of January 15th also began in the Song Dynasty. Apart from displaying festival lanterns and setting off fireworks, people also gave each other *yuanzi* (rice glue balls) as gifts, symbolizing family reunion on the first full-moon night of the new year.
元宵节是一个古老的节日，也是一个欢乐的节日。作为春节庆典的压轴活动，元宵节以其热闹、欢庆的气氛，表达了人们对新年幸福生活的美好祝愿。	The Lantern Festival is both an ancient and a cheerful holiday. As a **finale** of the Spring Festival celebration, the lively and joyous Lantern Festival reveals people's best wishes for a happy life in the new year.

词汇

gauze [gɔ:z] *n.* 纱布；薄纱

grant [grɑ:nt] *v.* 授予；承认

dowager ['daʊədʒə(r)] *n.* 贵妇；继承亡夫爵位的遗孀

elusive [ɪ'lu:sɪv] *adj.* 难懂的；易忘的

indispensable [ˌɪndɪ'spensəbl] *adj.* 不可缺少的；绝对必要的

entertaining [ˌentə'teɪnɪŋ] *adj.* 令人愉快的

glue [glu:] *n.* 胶；胶粘物

finale [fɪ'nɑ:li] *n.* 终曲；最后一场；最后乐章；尾声

1.2.5　讨论问题

(1) 春节为什么又叫过年？你能用英文向外国人介绍关于年的故事吗？

(2) 英美国家最重要的节日是什么？与之相比，我国的春节有什么独特之处？

(3) 汉译英的过程中，增补连词和介词的主要原因是什么？你能举出更多的例子吗？

1.3　中秋节（增补冠词）

本节将介绍中国的传统节日中秋节以及增补冠词这一翻译技巧。

每年农历八月十五我们会迎来中国第二大传统节日——中秋节。和春节一样，在中国人心中，中秋节意味着一家人团圆。历代都有很多吟咏中秋节的诗歌，如广为人知的一句诗："海上生明月，天涯共此时"，以及孩童都会诵读的"明月几时有，把酒问青天"。与中秋节相关的诗句大多体现出中秋节明月之夜正是背井离乡的人们遥望故乡、思念亲人的美妙时光，人们常以中秋节夜月之圆以兆人之团圆。

1.3.1　例句讲解

本节将通过翻译下面与中秋有关的文段来讲解增加冠词这一翻译技巧。

① 每年农历八月十五日，中国人都会庆祝中秋节。② 中秋节最广为流传的神话是月仙嫦娥的故事。③ 这一天，全家人聚在一起，边赏月色边分吃月饼。美味可口的月饼象征阖家团圆、欢乐。④ 在一些地区，人们会挂起纸灯笼，或将它们放飞到夜空中。⑤ 如今，中秋节已被列为国家法定节假日。很多人会借中秋小长假探访亲朋好友。

① 每年农历 | 八月 | 十五日，中国人都会庆祝中秋节。

在这句话中，"农历"是指中国传统历法，"中秋节"是中国传统节日。西方节日前面一般不会加冠词"the"，例如，我们经常说"Christmas"，而不是"the Christmas"；但是在表达中国传统节日时，却常常需要在节日前面加上冠词"the"，如"the Spring Festival"（春节），"the Dragon Boat Festival"（端午节）以及"the Double Seven Festival"（七夕节）。然而如果使用了"day"这个词语表示节日，则一般不再加冠词"the"，如"New Year's Day"，"Mid-Autumn Day"以及"Tomb-Sweeping Day"。

同时，在第一个分句中出现了序数词“十五”以及农历的第八个月，按英文文法需要在序数词前面加定冠词“the”。这句话可翻译如下：

Every year, Chinese people celebrate the Mid-Autumn Festival (中国传统节日) on the 15th (序数) day of the 8th (序数) month in the Chinese lunar calendar (农历).

② 中秋节最广为流传的神话是月仙嫦娥的故事。

在这个句子中，首先传统节日“中秋节”前面应增加冠词“the”。由于“中秋节”在全文已经是第二次提及，因此在翻译的时候可以将其简化为“the festival”。用英语表达“……的神话”和“……的故事”时，“神话”和“故事”前面应加上冠词“the”，翻译成“the myth of something”和“the tale of something”，因为这两个词语都分别带有后置限定成分。当翻译“月亮”时，因为月亮是世界上独一无二的东西，因此需要在“moon”前面增加冠词“the”。翻译“某某人是神仙”时，需要在“god”或者“goddess”前面添加不定冠词“a”来表示泛指，表明一类人或者事物中的一个。

The most widespread myth (后置修饰语) of the festival (上文提及) is the tale (后置修饰语) of Chang'e, a goddess (泛指类别) who lives on the moon (独一无二的事物).

③ 这一天全家人聚在一起，边赏月色边分吃月饼。

在第三句里，我们仍然需要在“moon”前加上冠词“the”，表示独一无二的事物。

On this day, extended families get together to appreciate the moon (独一无二) while sharing and eating moon cakes.

④ 在一些地区，人们会挂起纸灯笼，或将它们放飞到夜空中。

第四句话里，“空”指的是天空（sky），是独一无二的东西，因此需要在前面加上冠词“the”，全句翻译如下：

In some regions, people put paper lanterns on display or release them into the (独一无二的事物) evening sky.

⑤ 如今，中秋节已被列为国家法定节假日。

第五句话里提到了中秋节，正如前文提到的，在翻译中国传统节日时，前面需要增加冠词 "the"。其次，本句提到的 "节假日" 表示泛指。如前所述，在表示泛指类别的词语前应增加不定冠词 "a" 或者 "an"，泛指某类别中的一员。本句译文如下：

The Mid-Autumn Festival（中国传统节日）is listed as an（泛指类别中的一员）official holiday in China.

1.3.2　双语对照

中秋节 /The Mid-Autumn Festival	
每年Ø农历Ø八月Ø十五日，中国人都会庆祝Ø中秋节。Ø中秋节Ø最广为流传的Ø神话是Ø月Ø仙嫦娥的Ø故事。这一天全家人聚在一起，边赏Ø月色边分吃月饼。美味可口的月饼象征阖家团圆、欢乐。在一些地区，人们会挂起纸灯笼，或将它们放飞到夜空中。如今，Ø中秋节已被列为国家法定Ø节假日。很多人会借中秋小长假探访亲朋好友。	Every year, Chinese people celebrate the Mid-Autumn Festival on the 15th day of the 8th month in the Chinese lunar calendar. The most widespread myth of the festival is the tale of Chang'e, a goddess who lives on the moon. On this day, extended families get together to appreciate the moon while sharing and eating moon cakes. These yummy treats symbolize reunion and happiness. In some regions, people put paper lanterns on display or release them into the evening sky. The Mid-Autumn Festival is listed as an official holiday in China. Many people use this "mini-holiday" to visit relatives and friends.

1.3.3　译技总结

通过上面短文的英译，我们可以看出冠词是英文特有词类，且使用特别频繁，几乎句句必用。故而在汉译英时我们应特别注意是否应该在名词成分前增加冠词，以使译文符合英文文法和使用习惯，这是汉译英频繁使用的一个基本技巧。

英文中，冠词分为两类：定冠词 "the" 和不定冠词 "a/an"。[1] 在很多情况下我们都需要使用冠词，特别是遇到名词时，都要考虑是否应在名词前面增加冠词，否则译文就有可能不符合英文的语法要求。增补冠词的常见情况如下：

---

[1] 另外一种分类法是冠词有三类，除了定冠词 "the" 和不定冠词 "a/an" 外，第三类叫零冠词，即不使用冠词的情况。

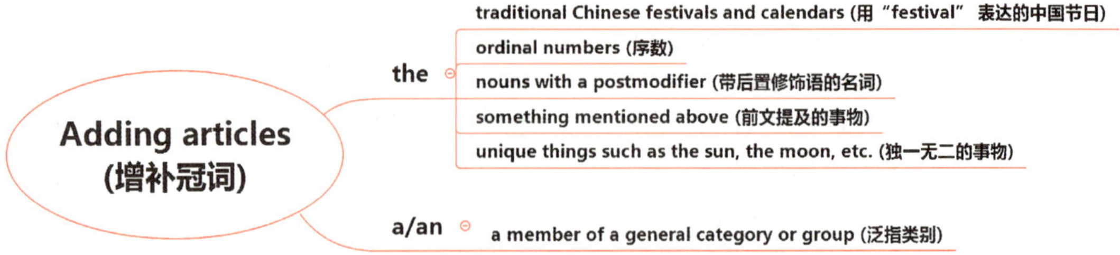

1.3.4 文化表达

(1) 文化基本知识与表达

一说到中秋节，中国人都会想到吃月饼。月饼(mooncake)是中国人在过中秋节时必吃的食物。月饼通常包含两个部分，外面的饼皮(crust)和中间的馅料(filling)。馅料又分很多种，如蛋黄(egg yolk)、五仁(five kinds of nut)、莲蓉(lotus seed paste)、豆沙(red bean paste)等。

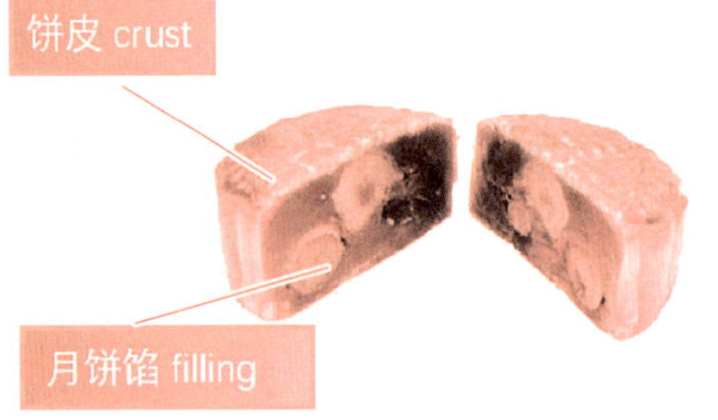

蛋黄月饼 egg yolk mooncake

五仁月饼 five kinds of nut mooncake

莲蓉月饼 lotus seed paste mooncake

红豆沙月饼 red bean paste mooncake

中秋节是一个皆大欢喜、阖家团圆的好日子。这一天，除了最重要的家人团圆外，还有很多传统活动，如赏月(admire the full moon)、拜月(worship the moon)、祭月(offer sacrifice to the moon)、猜灯谜(guess lantern riddles)、饮桂花酒(drink wine fermented with Osmanthus flowers)和观潮(watch the tide)等，这些活动流传至今，经久不衰。

家人团圆 family reunion
赏月 admiring the full moon

烧香 burning incense
祭品 sacrificial offering

灯谜 lantern riddle

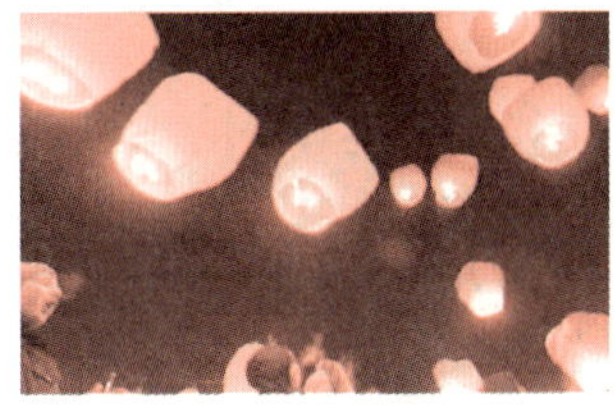

孔明灯 sky/kongming lantern

(2)文化知识延伸与翻译

中秋节/The Mid-Autumn Festival	
中秋节时间是农历八月十五日，是春节后的第二个重要节日。八月的月亮最圆、最亮。人们赏月活动的历史已经很悠久。如遇到丰收年，节日里更是“灯火家家市，笙歌处处楼”，天上月圆，人间家庭团圆。《红楼梦》里有两句诗描写中秋节盛况：“天上一轮才捧出，人间万姓仰头看”。在中秋节，人们一边赏月，一边吃月饼。	The Mid-Autumn Festival falls on lunar 15th August and is the second most important festival for Chinese people. The moon turns out to be at its fullest and brightest in August compared to all other months. The custom of the moon appreciating activity on Mid-August Festival boasts to have a long tradition. In **bumper** years, “Every house’s **floodlit**; every family is filled with happy music”, and “The round moon hangs over the sky; the reuniting families celebrate in the earth”. There are two poetic lines from the novel *A Dream of Red Mansions* that described the grand occasion of the festival: “As soon as the moon rises, thousands of people **crane** their necks watching”. On the festival, people watch the moon, and at the same time eat mooncake.
传说月亮里边有座广寒宫，住着一个美丽仙女嫦娥，嫦娥的名字在民间家喻户晓，所以中国登月卫星也被命名为嫦娥号。嫦娥是中国史前社会里一个部族首领的女儿，嫁给另外一个部族的勇士后羿为妻。后羿在西王母处得到一种不死药。有一天，嫦娥趁后羿不在，出于好奇，就把不死药偷吃了，后羿回家时只见嫦娥在院子里腾空飞起，一直飞进了月宫，从此两人人仙异途。	Legend has it that a beautiful goddess Chang’e lives in the Moon Palace. Chang’e was a household name among Chinese people; therefore, China’s **moon-probing** satellite is named after her. She was a daughter of a pre-historical tribal leader, and married Hou Yi, a brave warrior of another tribe. He had been given an immortality pill by the Celestial Heaven Mother. One day, out of curiosity, Chang’e stealthily took the pill. When Hou Yi returned home, he saw his wife elevate from the ground and fly directly to the moon, and the couple since then have been kept separate from each other.

（续表）

中秋节/The Mid-Autumn Festival	
历代诗人写了大量的关于月亮的诗歌，所以月亮也是中国文化中不可缺少的一部分。关于中秋节明月的诗歌，现在人们说得最多的是苏轼的“但愿人长久，千里共婵娟”。	Throughout Chinese history, many poets have composed a lot of excellent verses in praise of the moon, which has become an indispensable part of Chinese culture. Among the verses about the moon festival, the most popular and widely-read are from Su Shi (in the Song Dynasty): “Wish my dear ones live longer years; Share with me the same moon though thousand miles apart.”

词汇

bumper ['bʌmpə(r)] *adj.* 丰收的

crane [kreɪn] *v.* 伸长脖子看；用起重机起吊

floodlit ['flʌdlɪt] *adj.* 照明的，泛光灯照明的

probe [prəʊb] *v.* 调查；探测

1.3.5　讨论问题

（1）你能用英文简单介绍嫦娥奔月的美丽传说吗？

（2）你知道哪些关于中秋节的美妙诗句？你能用英文将这些诗句介绍给外国友人吗？

（3）汉译英时为什么经常需要增补冠词呢？你能举出一些例子吗？

1.4　十二生肖（增补代词、名词）

本节将介绍中国的十二生肖以及翻译技巧之增加代词、名词。

在中国，人们常会根据一个人的生肖属相来判断他的性格和运势。十二生肖，又叫属相，是中国与十二地支相配用于标记人出生年份的十二种动物，包括鼠、牛、虎、兔、龙、蛇、马、羊、猴、鸡、狗、猪。十二生肖是中国传统文化的重要组成部分。

1.4.1　例句讲解

我们通过翻译下面这篇关于十二生肖的短文来练习增加代词、名词的翻译技巧。

中国人有十二生肖，是以动物命名的，12年为一个循环，以鼠开始，以猪结尾。中国的老祖先以阴阳、五行和十二生肖为基础建立了一套非常复杂的理论框架。千百年来，这种流行文化影响着人们的一些决定，比如起名、婚姻、生产和对彼此的态度。① 甚至谈恋爱时也会参考生肖。 十二种象征性的动物拥有各自的性格特

点。② 龙年或虎年常说“生龙活虎”，马年会说“马到成功”。

① 甚至谈恋爱时也会参考生肖。

这个汉语例句的主语被省略了。汉语注重意合，允许主语省略，句间关系隐含。英语注重形合，一般不省略主语，句间关系明示（陈楪可、许希明，2013）。

在英译时需要把这个省略的主语补充出来，使译文语法结构更加完整，意思更加明确。从上下文来看，这句话是延续前一句话，暗含的主语是“人们”，因为只有人才会“恋爱”和“参考”。因此，在翻译成英文时，可以添加“we”或“Chinese people”作为主语，本句翻译如下：

Ø甚至谈恋爱时也会参考生肖。

We even refer to the zodiac when entering a romantic relation.

在汉译英的过程中，很多情况下，汉语允许省略主语，译成英文的时候我们需要增加相应的名词或者代词作为主语。和汉语相比，英文中代词的使用频率更高，翻译时应根据不同情形添加代词。

② 龙年或虎年常说“生龙活虎”，马年会说“马到成功”。

这句话中“龙年”“虎年”“马年”都是时间副词，不是主语。隐含的意思是在龙年或者虎年，人们经常说“生龙活虎”，在马年人们会说“马到成功”。英译时亦需增加合适的名词或者代词作为主语，翻译如下：

龙年或虎年Ø常说“生龙活虎”，马年Ø会说“马到成功”。

In the Year of the Dragon or the Year of the Tiger, **people** will say *shenglonghuohu* — full of vim and vigor; in the Year of the Horse, **people** will say *madaochenggong* — to gain an immediate success.

1.4.2　双语对照

十二生肖 /The Chinese Zodiac	
中国人有十二生肖，是以动物命名的，12年为一个循环，以鼠开始，以猪结尾。Ø中国的老祖先以阴阳、五行和十二生肖为基础建立了一套非常复杂的理论框架。	There are twelve animals in the Chinese Zodiac, which is a 12-year cycle labeled with animals, starting with Rat, and ending with Pig. **Our** Chinese ancestors constructed a very complicated theoretical framework based on *Yin-yang*, the five elements and the 12 zodiac animals. Over thousands of years,

（续表）

十二生肖/The Chinese Zodiac	
千百年来，这种流行文化影响着人们的一些决定，比如起名、婚姻、生产和对彼此的态度。Ø甚至谈恋爱时也会参考生肖。十二种象征性的动物拥有各自的性格特点。龙年或虎年Ø常说"生龙活虎"，马年Ø会说"马到成功"。	this popular culture has affected some of people's decisions, such as naming, marriage, giving birth and attitude towards each other. We even refer to the zodiac when entering a romantic relation. By revealing your zodiac sign, you are being evaluated. The twelve symbolic animals have their own characteristics. In the Year of the Dragon or the Year of the Tiger, people will say *shenglonghuohu* — full of vim and vigor; in the Year of the Horse, people will say *madaochenggong* — to gain an immediate success.

1.4.3 译技总结

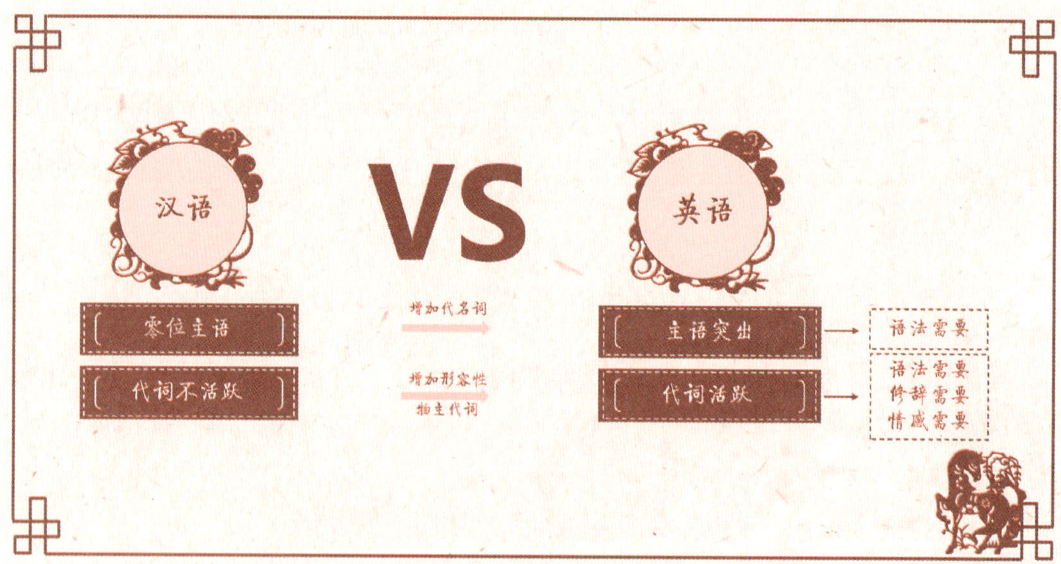

汉语重意合，句子在形式上比较松散，经常会省略掉一些句子成分。而英语重形合，比较强调句子形式上的完整和句子成分之间的显性连接。因此，汉译英时，对原文亦步亦趋，进行逐词逐句的翻译是不合适的，双语间的转换经常有增有减。作为译者应发挥主观能动性，在翻译时根据原文的上下文语境，考虑译入语文法和语言偏好，适当增加代词和名词以及前面所讲的连词和介词，以使译文形式正确，语意忠于原文。

1.4.4 文化表达

（1）文化基本知识与表达

十二生肖是十二地支的形象化代表，即子（鼠）、丑（牛）、寅（虎）、卯（兔）、辰（龙）、

巳(蛇)、午(马)、未(羊)、申(猴)、酉(鸡)、戌(狗)、亥(猪)。生肖文化不仅深深植根于历史,而且经常出现在现代人的生活中,有种种丰富的表现。优美的神话传说中不乏生肖的形象,如牛郎织女、玉兔捣药、龙女牧羊、老鼠娶亲、白蛇传、神猴孙悟空、猪八戒等,不胜枚举。历代宫廷的铜镜、民间的窗花、碑碣墓志上都可以看到生肖的踪影。生肖图案、纹样成为吉祥的象征。有关生肖的篆字、绘画、书法和工艺品使人们得到艺术的享受。民间流行的生肖剪纸、生肖卡、生肖游戏为民众的生活增添了无穷乐趣(常峻,2004)。

在我国和东南亚一些国家与地区,一些民族用生肖也称属相来代表年份和人的出生年。人们认为不同年份出生的人由于生肖属相不同,性格特征也就不同。例如,猴年出生的人通常会被认为很聪明灵活,如猴子一般;虎年出生的人通常会被认为比较勇猛,如猛虎一般。

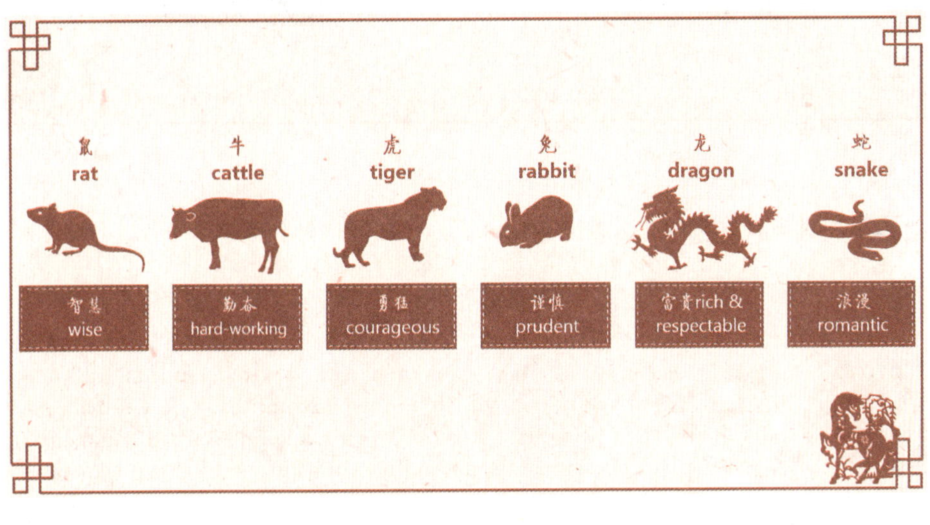

由于中西方文化的差异，人们对这些动物的看法也不太一样。例如，在汉文化中龙是财富和权力的象征，而在西方文化中龙却代表邪恶。

(2) 文化知识延伸与翻译

生肖/The Chinese Zodiac	
大多数西方人听说过古希腊、古罗马十二星座，这些星座把一年分成12个月。中国生肖不同，是以动物命名的，12年为一个循环，以鼠开始，以猪结尾，它们与星座没有任何联系。比如，1975年你出生，你就属兔。	Most Westerners know Greco-Roman **zodiac**, which divides the signs into 12 months. The Chinese zodiac is different. It is a 12-year cycle **labeled** with animals, starting with Rat and ending with Pig, and has no association with **constellations**. For example, if you were born in 1975, you are a Rabbit.
中国的老祖先以阴阳、五行和十二生肖为基础建立了一套非常复杂的理论框架。千百年来，这种流行文化影响着人们的大部分决定，如起名、婚姻、生产，甚至对彼此的态度。其中一些含义可以说令人称奇。中国人相信某些生肖较其他更好，所以有些夫妇选择特定的年份生孩子，因为他们相信特定的生肖组合会让家族更加繁荣。甚至谈恋爱时也会参考生肖。	Our Chinese ancestors constructed a very complicated theoretical framework based on *Yin-yang*, the five elements and the 12 zodiac animals. Over thousands of years, this popular culture has affected people's major decisions, such as naming, marriage, giving birth and attitude towards each other. And some of the **implications** are quite amazing. The Chinese believe certain animals get on better than the others. So, some parents choose specific years to give birth to babies, because they believe the team effort by the right combination of animals can give prosperity to families. We even refer to the zodiac when entering a romantic relation.

（续表）

生肖/The Chinese Zodiac	
有些人相信有些生肖更加好运，如生肖龙。不同于西方传统，在中国龙是权力、力量和财富的象征。几乎每个人都希望有一个龙宝宝。2012是龙年，中国的婴儿出生率提高了5%，比正常多出了一百万新生儿。当属龙的男孩长大，他们会面临更加激烈的婚姻和职场挑战。	Some people believe some animals, such as the Dragon, are luckier than the others. Unlike the Western tradition, the Chinese Dragon is a symbol for power, strength, and wealth. It is almost everyone's dream to have a Dragon baby in 2012, the Year of the Dragon, the birthrate in China increased by five percent. That means another one million more babies. When those Dragon boys grow up, they will face much more severe competition in marriage and job markets.

词汇

zodiac ['zəʊdɪæk] *n.* 黄道带；十二宫图；属相；生肖

label ['leɪbl] *n.* 标签；商标；*v.* 贴标签于；把……归类

constellation [ˌkɒnstə'leɪʃn] *n.* 星座

implication [ˌɪmplɪ'keɪʃn] *n.* 含义；暗示

1.4.5　讨论问题

（1）中国的生肖和西方的星座有什么异同？

（2）你的属相是什么？你能用英文向外国友人介绍你的属相和该属相典型的性格特征吗？

1.5　单元练习

1. 从两个备选项中选出对汉语原句翻译得较好的一个选项。

① 七夕节被称为“中国的情人节”。

A. Double Seventh Festival is called Chinese Valentine's Day.

B. The Double Seventh Festival is called Chinese Valentine's Day.

② 重阳节是根据阴阳论而得名的。

A. The Double Ninth Festival is named according to the theory of *Yin* and *Yang*.

B. Double Ninth Festival is named according to theory of *Yin* and *Yang*.

③ 元宵夜，吃元宵，赏花灯。

A. On the night of the Lantern Festival, we usually eat rice dumplings and enjoy watching lanterns.

B. The night of the Lantern Festival usually eat rice dumplings, enjoy watching lanterns.

④ 知道了十二生肖的排序以后，就能判断那一年是什么年了。

A. If you grasp the order of those twelve animals, you can know the zodiac animal of a certain year.

B. Grasp order of twelve animals, can know zodiac animal of a certain year.

⑤ 中秋节的传统食物是月饼，一种有馅的圆烤饼。

A. Traditional food of Mid-Autumn Festival is mooncake, a round baked-cake with fillings in.

B. The traditional food of the Mid-Autumn Festival is mooncake, a round baked-cake with fillings in it.

2. 翻译下面的句子，注意运用本单元所学的翻译技巧。

① 端午节喝雄黄酒（realgar wine），悬挂艾草（mugwort）和菖蒲（calamus）。

____

② 火把（torch）节是彝族人民最隆重的节日。

____

③ 腊八节是中国农历最后一个月的第八天。

____

1.6 单元测验

1. 从两个备选项中选出对汉语原句翻译得较好的一个选项。（5×5 分=25 分）

① 春节在阴历正月初一，是我国汉族和许多少数民族的传统佳节。

A. The Spring Festival is a traditional festival joyously celebrated by the Hans and many of the minority nationalities of China on the first day of the first lunar month.

B. Spring Festival is traditional festival joyously celebrated by Hans and many of minority nationalities of China first day of first lunar month.

② 在元宵节期间，还有舞龙、拔河、扭秧歌等文化体育活动。

A. Lantern Festival is also marked by sports and other entertainments, such as tug-of-war, Dragon Dance, Lion Dance, Yanko Dance.

B. The Lantern Festival is also marked by sports and other entertainments, such as the tug-of-war, the Dragon Dance, the Lion Dance, and the Yanko Dance.

③ 民间传说月亮上有广寒宫，宫里住着嫦娥和玉兔。

A. According to a Chinese folktale, Fairy Chang'e lives with her rabbit in the moon palace.

B. According to Chinese folktale, palace lives Fairy Chang'e and her rabbit.

④ 明代的皇宫里从农历九月初一起就开始吃重阳饼。

A. In the Ming Dynasty, the imperial families customarily began to eat the Double Ninth cake on the first day of the ninth lunar month.

B. Ming Dynasty customarily began to eat Double Ninth cake first day of ninth lunar month.

⑤ 重阳节登高习俗与季节有密切的关系。

A. Chongyang climbing mountain custom is closely associated with season.

B. The custom of climbing mountains during the Chongyang Festival is closely associated with the season.

2. 翻译下面的句子，注意运用本单元所学的翻译技巧。(3×10分=30分)

① 清明节主题一是认祖归宗、怀念亲人，二是亲近大自然。

____

② 在除夕夜来临之前打扫房屋的古老习俗可以追溯到几千年前。

____

③ 在重阳节前后，中国各地都要举办菊花(chrysanthemum)展和游园赏菊活动。

____

3. 将下面短文翻译成英文，注意运用本单元所学的翻译技巧。(45分)

节日的高潮(climax)就是除夕夜。离家在外的人们无论多远都要回家团聚。全体家庭成员要聚在一起吃丰盛的年夜饭。餐中有道菜是鱼，而且有人讲究不能把它吃完，图个“年年有余”。

婚嫁丧葬

Wedding and Funeral

2.1 背景介绍

Lead-in Questions

(1) What are the customs of traditional Chinese weddings and funerals?

(2) Why are weddings and funerals considered the "red and white happy events" in China?

Weddings and **funerals** are the "red and white happy events" celebrated in Chinese culture. Traditional Chinese weddings and funerals reflect Chinese **philosophy**.

Traditional Chinese wedding customs are considered one of the foundations of traditional Chinese **rituals**. There are eight major procedures before and during a wedding: **proposal** making, birthday matching (An **fortune teller** is invited to predict whether the couple-to-be's eight characters① of birth are **compatible**.), marriage **divination**, **betrothal** gifts presenting, wedding date fixing, **dowry** preparation, fetching the bride on a big day and performing the formal wedding ceremony (performing the formal bows). Performing the formal bows② is one of the important parts of Chinese wedding ceremony, the process of which is like this: the newly-married bow first to the heaven and earth, second to parents, and third to each other. The first bow reflects the philosophic idea of the unity of heaven and man. Although man dominates the world, the heaven and earth are the **cradle** of our lives.

Meanwhile, the **burial** of the dead is a matter taken very seriously by the Chinese. They regard a person's death as the "returning to heaven", which means going back to mother nature's body. At traditional Chinese funerals, white and black are the dominant colors. And the **keynote** for funeral and memorial services is spiritual **eternity** and continuation of life after death. **Improper** funeral arrangements, it is believed, can **wreak** ill fortune and disaster upon the family of the deceased. To a certain extent, Chinese funeral rituals and burial customs are determined by the age of the deceased, the manner of his or her death, the social status and roles, and the **marital** status of the deceased.

Traditional Chinese wedding and funeral customs have been popular for thousands of years, and they are still commonly practiced. They may vary from place to place and from time to time, but they have been playing an important role in the life of Chinese people, with far-reaching impacts on Chinese people's lifestyle.

Tomb-Sweeping Day③ is the most important day of **sacrifice** in China; it is a day to pay respect to **ancestors**. It began more than 2,500 years ago in the Zhou Dynasty. The Cold Food Day④ is an ancient Chinese Day. On this day only cold dishes are served (making fire is **prohibited**) and **tombs** are visited. This **coincides** with the custom of Tomb-Sweeping Day, and sometimes the terms are used **interchangeably**. **Playing on swings** is a custom of Tomb-Sweeping Day. It is also a favored leisure activity for children. The young can have fun on swings and **nurture** a courageous mind at the same time.

词汇

funeral ['fju:nərəl] *n.* 葬礼

philosophy [fɪ'lɒsəfi] *n.* 哲学

ritual ['rɪtʃʊəl] *n.* 仪式

proposal [prə'pəʊzl] *n.* 求婚

astrological [ˌæstrə'lɒdʒɪkl] *adj.* 占星学的；占星术的

compatible [kəm'pætəbl] *adj.* 能共处的

divination [ˌdɪvɪ'neɪʃn] *n.* 预测；占卜

betrothal [bɪ'trəʊðl] *n.* 婚约

dowry ['daʊrɪ] *n.* 嫁妆

cradle ['kreɪdl] *n.* 摇篮

burial ['berɪəl] *n.* 葬礼

keynote ['ki:nəʊt] *n.* 主旨

eternity [ɪ't3:nətɪ] *n.* 永恒

improper [ɪm'prɒpə] *adj.* 不适当的

wreak [ri:k] *v.* 造成（巨大的破坏或伤害）

marital ['mærɪtl] *adj.* 婚姻的

sacrifice ['sækrɪfaɪs] *n.* 祭祀；供奉

ancestor ['ænsestə] *n.* 始祖；祖先

prohibit [prə'hɪbɪt] *v.* 阻止；禁止

tomb [tu:m] *n.* 坟墓

coincide [ˌkəʊɪn'saɪd] *v.* 一致；符合

interchangeably [ˌɪntə'tʃeɪndʒəbli] *adv.* 可交换地

play on swings 荡秋千

nurture ['n3:tʃə(r)] *v.* 培育

文化注释

① eight characters 八字（八字是用天干地支表示人出生的年、月、日、时，合起来是八个字。八字命理学是一种根据八字推命的方法。）

② performing the formal bows 拜堂（中国旧式婚礼仪式，起源约在北宋时期，流行于全国各地。在举行婚礼时，将拜天地、拜祖先及父母和夫妻对拜都统称为拜堂。）

③ Tomb-Sweeping Day 清明节（中国四大传统节日之一，节期在仲春与暮春之交。它既是一个扫墓祭祖的肃穆节日，也是人们亲近自然、踏青游玩、享受春天乐趣的欢乐节日。）

④ the Cold Food Day 寒食节（在夏历冬至后105日，清明节前一两日。两千多年前，为逼介子推出山为官，晋文公下令放火烧山，介子推不幸被烧死。为了纪念介子推，晋文公把这一天定为寒食节，晓谕全国，每年这天禁忌烟火，只吃寒食。寒食节是汉族传统节日中唯一以饮食习俗来命名的节日，后来寒食与清明渐渐合二为一。）

2.2 婚嫁（增补隐含语义）

我国历史源远流长，有许多古老的传统，也有很多相关的仪式。“四礼”（Four Major Rituals）就是其中比较重要的仪式，即“加冠、婚嫁、治丧、祭祀礼”（cappings, weddings, funerals and sacrificial ceremonies）的合称。隋朝王通在《中说·关朗》中曾提到“正家以四礼，冠婚丧祭”。

中国文化中，“婚嫁”和“治丧”常被称为“红白喜事”。男女结婚是喜事，高寿的人病逝的丧事叫喜丧，统称红白喜事。清朝杨静亭在《都门杂咏·时尚门·知单》写道：“居家不易是长安，俭约持躬稍自宽；最怕人情红白事，知单一到便为难。”为何称婚礼为“红喜事”？中国葬礼背后蕴含怎样的哲学？中国人如何过清明节？

中国色彩文化历史非常悠久。我们的祖先之所以崇拜红色，是因为它和太阳、火及血液的颜色一样。后来孔子在《论语》中提到“恶紫之夺朱也”，指的是红色是大雅之色（the color of elegance），代表正统。此后，红色正式获得帝王的认同和喜爱。唐宋时期，中国制瓷技术达到鼎盛，红色瓷器流传到世界各地，外国人称之为“中国红”（China Red）。明朝时期，红色逐渐走入寻常百姓的生活，被用于婚礼等许多场合。接下来我们将了解“红喜事”，即中国的婚礼。

2.2.1 例句讲解

下文介绍了传统中式婚礼上的幸运色和新娘所吃的幸运食物，请仔细阅读，并注意标号部分的内容。

中国传统婚礼是华夏文化的精粹。中国人喜爱红，将红色看作幸福、好运、忠诚和繁荣的象征。① 红色是婚礼的主色——屋内遍布着“红双喜”剪纸、红色缎带、红色蜡烛和红色嫁妆。新郎戴红花，新娘着红装和红盖头。② 这不仅增加了欢乐感，也表明了夫妻俩向往幸福婚姻的愿望。新娘吃的食物也是一种文化象征。③ 新娘一般会吃红枣（red date）、花生、桂圆（longan）和莲子，其中的象征意义可以从它们的读音中看出。当它们放在一起读时就是“早生贵子”。

我们来看第一个例句：

① 红色是婚礼的主色——屋内遍布着“红双喜”剪纸、红色缎带、红色蜡烛和红色嫁妆。

首先，“红色是婚礼的主色”这句话与前面两句存在隐含的因果关系，因为中国人喜爱红色，所以红色是婚礼的主色。英译时考虑是否添加一个连接词，明确表明这种因果关系，从而使译文易于理解。其次，原文中“婚礼”是指具体的某种婚礼，不能想当然地译为“wedding”，否则就会使读者产生困惑，不清楚这里的“婚礼”到底是中式婚礼还是西式婚礼，是现代婚礼还是传统婚礼。根据这段文字的上下文语境，我们需在“婚礼”前适当增添具体信息：

Red, **therefore** (增补逻辑关系词), is the dominant color at a **traditional Chinese** (增补细节词) wedding. There are paper-cuts of “red double happiness”, red ribbons, rcd candles as well as red dowries all around the house.

通过增补逻辑关系词和细节词，译文意思更加清晰，信息单元间也更加连贯了。

② 这不仅增加了欢乐感，也表明了夫妻俩向往幸福婚姻的愿望。

请注意这句话中的“欢乐感”一词。前面的动词是“增加”，这自然使我们想到了英文“add”一词，这个词语在英文中使用时，通常用在“add sth. to sth.”这种结构中。本段的欢乐感是增加到什么上呢？根据上下文，这里应该是增加婚礼庆典的“欢乐感”，翻译时宜添加“occasion”一词，使得“add sth. to sth.”的结构完整，意思也更清楚。

This not only adds a sense of merriment to the occasion (增补词语构成词组搭配), but also indicates the couple's desire for a happy and prosperous marriage.

③ 新娘一般会吃红枣(red date)、花生、桂圆(longan)和莲子,其中的象征意义可以从它们的读音中看出。

请注意第三个例句中的"读音"一词。翻译时如果简单地处理为"pronunciation",也容易造成误解。我们的译文是以英文读者为对象的,这里的读音是指汉语读音还是英语读音? 没讲清楚就容易引起混淆。很显然,这里是指汉语读音,汉语中"枣、生、桂、子"四个字的读音与"早生贵子"读音一样,暗指"子孙绵延,富贵吉祥";而这四类食物的英文单词读音与"早生贵子"毫无关系,也没有任何联想意义。因此,翻译时也需要增加上下文隐含的"Chinese"一词,明确这里的读音是指汉语的读音。

The bride usually eats red dates, peanuts, longans and lotus seeds, the symbolic meaning of which is evident in Chinese pronunciation.

2.2.2 双语对照

中国婚礼的红与吉 the Color Red and Auspicious Meaning in Traditional Chinese Wedding	
中国传统婚礼是华夏文化的精粹。中国人喜爱红,将红色看作幸福、好运、忠诚和繁荣的象征。红色是婚礼的主色——屋内遍布着"红双喜"剪纸、红色缎带、红色蜡烛和红色嫁妆。新郎戴红花,新娘着红装和红盖头。这不仅增加了欢乐感,也表明了夫妻俩向往幸福婚姻的愿望。新娘吃的食物也是一种文化象征。新娘一般会吃红枣、花生、桂圆和莲子,其中的象征意义可以从它们的读音中看出。当它们放在一起读时就是"早生贵子"。	Traditional Chinese wedding is the essence of Chinese culture. Chinese are fond of red color and regard red as the symbol of happiness, luck, loyalty, and prosperity. Red, therefore (增补逻辑关系词), is the dominant color at a traditional Chinese (增补细节词) wedding. There are paper-cuts of "red double happiness", red ribbons, red candles as well as red dowries all around the house. While the bridegroom wears big red flowers, the bride wears red dress and shoes and the red veil. This not only adds a sense of merriment to the occasion (增补词语构成词组搭配), but also indicates the couple's desire for a happy and prosperous marriage. The food the bride eats has cultural significance. The bride usually eats red dates, peanuts, longans and lotus seeds, the symbolic meaning of which is evident in Chinese (增补细节词) pronunciation. When they are pronounced together, it sounds like "*zao sheng gui zi* (Have a noble baby soon)".

2.2.3 译技总结

从上面的翻译案例中可以看出,为使译文意思清晰、准确、连贯,便于理解,翻译时须将原文语境里隐含的意义明确地翻译出来。那么应该如何“增补”原文中隐含的意义呢？主要有三种方式：增补隐含逻辑关系词、增补词语构成译入语常用搭配和增补细节词。

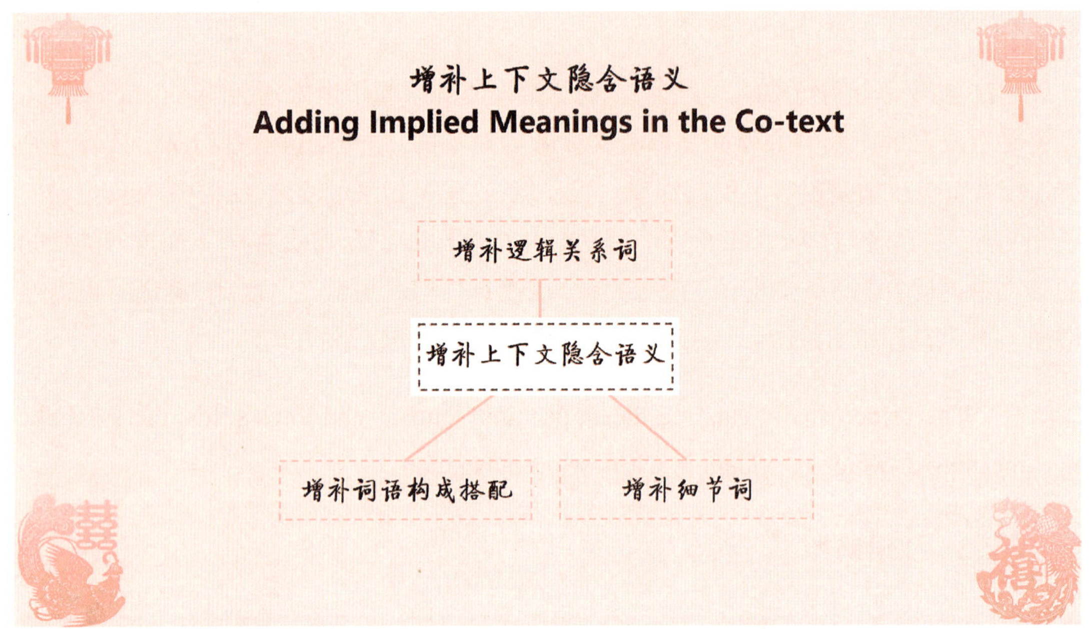

2.2.4 文化表达

(1) 文化基本知识与表达

与婚嫁相关的文化表达很多，如“红双喜”，两个红色的“喜”字，代表幸福美满和对新人的美好祝愿。翻译时，若简单逐字翻译，原文中的文化信息便无法传达到译文中。中国文化中还有许多类似的“双喜”现象，如绣一对鸳鸯表达美满吉祥之意，又如重复词语中的字来加强其积极意义，如“红火”和“红红火火”、“顺利”和“顺顺利利”、“平安”和“平平安安”等。我们国家也呼吁在世界上进行“双赢”合作，正如古话所言——“好事成双”。这些都是中国文化的独特之处。

此外，汉语中还有很多对婚礼美好祝福的表达。如参加婚礼时，中国人通常会把礼金放在红包里，并在红包上写下吉祥的话语，交给新郎和新娘，口中说着：“恭喜！愿百年好合/白头偕老/早生贵子！”

更多的祝福语列举如下：

比翼双飞

pair off wing to wing; fly side by side; (of loving husband and wife) keep each

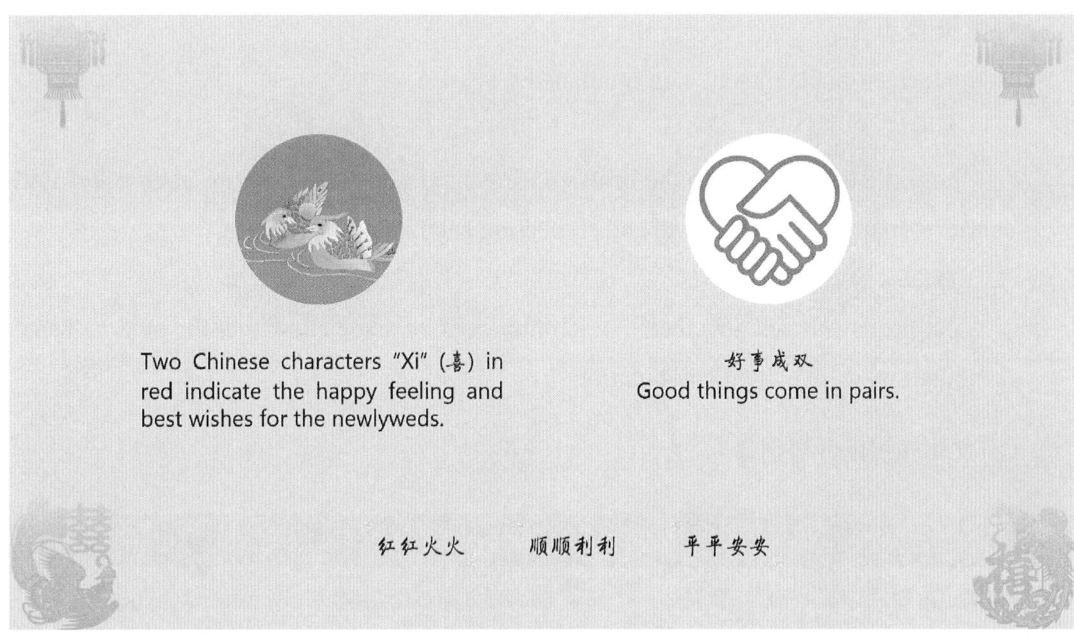

other company all the time; help each other to make progress

双宿双飞

Always keep each other's company (like birds flying and nesting together).

双喜临门

Two happy events come at the same time; good things come in pairs.

天作之合

a heaven-made match; a union made by heaven

举案齐眉

hold the tray level with the brows — husband and wife treating each other with courtesy; married couple loving and respecting each other

珠联璧合

put pearls and jade together — each improves by association with the other; a happy combination; an excellent combination

（2）文化知识延伸与翻译

婚礼礼物/Wedding Gifts

新郎、新娘双方家庭沟通过婚礼细节，以及算命先生根据新娘和新郎的生辰八字推算出两人是否合适之后，新郎家庭就要为新娘家庭送上一份彩礼了。传统上，彩礼包括以下项目：利是钱（即红包）、珠宝、龙凤饼、海鲜菌类和发菜干货、家禽、鱼、核桃、酒类以及装有干果、鲜果和茶的盒子。传统的婚礼礼物一般在典礼前几天就已经送到，传统意义上这些礼物用于祭祀祖先。传统上客人送给新人的礼物不会像彩礼那么铺张，这些送给新娘和新郎的礼物一般都是包在红包或信封里的现金。最后一种传统婚礼的礼物是新娘和新郎回送给客人的礼物。这些礼物一般都是小件物品，比如刻有花纹的银元宝、装满薰衣草的清酒杯、陶瓷茶杯、装在丝囊中的茉莉花茶、喜糖包、玻璃油灯以及其他一些非常漂亮的可以让来宾珍藏的小物件。

The **Grand Gifts** are wedding gifts that the Chinese **groom**'s family give to the bride's family after the terms of the marriage have been negotiated and a **fortune teller** has analyzed the date and hour of the **bride**'s birth with those of the groom to determine if they are compatible with each other. Traditional Grand Gifts include the following items: *lishi* money (red packets with money inside), **jewelries**, dragon-phoenix cakes, dried seafood, mushroom and fat choy, **poultries**, fish, walnut, wine or liquor, and a gift box with dried fruits, raw fruits and tea. Grand Gifts, used for the purpose of worshipping ancestors in the conventional sense, are sent to the bride's home a few days before the wedding. The traditional wedding gifts that guests give to the couple are not nearly as **extravagant** as the Grand Gifts. They customarily consist of cash, **stuffed** in red packets or envelopes. The last type of gift at a traditional Chinese wedding is the **wedding favors** that the bride and groom give to the guests. These gifts are usually small items such as **engraved** silver fortune cookies, sake cups filled with **lavender**, **porcelain** tea cups, **jasmine** tea in silk **pouches**, candy bags, glass oil lamps, and many more beautiful items that guests can treasure.

词汇

grand gift 大的礼物；彩礼

fortune teller 算命先生

groom [gruːm] *n.* 新郎

bride [braɪd] *n.* 新娘

jewelry ['dʒuːəlri] *n.* 珠宝

poultry ['pəʊltri] *n.* 家禽

extravagant [ɪk'strævəgənt] *adj.* 奢侈的；浪费的；过度的

stuff [stʌf] *v.* 塞满

wedding favor 结婚回礼的礼物

engrave [ɪn'greɪv] *v.* 雕刻；镌刻

lavender ['lævəndə(r)] *n.* 薰衣草

porcelain ['pɔːsəlɪn] *n.* 瓷；瓷器

jasmine ['dʒæzmɪn] *n.* 茉莉花

pouch [paʊtʃ] *n.* 小袋子；荷包

2.2.5　讨论问题

（1）你怎样看待天价彩礼呢？

（2）为什么翻译时常需要增补上下文中隐含的语义呢？

2.3　葬礼（增补文化信息）

隋·王通《中说·关郎》有言："正家以四礼，冠婚丧祭。"中国古代的四礼之说足以证明丧葬之事虽属沉重话题，却对中国人至关重要。孔子甚至认为，"四礼"之中，"治丧、祭祀礼"最为重要。《论语·阳货篇》中曾记载了这样一则故事：孔子弟子宰我曾质疑服丧三年的时间太长，问孔子道："三年之丧，期已久矣！"子曰："子生三年，然后免于父母之怀。"孩子生下来三年后才能脱离父母的怀抱，因此当先辈逝去，子女应服丧三年。

宰我问："三年之丧，期已久矣！君子三年不为礼，礼必坏；三年不为乐，乐必崩。旧谷既没，新谷既升，钻燧改火，期可已矣。"子曰："食夫稻，衣夫锦，于女安乎？"曰："安！""女安则为之！夫君子之居丧，食旨不甘，闻乐不乐，居处不安，故不为也。今女安，则为之！"宰我出，子曰："予之不仁也！子生三年，然后免于父母之怀。夫三年之丧，天下之通丧也，予也有三年之爱于其父乎！"

——《论语·阳货篇》

2.3.1 例句讲解

以下文字介绍了中国传统葬礼习俗，请仔细阅读并思考：如果对画线部分的内容逐字翻译，译文读者能否理解其意义？

中国传统土葬通常繁复冗长。① 直至出殡前一天，灵柩停放在灵棚内，花圈、挽联、出殡车等所有悼念物品排放规矩。亲朋好友焚香烧纸吊唁死者；和尚、道士、乐队、哭丧者吟唱祭拜以慰死者之魂。出殡日，棺材被抬上灵车，后跟送葬人员，缓慢行驶过亡者生前熟悉的地方，最后驶向墓地。② 按传统习俗，墓址须根据风水理论谨慎选择；③且棺材抵达墓地后，要等待黄道吉时才能下葬。只有等棺材安放妥帖、所有丧葬品都掩埋或焚烧了，整个葬礼才算结束。

① 直至出殡前一天，灵柩停放在灵棚内，花圈、挽联、出殡车等所有悼念物品排放规矩。

第一句话中，“花圈”和“挽联”是中国丧葬文化中的特有物品，无法在英文中找到对应词，因此翻译时，我们宜使用“huge paper-made wreath”和“elegiac-couplet cloths”，将这两类悼念物品的具体尺寸、材质、样式或用途等描述给读者，使其能够形象地感受到何为“花圈”和“挽联”。

All the memorial supplies like **huge paper-made wreaths**, **elegiac-couplet cloths**, and funeral vehicles are arranged in special dispositions there.

② 按传统习俗，墓址须根据风水理论谨慎选择。

“风水”文化是独特的中国文化，想当然地将之译为“wind and water”易导致误解，显然是不可取的。该词可直接使用音译法，译为“*Fengshui*”。维基百科上也已经有*Fengshui*的介绍，说明这个音译词在一定程度上已被国外读者理解和接受，但为了便于读者更好理解，可在音译后增添geomancy（地相术）一词作进一步释译。

According to the traditional customs, the tomb site is strictly chosen following the ***Fengshui*** **theory (also known as Chinese geomancy)**.

③ 且棺材抵达墓地后，要等待黄道吉时才能下葬。

黄历是中国传统历法，也称万年历，我们祖先依据天体星象运行变化对人类影响的规律制定了黄、黑道日，为国人用事择日、趋吉避凶提供参考与选择。中国人

用“黄道吉时”表示适宜出门办要事的好日子。婚嫁、丧葬、诞辰等都喜欢找算命先生卜算“黄道吉时”。故翻译时需增添文化信息“calculated”，将其核心意思表达出来。

When the coffin arrives, it will still have to wait for **a calculated auspicious time of the zodiac** to be moved underground.

2.3.2　双语对照

中国传统葬礼/The Traditional Chinese Funeral	
中国传统土葬通常繁复冗长。直至出殡前一天，灵柩停放在灵棚内，**花圈**、**挽联**、出殡车等所有悼念物品排放规矩。亲朋好友焚香烧纸吊唁死者；和尚、道士、乐队、哭丧者吟唱祭拜以慰死者之魂。出殡日，棺材被抬上灵车，后跟送葬人员，缓慢行驶过亡者生前熟悉的地方，最后驶向墓地。按传统习俗，墓址须根据**风水**理论谨慎选择；且棺材抵达墓地后，要等待**黄道吉时**才能下葬。只有等棺材安放妥帖、所有丧葬品都掩埋或焚烧了，整个葬礼才算结束。	The traditional Chinese burial ceremonies are usually complex and lengthy. The coffin is kept in the mourning hall until the day before the burial. And all the memorial supplies like **huge paper-made wreaths**, **elegiac-couplet cloths**, and funeral vehicles are arranged in special dispositions there. Family members and friends burn joss paper and incense to express condolence to the deceased. Monks, Taoists, folk musical players, and professional mourners chant and worship to relieve the dead soul. On the burial day, the coffin is carried to the hearse. And then the hearse is accompanied by the mourners, moving slowly around the familiar surroundings of the diseased person and all the way to the tomb site. According to the traditional customs, the tomb site is strictly chosen following the ***Fengshui* theory (also known as Chinese geomancy)**. When the coffin arrives, it will still have to wait for **a calculated auspicious time of the zodiac** to be moved underground. Only when the coffin is placed properly and all the burial objects are buried or burned is the whole funeral finished.

2.3.3　译技总结

综上，在原文包含特有文化意义的情况下，简单直译有时会导致理解困难。这时译者需在译文中增补原文所包含的文化背景信息，便于目标读者理解。

具体来讲，翻译具有文化内涵或联想意义的文化负载词（culturally loaded words）主要有三种方法：① 译意，如案例中“花圈”“挽联”的翻译；② 译音，如将“风水”译为“Fengshui”；③ 增加注释，如“黄道吉时”。翻译中的文化差异常常导致译入语读者理解困难，译者可增补关于术语概念、成语典故起源、社会文化背景、经典人物形象、性质特征、功能功用等说明性词句。

翻译文化负载词时，除了单独使用上述三种方法外，也可将多种翻译方法进行有机

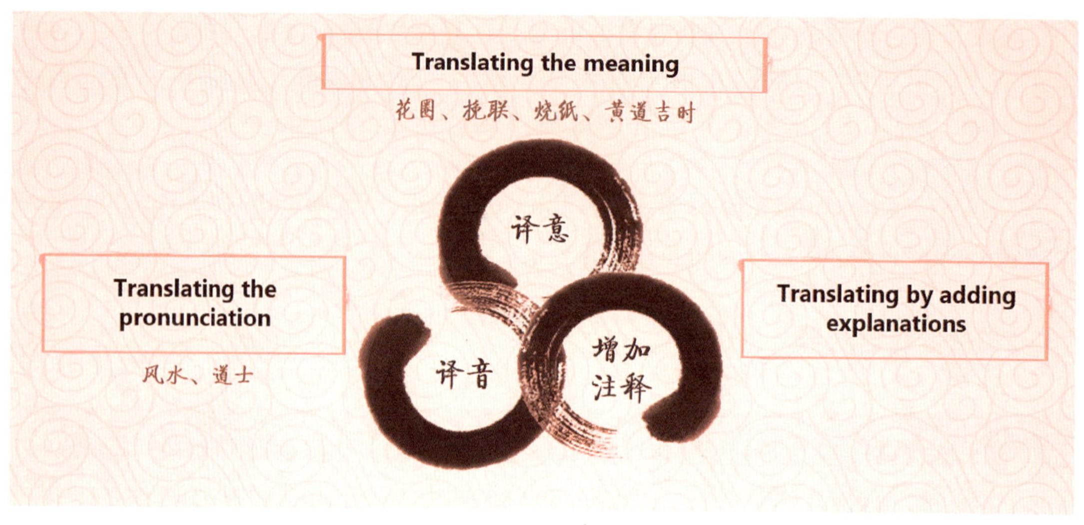

结合，最大程度克服翻译中的文化障碍。很多情况下，单纯的译意或译音不足以传达原文文化信息，比如并非所有目标读者都能理解"Fengshui"，那么这时我们就需进一步增加解释，使读者易于理解。

例：风水

Fengshui, also known as Chinese geomancy (地相术), is an important Chinese belief to create a spiritual balance between one's home and workplace. It has been widely used to direct the construction of dwellings, office buildings, tombs, etc. in a particular way, which will bring you good or bad luck.

下图总结归纳了一些汉语文化负载词英译的方法和例子。

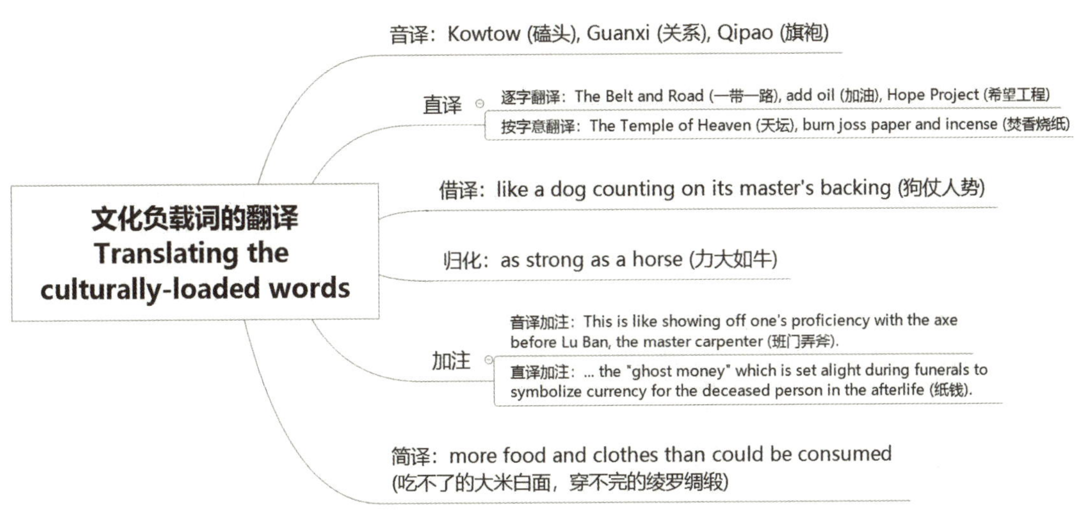

2.3.4　文化表达

(1) 文化基本知识与表达

位于西安的秦始皇帝陵(Emperor Qinshihuang's Mausoleum Site)发现于1974年，拥有恢宏庞大的地下墓室(vast underground chambers)。

秦始皇陵兵马俑(Terracotta Army)是秦始皇帝陵的重要组成部分，这座包含8 000多个真人大小的泥塑士兵、战车、马(clay soldiers, chariots and horses)，个个制作精良。修建这些兵马俑的最初目的是保护秦始皇陵墓，并帮助他获得永生(achieve immortality)，这是中国古人追求的理想的来世生活方式。秦始皇陵兵马俑是中国古代灿烂文明的鲜活象征，1987年被联合国教科文组织列入世界文化遗产名录(World Cultural Heritage List)，并被称为世界第八大奇迹(the Eighth Wonder of the World)。

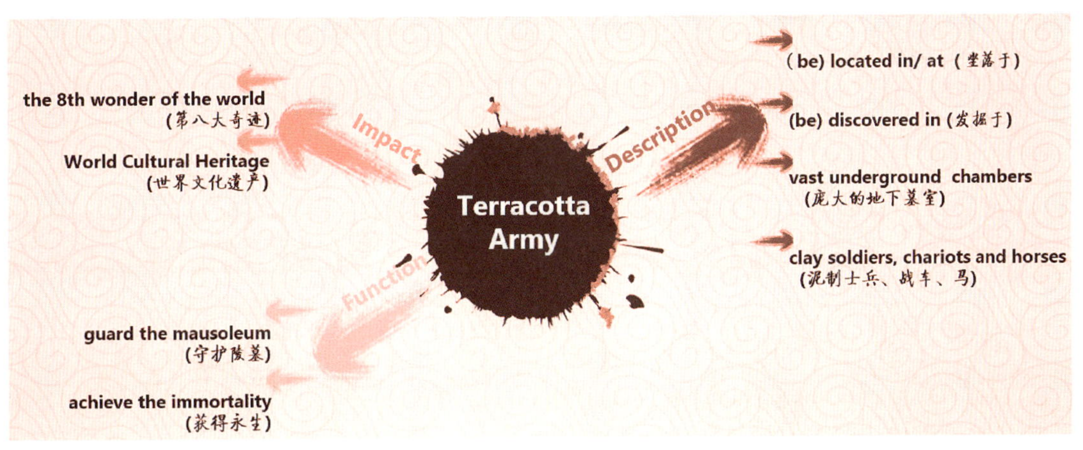

附加相关文化词

陪葬品	burial objects
非物质文化遗产	intangible cultural heritage
文物古迹	cultural relics and historic sites
全国重点文物保护单位	key cultural relics sites under the protection of the state/key national cultural relics protection unit
保护和传承	protection and inheritance

（2）文化知识延伸与翻译

短文 1

纸钱，也称冥币，是葬礼和其他祭拜仪式上用来焚烧的一种纸张，代表着死者使用的货币。黑龙江省省会城市哈尔滨市政府周三表示，焚烧纸钱是一种导致空气污染的“封建迷信”。哈尔滨市政府在其官网发声明称，政府禁止居住在市区及周边农村地区的960万居民生产、销售和燃烧纸钱。该禁令将根绝不良殡葬习俗、倡导文明祭祖、净化城市环境。在过去4年里，环保局一直在倡导文明殡葬，用献花等方式替代烧纸钱的祭奠习俗。烧纸钱是一种传统，当今社会是否应该继承这一传统应该取决于当代人的考量。

Joss paper, also known as **ghost money**, is set alight at funerals and other sacrificial ceremonies, and is intended as currency to be burned for deceased persons for their use in the afterlife. The municipal government of Harbin, capital of Heilongjiang province, said on Wednesday that it is a “**feudal superstition**” that is causing air pollution. In a statement on its website, the government banned the 9.6 million people from producing, selling and burning joss paper in the city and its surrounding rural areas. The ban will eradicate bad funeral practices, advocate **civilized ancestor worship**, and purify the urban environment. In the past four years, the environmental protection bureau has been advocating civilized funerals and ancestor worship with **alternatives** to burning joss paper, such as offering flowers. The burning of joss paper is a tradition, but it should be up to people whether it is inherited or not in today’s society.

词汇

joss paper 纸钱

ghost money 冥币

feudal superstition 封建迷信

civilized ancestor worship 文明祭祖

alternative [ɔ:l'tɜ:nətɪv] *n.* 选择；替代物

短文 2

葬礼是送走逝者、宴请生者的一个仪式。对于中国人来说，葬礼是非常重要的一个习俗。中国的各个地区都有着不同的风俗，而土葬是最普遍的形式。在这种葬礼中，死者的家庭成员需要穿丧服。丧服根据材料分为五种，视亲属关系远近而分别穿戴。在某种程度上，中国的葬礼仪式和葬礼习俗都由逝者的年龄、死因、社会地位及婚姻状况决定。

Funerals are a ritual for **lamenting** the deceased and an occasion for treating the living. Funeral customs are very important to the Chinese and they are varied in different regions of China. **Inhumation** is the most popular practice. Usually for this kind of funeral, the family members of the dead shall wear mourning dresses, which shall be made in five different materials according to how close the relationship is with the dead. To a certain degree, Chinese funeral rites and burial customs are determined by the age of the deceased, cause of death, status and position in society, and **marital status**.

词汇

lament [lə'ment] *v.* 哀悼；恸哭

marital status 婚姻状况

Inhumation [ˌɪnhjuː'meɪʃn] *n.* 土葬

2.3.5　讨论问题

（1）你如何看待在网络上烧纸钱、祭奠祖先和去世亲人的做法？

（2）汉译英时，为什么有时候需要增补文化信息？在增补文化信息时，我们应遵循什么原则？

2.4　清明节（增补技巧总结）

清明节是最重要的祭祀节日，约始于周代，距今已有2 500多年的历史。一提到清明节，国人都会想到杜牧著名的《清明》："清明时节雨纷纷，路上行人欲断魂。借问酒家何处有？牧童遥指杏花村。"这首诗呈现了清明春雨中所见，色彩清淡，心境凄冷，广为传诵。本节将通过翻译一篇有关清明节的短文，继续讲解增译技巧。

2.4.1　例句讲解

首先，请认真阅读原文。

① 清明是我国的二十四节气之一，在每年的4月5日左右，是祭祖和扫墓的

日子。② 在清明这天，成千上万的中国家庭前往陵园扫墓。③ 人们在坟前供上食物、酒水、鲜花，焚香烧纸，拜祭祖先；④ 并在此过程中祷告和祈求保佑。⑤ 除此之外，春季到来，万物复苏，人们常趁此机会外出野餐、荡秋千、放风筝、赏花和插柳。⑥ 清明既有祭扫的悲酸泪，又有踏青的欢笑声，是一个富有特色的节日。

① 清明是我国的二十四节气之一，在每年的4月5日左右，是祭祖和扫墓的日子。

翻译“我国”时应遵循英语表达习惯，在表示地点的名词前增添介词。“二十四节气”是我国独有的节气划分法，承载着中国独有的文化信息。翻译时为便于读者理解，须增添相应的文化内容。此外，与英语不同，汉语中的名词没有单复数之分。但是对汉语中具有单数意义的名词（如本句中的“日子”一词），翻译时应在其前增添不定冠词“a”。根据语境，扫墓的对象是已故之人，翻译时也可将这一隐含意义翻译出来。

本例最后一小句是汉语中典型的无主句。汉语中存在许多没有主语的句子，而英语重形合，句子一般不能缺少主语。英译时需增添主语“it”，使译文语法正确。全句翻译如下：

In China Tomb-Sweeping Day is one of **the 24 solar terms used in the traditional Chinese calendar and divided according to the relationship between the sun and the earth**, falling around April 5 each year. **It** is **a** day to offer sacrifices (祭品) to their ancestors and tend the tombs **of the deceased**.

② 在清明这天，成千上万的中国家庭前往陵园扫墓。

根据这句话的语境，可判断“扫墓”的对象通常是已故的家人，故翻译时须将这一意义增补出来，使译文意义更明确：

On Tomb-Sweeping Day, thousands of Chinese families will head to cemeteries to sweep the tombs **of deceased family members.**

③ 人们在坟前供上食物、酒水、鲜花，焚香烧纸，拜祭祖先……

本例中“食物、酒水、鲜花”是“供上”的宾语，为三个并列成分；而“焚香”“烧纸”又是一个并列结构。汉语中，多个并列成分同时出现，可不用连接词，直接用顿号或逗号表示，而英语中则需使用并列连词。因此，翻译时需增添并列连词“and”。

People offer food, spirits and flowers at the gravesites, burning incense (香) and joss paper (纸钱) to worship.

④ ……并在此过程中祷告和祈求保佑。

本小句没有主语，但从语境可判断，主语为前面的“人们”，翻译时为使译文语法正确和避免重复，需增添代词“they”作为句子主语；同时我们可以判断，祷告的地点是先人墓前，人们祈求的是先人的保佑，保佑的对象是家人，翻译时也宜将这些隐含意义表达出来，充分传达原文意义。

They pray before their ancestors' graves and beseech (恳求) them to bless their families.

⑤ 除此之外，春季到来，万物复苏，人们常趁此机会外出野餐、荡秋千、放风筝、赏花和插柳。

这句话中的“春季到来”“万物复苏”是两个并列结构，翻译时需增添表示并列关系的连词“and”。而后面人们的一系列活动都发生在这个时间段，英语中表示某个时间段发生了某事时，一般可使用连词“when”或“as”，此处我们需增添表示时间关系的连词。而“插柳”这一活动在中国人眼中具有驱魔辟邪的文化内涵，翻译时我们也须将这一文化意义译出。

In addition, as spring comes and everywhere gets green, people often go picnicking, swing, fly kites, enjoy blooms, and carry willow branches that are believed to scare away dead spirits.

⑥ 清明既有祭扫的悲酸泪，又有踏青的欢笑声，是一个富有特色的节日。

该句位于段落末尾，与前面的所有内容暗含因果关系，翻译时可增添表因果关系的连接词，使句子之间逻辑关系更明确。而本句话的第3小句又是对前面两个小句的概括，宜作为英文的主句，然后将“祭扫的悲酸泪”“踏青的欢笑声”这类动宾结构转化为“with+名词词组”作附带状语，并适时增添定冠词“the”。

Therefore, Tomb-Sweeping Day is a distinctive festival with both the sad tears of mourning the dead and the happy laughter from spring outings.

2.4.2 双语对照

清明节/Tomb-Sweeping Day	
清明是我国的二十四节气之一，在每年的4月5日左右，是祭祖和扫墓的日子。在清明这天，成千上万的中国家庭前往陵园扫墓。人们在坟前供上食物、酒水、鲜花，焚香烧纸，拜祭祖先；并在此过程中祷告和祈求保佑。除此之外，春季到来，万物复苏，人们常趁此机会外出野餐、荡秋千、放风筝、赏花和插柳。清明既有祭扫的悲酸泪，又有踏青的欢笑声，是一个富有特色的节日。	In China Tomb-Sweeping Day is one of the 24 solar terms used in the traditional Chinese calendar and divided according to the relationship between the sun and the earth, falling around April 5 each year. It is a day to offer sacrifices to their ancestors and tend the tombs of the deceased. On Tomb-Sweeping Day, thousands of Chinese families will head to cemeteries to sweep the tombs of deceased family members. People offer food, spirits, and flowers at the gravesites, burning incense and joss paper to worship. They pray before their ancestors' graves and beseech them to bless their families. In addition, as spring comes and everywhere turns green, people often go picnicking, swing, fly kites, enjoy blooms, and carry willow branches that are believed to scare away dead spirits. Therefore, Tomb-Sweeping Day is a distinctive festival with both the sad tears of mourning the dead and the happy laughter from spring outings.

2.4.3 译技总结

本节将增补的各种技巧与语言、文化差异的关系总结如下：

首先，如下页图①所示，汉语重意合（parataxis），行文上的连贯（coherence）多通过词序和内在语义实现，句子成分之间的功能辅助词用得少。而英语重形合（hypotaxis），注重形式上的衔接（cohesion）。因此，汉译英时，为使译文语法正确和语义连贯，需增补代词、连接词、冠词、介词等。

其次，如下页图②所示，为充分传达原文语境，便于目标读者理解，译者还须在译文中增添原文语境中的隐含语义或文化语义。

2.4.4 文化表达

（1）文化基本知识与表达

清明节主要的纪念仪式是扫墓。扫墓既可表达对已故亲人的孝心（filial piety），也可让人们感悟人生的价值和意义（the value and meaning of life）。下图（见44页）是与清明节相关的祭祀活动与习俗。

清明节不仅是祭祀的节日，也是户外踏青的时节。人们在这一天或放飞风筝，或爬高登山，或荡秋千，或赏花怡情。古时候，人们还在这一天玩蹴鞠，强身健体。

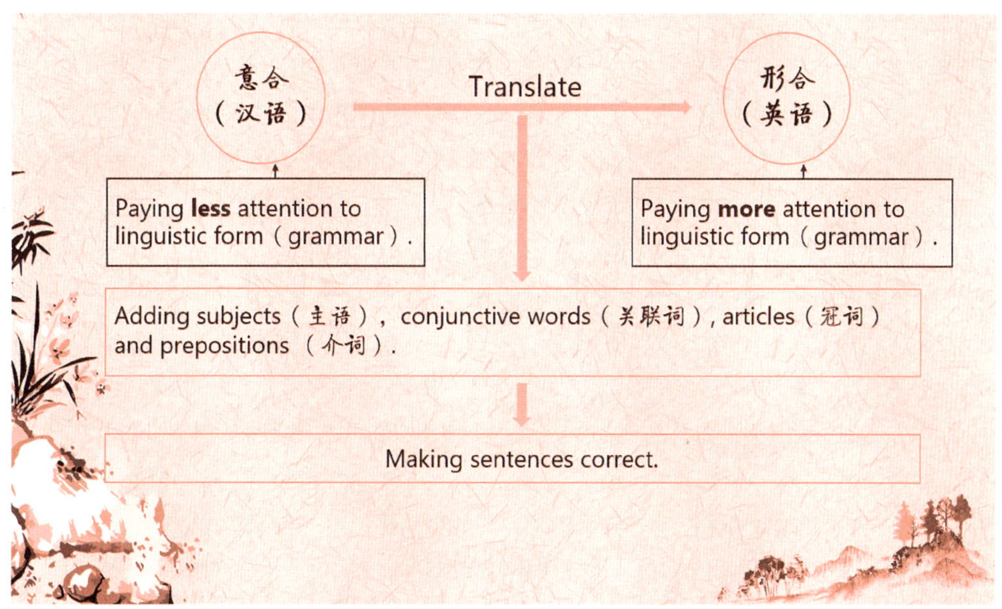

图①

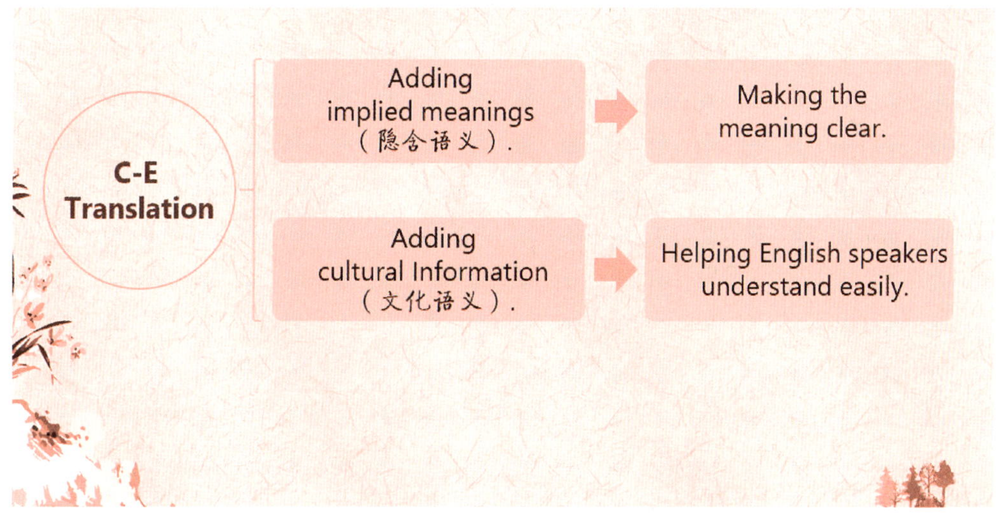

图②

清明节和寒食节(the Cold Food Day)日期相近,常被联系在一起。寒食节一般在清明节前一两日,在此期间人们不生火,吃冷饭。寒食节的一些习俗也融入清明节。人们会准备各类清明节的美食,如青团(green rice balls/Qingtuan)、薄饼(thin pancake)、子推馍(Zitui bun, named after Jie Zitui, a famous hermit of the Spring and Autumn Period [770 ~ 476 BC])等。这些清明节的食物往往承载着一定的文化含义,如青团是长江以南地区人们在清明节吃的一道传统点心,人们认为食之可防毒虫叮咬。

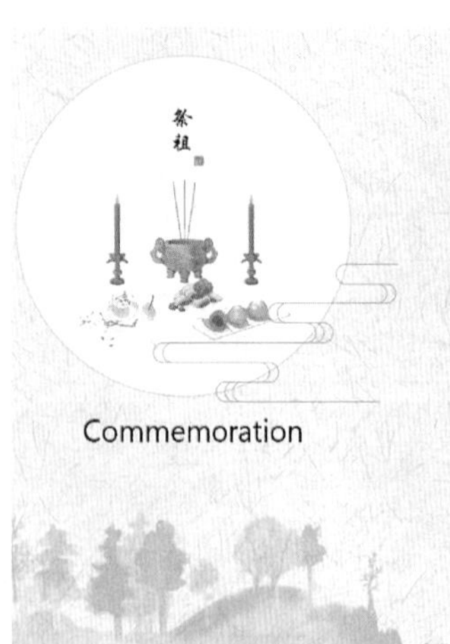
Commemoration

祭祖 worship ancestors
扫墓 sweep the tombs
向祖先献祭品 offer sacrifices to ancestors
焚香烧纸 burn incense and joss paper
磕头 perform kowtows
整修坟墓 renovate tombs

Activities

have an outing in spring

go hiking

fly kites

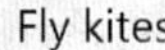

Fly kites

Cutting kites' string indicates chasing away bad luck and diseases.

carry willow branches

enjoy the blooming flowers

play Cuju

Cuju

Cuju literally means "kick-ball", a type of ancient Chinese football.

Delicacies

the Cold Food Day

Sanzi

green rice balls/Qingtuan

The Cold Food Day

A memorial day for Jie Zitui and one day before Tomb-sweeping Day.

Green rice balls/Qingtuan

Food believed to have the function of preventing toxic insect bites.

steamed rice with leaf mustard

thin pancake

Zitui bun

Zitui bun

Being named after Jie Zitui, a famous hermit of the Spring and Autumn Period (770-476 BC).

（2）文化知识延伸与翻译

短文 1

清明节和春秋时代的介子推有关。他曾割下自己腿上的肉让逃亡的晋国公子重耳充饥。重耳执政后要封赏他，但介子推隐居山林拒绝封赏。无奈，晋文公重耳放火烧山想逼他出山，不料却烧死了恩人。自此晋文公下令每年的这一天禁止生火，只吃冷食，这就是寒食节的来历。因寒食节恰好在清明前一两天，久而久之，寒食的习俗逐渐被移到清明中，清明便从单纯的农业节气变为一个重要的祭祀日。

The Qingming Day is popularly associated with Jie Zitui in the Spring and Autumn Period, who saved his starving lord's life by serving meat cut from his own leg. The lord, known as Duke Wen of Jin, later took power and decided to reward Jie but was declined. Duke Wen of Jin tried to force Jie out of the forest in which he lived in seclusion by setting the forest to fire, but instead Jie was burned to death. Deeply regretful for his misconduct, Duke Wen of Jin gave orders that on that day every year the use of fire be banned and only cold food be served so as to commemorate Jie. That is the origin of the Cold Food Day, which is one or two days before Qingming and later merges with it. The Qingming Day then becomes an important day of sacrifice from an originally simple solar term for guiding farming.

短文 2

为表达全国各族人民对抗击新冠肺炎疫情牺牲烈士和逝世同胞的深切哀悼，国务院发布公告，决定于2020年4月4日举行全国性哀悼活动。在此期间，全国和驻外使领馆下半旗志哀，全国停止公共娱乐活动。4月4日10时起，全国人民默哀3分钟，汽车、火车、舰船鸣笛，防空警报鸣响。

China will hold a national mourning for the **martyrs** who died in the fight against the novel coronavirus disease (COVID–19) outbreak and the **compatriots** who died of the disease, according to the State Council. During the commemoration, national **flags will fly at half-mast** across the country and in all Chinese embassies and consulates abroad, and public recreational activities will be suspended across the country. At 10:00 a.m. Saturday, Chinese people nationwide will **observe three-minute silence to mourn** for the deceased, while air raid sirens and horns of automobiles, trains and ships will wail in grief.

词汇

martyr ['mɑːtə(r)] *n.* 烈士

compatriot [kəm'pætrɪət] *n.* 同胞

flags fly at half-mast 下半旗（也可用 flags fly at half-staff）

observe (three-minute) silence to moum (for someone) 默哀（也可用 pay silent tribute to someone）

2.4.5　讨论问题

（1）2020年4月4日清明节这天，全国为在新冠疫情中逝去的公民举行了国家公祭。

当公祭鸣笛声响起的时候你想到了什么？

(2)汉译英时我们经常需要增添哪些词类？为什么？

2.5 单元练习

1. 从两个备选项中选出对汉语原句翻译得较好的一个选项。

① 在汉语中“wine”写作“酒”,“酒”是“久”的谐音,寓意着长寿。

A. The Chinese word for wine is *jiu*, a homonym of the Chinese word for “long”, symbolizing longevity.

B. The Chinese word for wine is *jiu*, a homonym for “long”, symbolizing longevity.

② 偶数属阴,奇数属阳。

A. Even numbers belong to *Yin*, while odd numbers belong to *Yang*.

B. Even numbers belong to *Yin* (the feminine and negative principle), while odd numbers belong to *Yang* (the masculine and positive principle).

③ 清明节是中国人扫墓的日子。

A. Tomb-Sweeping Day is the day for Chinese people to sweep the tombs of their deceased families.

B. Tomb-Sweeping Day is the day for Chinese people to sweep tombs.

④ “九九”和“久久”同音。

A. “Double Ninth” is identical in sound to “forever”.

B. “Double Ninth” is identical in sound to “forever” in Chinese.

⑤ 当一起读时就是“早生贵子”。

A. When pronounced together, it sounds like *zao sheng gui zi*.

B. When pronounced together, it sounds like *zao sheng gui zi* (having a noble baby soon).

2. 翻译下面的句子,注意运用本单元所学的翻译技巧。

① 人的生命受之于父母,延续于子女。

___

② 春节期间,“福”字经常倒贴在门上,表达人们对“福到”的期盼。

③ 清明节与寒食节临近。

2.6 单元测验

1. 单项选择。从两个备选项中选出对汉语原句翻译得较好的一个选项。(5×5 分=25 分)

① 蹴鞠是古代清明节人们喜爱的一种游戏。

A. *Cuju*, a kick-ball game, was popular to play on Tomb-Sweeping Day in ancient China.

B. *Cuju* was a popular game to play on Tomb-Sweeping Day in ancient China.

② 百日剃发是满族的传统丧葬习俗。

A. The traditional funeral custom of Manchu is the haircut system of a hundred days.

B. The traditional funeral custom of Manchu is that no haircut shall be had until a hundred days later after the funeral.

③ 清明节是传统节日,也是最重要的祭祀节日。

A. Tomb-Sweeping Day is not only a traditional Chinese holiday, but also the most important day of sacrifice in China.

B. Tomb-Sweeping Day is a traditional holiday, the most important day of sacrifice.

④ 汉族和一些少数民族大多在清明节扫墓。

A. The Han people and some ethnic minorities mostly sweep tombs on Tomb-Sweeping Day.

B. Han people and some ethnic minorities mostly sweep tombs on the Tomb-Sweeping Day.

⑤ 中国传统婚礼是华夏文化的重要部分。

A. Traditional Chinese weddings are important part of Chinese culture.

B. Traditional Chinese weddings are an important part of Chinese culture.

2. 翻译下面的句子，注意运用本单元所学的翻译技巧。(3×10分=30分)

① 只羡鸳鸯不羡仙。

____

② 红色象征着喜庆、吉祥，在中国，美丽的女子称为红颜。

____

③ 回门是指女子出嫁后首次回娘家探亲。

____

3. 将下面短文翻译成英文，注意运用本单元所学的翻译技巧，增补必要信息以帮助目的语读者理解。(45分)

“婚”在古代是“昏”(黄昏)的意思，因此夫妻结合的礼仪称为“昏礼”。中国传统婚礼反映着中国的哲学思想。婚礼上总是用红色的东西来表达祝福和尊重。这是因为中国人将红色看作幸福、成功和好运的象征。婚姻不仅是一对新人的结合，也象征着两个家庭的结合。邀请亲朋好友来参加婚礼体现着人与人之间的关系和礼节(formality)。婚礼上奏乐的声音通常很响，响到足以让自然“听到”，同时也证明婚姻的重要性。

____

____

____

____

____

____

____

____

____

____

第3单元

生物地理

Biology and Geography

3.1 背景介绍

Lead-in Questions

(1) What is the biggest offshore island in China?

(2) Could you offer some suggestions about how to realize a harmonious relationship between human and nature?

Situated in eastern Asia and on the west coast of **the Pacific Ocean**, China is the world's third largest country with a total area of 9.6 million square kilometers. Extending about 5,500 kilometers from north to south and 5,200 kilometers from west to east, the shape of China on the map is like a rooster. Its **terrain** is higher in the west and lower in the east with great varieties, including mountains, **plateaus**, **foothills**, **basins,** and **plains**. China's mountainous areas, broad and vast, occupy nearly two-thirds of the land area and have **abundant mineral** resources. China's mainland has a **coastline** of 18,000 kilometers and a large number of **offshore** islands, with Taiwan Island the biggest one. There are numerous rivers and lakes in China, which make up an important part of China's **geographical** environment.

From vast deserts to **steaming** rainforests, China is harboring different kinds of **rare creatures**. However, its **biodiversity** has **deteriorated** in recent years and it is a difficult task to **arrest** the process. China today is faced with a challenge: how to protect nature in an increasingly crowded space? Like the rest of the world, China is still feeling its way towards a **harmonious** relationship with nature.

词汇

the Pacific Ocean 太平洋
terrain [tə'reɪn] *n.* 地形,地势
plateau ['plætəʊ] *n.* 高原
foothill ['fʊthɪl] *n.* 山麓小丘;丘陵地带
basin ['beɪsn] *n.* 盆地
plain [pleɪn] *n.* 平原
abundant [ə'bʌndənt] *adj.* 丰富的;充裕的
mineral ['mɪnərəl] *adj.* 矿物的;矿质的
coastline ['kəʊstlaɪn] *n.* 海岸线
offshore [ˌɒf'ʃɔ:(r)] *adj.* 离岸的
geographical [dʒɪə'græfɪkl] *adj.* 地理的
steaming ['sti:mɪŋ] *adj.* 非常热的;热气腾腾的
rare creatures 珍稀动物
biodiversity [ˌbaɪəʊdaɪ'vɜ:səti] *n.* 生物多样性
deteriorate [dɪ'tɪərɪəreɪt] *v.* 恶化;变坏
arrest [ə'rest] *v.* 阻止
harmonious [hɑ:'məʊnɪəs] *adj.* 和谐的;谐调的

3.2 喜马拉雅(删减重复)

本节我们将介绍世界名山喜马拉雅,同时学习删减重复这一常用翻译技巧。

我国位于亚洲东部、太平洋西岸,地大物博,领土面积约960万平方公里,居亚洲第一,世界第三。地形地貌多种多样,既有北方的戈壁沙漠,也有南方的亚热带雨林;既有雄伟的高原,亦有广阔的平原;既有起伏的山岭,亦有四周群山环抱、中间低平的大小盆地。其中,位于青藏高原南巅边缘的喜马拉雅山脉是世界海拔最高的山脉,其主峰就是世界最高峰——珠穆朗玛峰。

删减,又称减译法或省略法,指原文有些词不必译出,因为译文中虽无其词已有其意,或者在译文中是不言而喻的。换言之,省略是删去一些可有可无,或者有了反嫌累赘或违背译文语言习惯的词(方梦之,2004:112)。在汉译英中,我们经常会删减一些词语,如重复的词语、范畴词。

3.2.1 例句讲解

我们将通过翻译下面这段关于喜马拉雅的故事来学习删减重复。

① 中国与印度的交界处,巨大的岩石被推挤至海平面以上8 000米处之高,造

就了世界最高大宏伟的山脉——喜马拉雅山。② 对东部来说，岩石被皱褶进了南北走向的绵延陡峭的山脊，同时也切进了云南的心脏地带，形成了平行的横断山脉。这些天然屏障守护着隔绝在云南各自毗邻的河谷中的动植物。雪峰与斜坡间巨大的温差所创造的足够的优厚条件，使得这儿生命彰显无限生机。③ 在春的岁月，横断山脉的斜坡上上演了中国最为恢宏壮绝的自然景致。此处的森林是世界上植被及物种最多样化的区域。这里生长着超过18 000种植物，其中约3 000种植物是这儿特有的。

① 印度与中国的交界处，巨大的岩石被推挤至海平面以上8 000米处之高，造就了世界最高大宏伟的山脉——喜马拉雅山。

在这句话里，8 000米已经暗示了高度 "height"，因此翻译时为了避免重复，后文的 "处之高" 宜省略，如果按照汉语一字一词地全部译出，译文就会显得啰唆。

另外，汉语喜欢使用四字结构，形象生动，比一般词语更具表现力，如 "胡言乱语" "能说会道" "耀武扬威" "见多识广" "千辛万苦" "和颜悦色" 等。但是有一些四字结构是为了音律整齐而使用的两组同义词，因此在翻译的时候，为了避免重复，译出一组的意思即可。在这句话里出现了 "高大宏伟" 一词，"高大" 与 "宏伟" 意思相近，在汉语中经常一起使用，但在翻译成英文时，为了简洁只需翻译成 "high" 即可。整句话的翻译如下：

On the border between China and India, the giant rocks have been raised eight kilometres **above sea level**, creating the world's **highest** mountain range, the Himalayas.

② 对东部来说，岩石被皱褶进了南北走向的绵延陡峭的山脊，同时也切进了云南的心脏地带，形成了平行的横断山脉。

"南北" 一词已经指代了方向，因此在翻译成英文的时候，为了避免重复，应该省略掉后面的 "走向"。"心脏" 就是指 "中心地带"，英译时后面的 "地带" 二字也应该省略掉。整句话的翻译如下：

To the east, the rocks have buckled into a series of steep **north-south** ridges, cutting down through the **heart** of Yunnan, the parallel mountains of the Hengduan Shan.

③ 在春的岁月，横断山脉的斜坡上上演了中国最为恢宏壮绝的自然景致。

在汉语里，"春" 指春天这一段时间，后面紧跟的 "岁月" 一词指年月、日子，也是指时间，在翻译成英文的时候，为避免重复，应省略掉。四字成语“恢宏壮绝”里“恢宏”和“壮绝”意思相近，只需要翻译其中一组词的意思即可，以免重复。整句翻译如下：

Through **spring**, the Hengduan slopes stage China's **greatest** natural scenery.

我们再来看一个词语重复的例子：

中国位于亚洲东部、太平洋的西岸，陆地边界长达2万余千米，东**邻**朝鲜，北**邻**蒙古人民共和国，东北和西北与俄罗斯、哈萨克斯坦**接壤**，西和西南**邻**阿富汗、巴基斯坦、印度，南**邻**缅甸、老挝和越南。

在这个长句子里，“邻”反复出现了四次。另一个词语“接壤”和“邻”所表达的意思几乎是一样的，它们是近义词，可以翻译成“adjoin”，并且只翻译一次，以避免不必要的重复。否则译文累赘冗长，不符合英语的表达习惯。本句翻译如下：

It has a continental land boundary of more than 20,000 kilometers and **adjoins** DPRK in the east, the People's Republic of Mongolia in the north, Russia and Kazakhstan in the northeast and northwest, Afghanistan, Pakistan, India in the west and southwest, and Myanmar, Laos and Vietnam in the south.

3.2.2 双语对照

喜马拉雅/The Himalayas	
中国与印度的交界处，巨大的岩石被推挤至海平面以上8 000米**处之高**，造就了世界最**高大宏伟**的山脉——喜马拉雅山。对东部来说，岩石被皱褶进了**南北走向**的绵延陡峭的山脊，同时也切进了云南的**心脏地带**，形成了平行的横断山脉。这些天然屏障守护着隔绝在云南各自毗邻的河谷中的动植物。雪峰与斜坡间的巨大的温差所创造的足够的优厚条件，使得这儿生命彰显无限生机。在春的**岁月**，横断山脉的斜坡上上演了中国最为**恢宏壮绝**的自然景致。此处的森林是世界上植被及物种最多样化的区域。这里生长着超过18 000种植物，其中约3 000种植物是这儿特有的。	On the border between China and India, the giant rocks have been raised eight kilometres **above sea level**, creating the world's **highest** mountain range, the Himalayas. But to the east, the rocks have buckled into a series of steep **north-south** ridges, cutting down through the **heart** of Yunnan, the parallel mountains of the Hengduan Shan. These natural barriers serve to protect plants and animals isolated in each adjacent valley in Yunnan. The huge temperature range between the snowy peaks and the warmer slopes below provides a vast array of conditions for life to thrive. Through **spring**, the Hengduan slopes stage China's **greatest** natural scenery. The forests here are among the most diverse botanical areas in the world. Over 18,000 plant species grow here, of which 3,000 are found nowhere else.

3.2.3　译技总结

从以上翻译我们可以看出汉语表达讲究平衡、对称和韵调节律，广泛使用叠词、四字结构、排比、对比和重复手段，读起来朗朗上口，铿锵有力；而英语则讲究简洁明了。若将汉语中的叠词、对称和重复结构等原原本本、一字一句地照搬翻译，英语译文就会显得累赘。在遇见诸如此类情况时，为了避免重复啰嗦，译者往往需要采用删减手段，使英文译文简洁流畅。

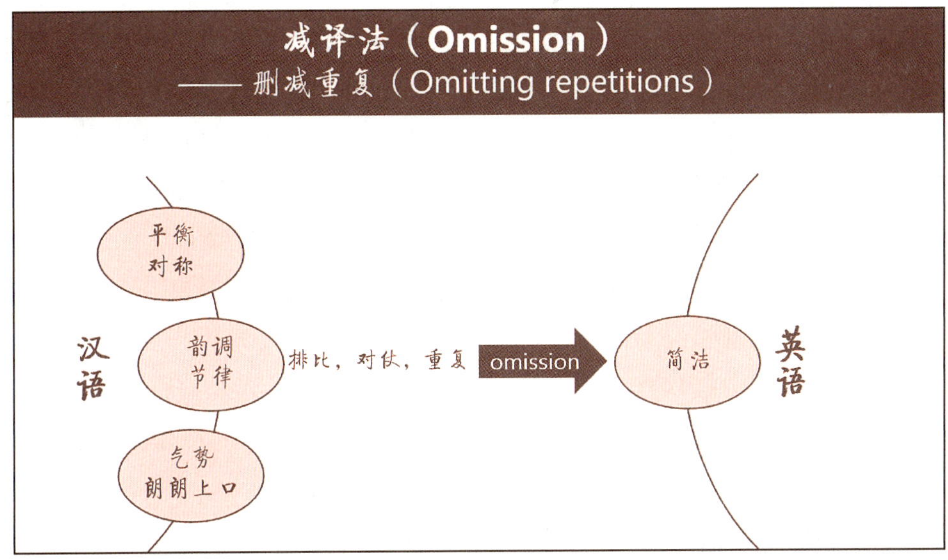

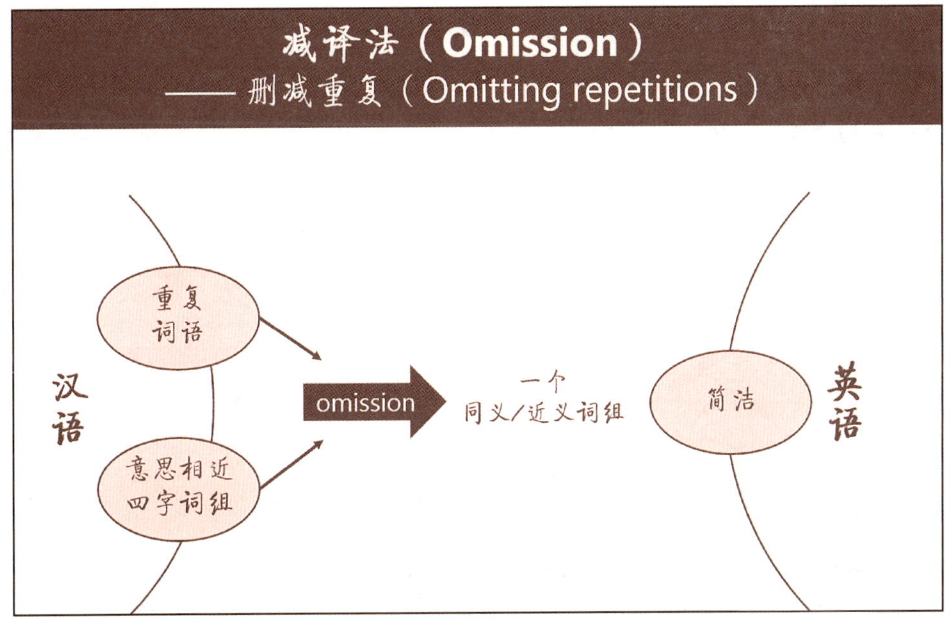

3.2.4 文化表达

(1)文化基本知识与表达

从地图上看,青藏高原西南喜马拉雅山地区呈浓重而单调的深褐色,这是因为其崇山峻岭海拔极高所致。其实走近这里看到的不仅是冰天雪地,荒草无际,而且有色彩极为丰富、斑斓多姿、奇异神秘、令人向往的景色,许多美丽的传说给这里增添了无穷的魅力。喜马拉雅山势雄伟,是我国西南边境上绵延最长、最壮丽的山脉,也是世界上最高最大的山脉,横穿我国西藏以及尼泊尔、不丹、印度等国家。

喜马拉雅在藏语中的意思是"冰雪之乡"。喜马拉雅山厚积着万年冰雪,冰河从山间的粒雪盆地中倾泻而出,或切割出万仞的山谷,或衍生出森林、草原、湖泊,形成奇丽的风光。喜马拉雅山全长约2 450公里,南北间的宽度为200 ~ 300公里,大抵中间一段较窄,东西两端宽。其东端延伸至我国境内的雅鲁藏布江大拐弯处,向西达帕米尔高原,南面是平坦的印度河和恒河冲积平原,北达青藏高原的雅鲁藏布江谷地和印度恒河谷地。广义的喜马拉雅山还包括四条几乎平行的山脉:外喜马拉雅山,小喜马拉雅山,大喜马拉雅山和泰迪斯喜马拉雅山。在这个广阔的范围内,海拔高度多在5 000米以上,海拔8 000米的高山有14座。作为喜马拉雅山脉的主干,喜马拉雅山大部分高出雪线,有9座8 000米以上的冰峰。世界最高峰的珠穆朗玛峰(8 848.13米)就是其中之一。在藏民的心中,喜马拉雅山是一座永恒的神山(李西宁,2001)。

在介绍山脉时,我们经常用到下图中的英文词汇。

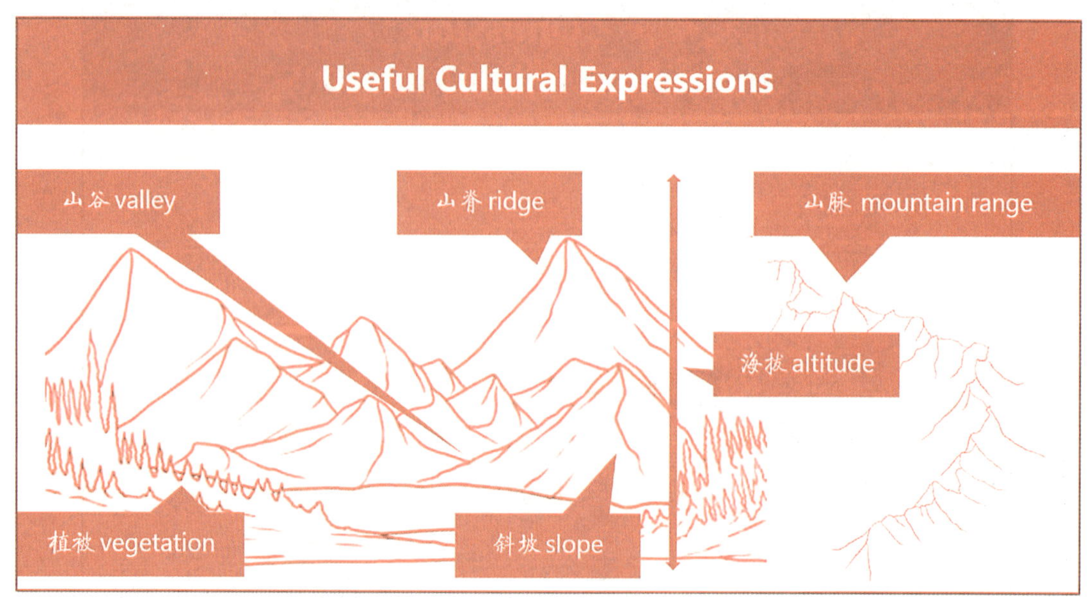

(2)延伸阅读与翻译拓展

拥有世界最高峰的喜马拉雅山脉还将继续"长高"吗？我国一些科学家认为"不会"。	Will the Himalaya Mountains, home to the world's highest peaks, continue to push up into the sky in future? Some Chinese scientists say no.
中科院地质与地球物理研究院的研究员边千韬说，喜马拉雅山脉已基本达到最高点，在未来几个世纪内，甚至可能会有所下降。	The Himalayas may have reached their highest altitude and in the centuries to come may even **shrink** a little, said Bian Qiantao, a researcher with the Institute of Geology and Geophysics of the Chinese Academy of Sciences.
喜马拉雅山脉位于青藏高原南侧，呈向南突出的弧形，山脉的主要部分位于中国境内。"喜马拉雅"在藏语中是"冰雪之乡"的意思。喜马拉雅山脉的平均高度在6 000米以上。	Located on the southern **rim** of the Qinghai-Tibet Plateau, the Himalaya Mountains form an **arc** protruding southward. The main part of the range lies in China. "Himalaya" means "**abode** of snow" in Tibetan. The average height of these mountains is more than 6,000 meters.
科学界普遍认为，青藏高原和喜马拉雅山脉是6 500万年前向北漂移的印度板块与欧亚板块相撞而形成的。	Scientists believe that 65 million years ago, the **Indian Plate** moving north **collided** with the **Eurasian Plate**, and the **upheaval** saw the emergence of the Qinghai-Tibet Plateau as well as the Himalayas.
边教授说："这两个板块之间的摩擦仍在继续，在这种力量的作用下，喜马拉雅山脉一直在慢慢升高。"	"**Friction** between the **tectonic plates** continues to this day, gradually pushing the Himalayas upward," said Bian.
"但同时，从下地壳一直到地幔上部在产生一种东西拉张的力量，这种拉力对喜马拉雅山脉的继续升高起到了阻碍作用。"	"But at the same time, a horizontal pulling power inside the lower continental **crust** and **mantle** of the earth counteracts this upward movement," said Bian.
2005年，科学家测出珠穆朗玛峰的海拔为8 844.43米，比1975年低3.7米。	According to measurements made by scientists in 2005, the **altitude** of Mount Qomolangma is 8,844.43 meters, 3.70 meters lower than the figure obtained in 1975.
测量结果表明，喜马拉雅山脉和青藏高原不会无限升高。边教授说，喜马拉雅山脉达到一定高度后，在重力和由板块碰撞产生的挤压力的作用下，山脉会向外扩展，而不会持续增高。	The result suggests that the Himalayas and the Qinghai-Tibet Plateau will not continue to move up indefinitely. After growing to a certain height, the effect of **gravity** and **collision**-generated **extrusion** will make them grow wider, but not higher, Bian said.

词汇

shrink [ʃrɪŋk] *v.* (使)缩小；(使)收缩　　**rim** [rɪm] *n.* 边，边缘；圆圈

arc [ɑːk] *n.* 弧(度);弧光;弧形物;*adj.* 圆弧的
abode [ə'bəʊd] *n.* 住处;营业所
Indian Plate 印度板块
collide [kə'laɪd] *v.* 碰撞;抵触,冲突
Eurasian Plate 欧亚大陆板块
upheaval [ʌp'hiːvl] *n.* 剧变;隆起;举起
friction ['frɪkʃn] *n.* 摩擦
tectonic plates (地球表面的)构造板块
crust [krʌst] *n.* 地壳;外壳
mantle ['mæntl] *n.* 地幔;斗篷;覆盖物
altitude ['æltɪtjuːd] *n.* 高地;高度;顶垂线;海拔
gravity ['grævətɪ] *n.* 重力;地心引力
collision [kə'lɪʒn] *n.* 碰撞;冲突;抵触
extrusion [ɪk'struːʒn] *n.* 挤出;推出;赶出;喷出

3.2.5 讨论问题

(1)珠穆朗玛峰坐落于世界屋脊之上,是世界最高峰,它是无数人魂牵梦绕的神圣坐标。每年都会有很多勇士攀登珠峰,可是攀登之路凶险万分,为什么还有那么多人要登顶主峰呢?请谈谈你对此的看法。

(2)汉译英的过程中我们为什么要删减汉语中的一些重复表达呢?你能自己举出一些例子吗?

3.3 中国龙(删减范畴词)

减译法除了上一节讲到的删减重复外,还包括删减范畴词。本节我们将以介绍中华民族的图腾、中国文化的象征——中国龙为例,讲解删减范畴词这一翻译技巧。首先来看下面这句话:

在中国人心中,龙具有开拓变化的寓意和团结凝聚的精神。

这句话大家会怎么翻译呢?你可能会进行如下翻译:

T1: To the Chinese, the dragons signify the spirit of innovation and cohesion.

从语法角度来讲,这样的翻译没有错误。那么还可以在此基础上作一些修改吗?例如:

T2: To the Chinese, the dragons signify innovation and cohesion.

这两种翻译在语法上都正确，也都表达出了原句的意思。区别就在于，第一句话把原句中的“精神”一词翻译出来了“the spirit of”，而第二句翻译却直接将其省略掉，使整个句子更加简洁明了。

在汉译英的过程中是不是什么词语都可以省略呢？当然不是。除了删减不必要的重复词语以外，范畴词也是常需删减的一类。

3.3.1 例句讲解

请先看下面这段关于中国龙的故事。

① 中国龙，也叫东方龙，是中国神话故事、民间传说以及东方文化中的动物形象。② 传统认为，它们是吉祥的化身，特别在治水、降雨、台风等方面有着神奇的力量。在东方文化中，中国龙也代表着那些拥有权力、实力和好运的人。③ 在帝王时代，中国的帝王通常用龙作为他帝国强权的象征。

在中国文化中，优秀杰出的人才被誉为龙，而那些少有成就的无能之人则被喻为其他诸如蝼蚁之类的被轻视的生物。很多中国谚语和成语都提到了龙，比如“望子成龙”。

① 中国龙，也叫东方龙，是中国神话故事、民间传说以及东方文化中的动物形象。

汉语中有一类四字格结构的词语，其词汇结构为“实词+虚词”。实词部分其实已经清楚地陈述了要表达的信息，虚词部分是为了补充四字格完整的结构而存在，其本身没有实际意义。如果按照汉语照搬直译，将虚词部分也翻译出来，译文会显得冗余，因此应省略不译。本句译文如下：

Chinese dragons, also known as East Asian dragons, are legendary **creatures** in Chinese mythology, Chinese folklore, and East Asian culture at large.

② 传统认为，它们是吉祥的化身，特别在治水、降雨、台风、洪水等方面有着神奇的力量。

这句话你可能会进行如下翻译：

They traditionally symbolize potent and auspicious powers, particularly control over the aspect of water, rainfall, typhoons, and floods.

在语法上译文并没有错，也表达出了原句的意思。但是在汉语中，由于行文结构的需要，会出现一些没有太大实际意义的抽象词汇。如果硬生生地把这些词汇直接翻译成英语，就无法保证译文简洁。本句核心意思是中国龙能够治水、降雨、控制台风，而“方面”一词在这一语境中没有太大实际意义，属于汉语范畴词，翻译时宜省略不译。

They traditionally symbolize potent and auspicious powers, particularly control over **water, rainfall, typhoons, and floods**.

③ 在帝王时代，中国的帝王通常用龙作为他帝国强权的象征。

这句话你可能会进行如下翻译：

During the days of Imperial China, the emperor usually used the dragon as a symbol of his imperial strength and power.

译文无误，也表达出了原句的意思。但是“时代”一词也属于范畴词，且“during”一词在英文中就是指“在……的期间”，已经明确表示了时间概念，因此在翻译时，最好省略“时代”，使译文更为简洁明了。

During Imperial China, the emperor usually used the dragon as a symbol of his imperial strength and power.

3.3.2 双语对照

中国龙/The Chinese Dragon	
中国龙，也叫东方龙，是中国神话故事、民间传说以及东方文化中的动物形象。传统认为，它们是吉祥的化身，特别在治水、降雨、台风、洪水等方面有着神奇的力量。在东方文化中，中国龙也代表着那些拥有权力、实力和好运的人。在帝王时代，中国的帝王通常用龙作为他帝国强权的象征。 在中国文化中，优秀杰出的人才被誉为龙，而那些少有成就的无能之人则被喻为其他诸如蝼蚁之类的被轻视的生物。很多中国谚语和成语都提到了龙，比如“望子成龙”。	Chinese dragons, also known as East Asian dragons, are legendary **creatures** in Chinese mythology, Chinese folklore, and East Asian culture at large. They traditionally symbolize potent and auspicious powers, particularly control over **water, rainfall, typhoons, and floods**. The dragon is also a symbol of power, strength, and good luck for people who are worthy of it in East Asian culture. **During Imperial China**, the emperor usually used the dragon as a symbol of his imperial strength and power. In Chinese culture, excellent and outstanding people are compared to dragons, while incapable people with no achievements are compared to disesteemed creatures, such as worms. A number of Chinese proverbs and idioms feature references to a dragon, such as “Hoping one’s son will become a dragon”.

3.3.3　译技总结

汉英两种语言在表达方式上存在着一定的差异，有时一种语言中使用的某些词语在另一种语言中可能显得多余。如果机械地、一字一字地照搬保留，译文读起来会累赘冗长。本节我们学习的就是汉译英省略法的一种——删减范畴词。范畴词是指表示事物属性的比较抽象的词语，如“任务”“工作”“情况”“问题”“事业”“局面”等。汉语更偏好使用此类词语，它们虽然能使句子更加流畅，在语法或语气上不可或缺，但通常没有太大实质意义。因此，英译时常可删除不译，这样英语译文更简洁明了，严谨精炼。

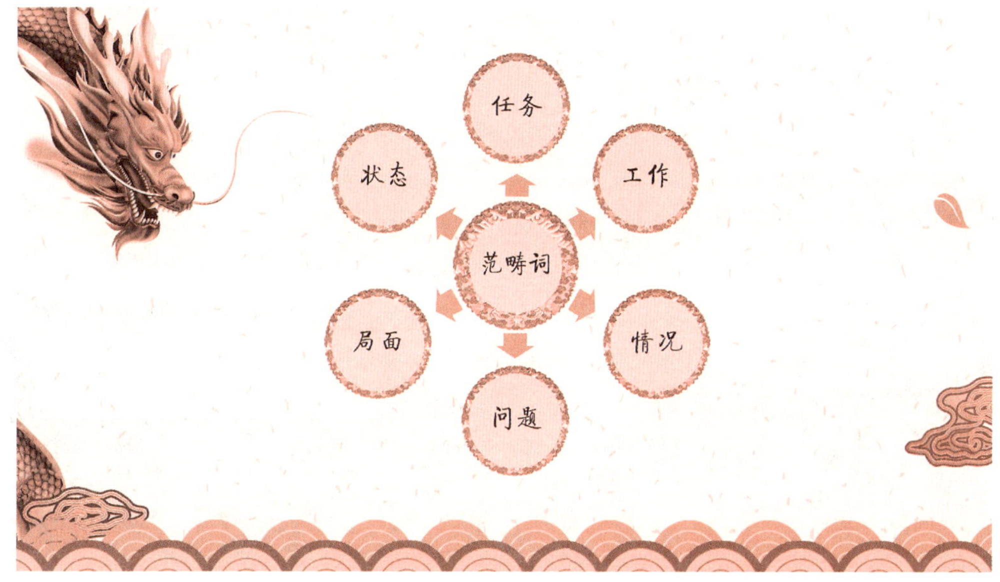

我们再来看下面的例子：

加快经济改革的速度。

To accelerate ~~the speed of~~ economic reform.

在这句话里，“速度”就是一个范畴词，与“加快”搭配，构成汉语中常用的表达方式“加快……速度”；但本句话实际就是指加快经济改革，“速度”一词本身意义不大，其语义也已经包含在“加快”一词中。英译时删减该词，原文意思不会受到影响，反而更简洁。

3.3.4　文化表达

（1）文化基本知识与表达

龙是古代中国人把蛇、鳄、鱼、蜥蜴、鲵、猪、马、牛、鹿、虎、熊等动物和雷电、云、虹霓、龙卷风、星宿等自然天象多元融合而产生的一种动物。动物崇拜和天象崇拜是自然崇拜的主要内容。龙崇拜是以自然崇拜为基础，是自然崇拜的升华（庞进，2007）。

千百年来，龙文化已经渗透到中国社会的各个角落，成为中国文化和传统的象征，也成为中华民族的象征。在中国，龙象征着权力、吉祥、富强、卓越、皇权等。至今在很多成语和谚语的表达中都能看到“龙”的影子。下图列举了四个常用的包含“龙”的四字成语及其译文。

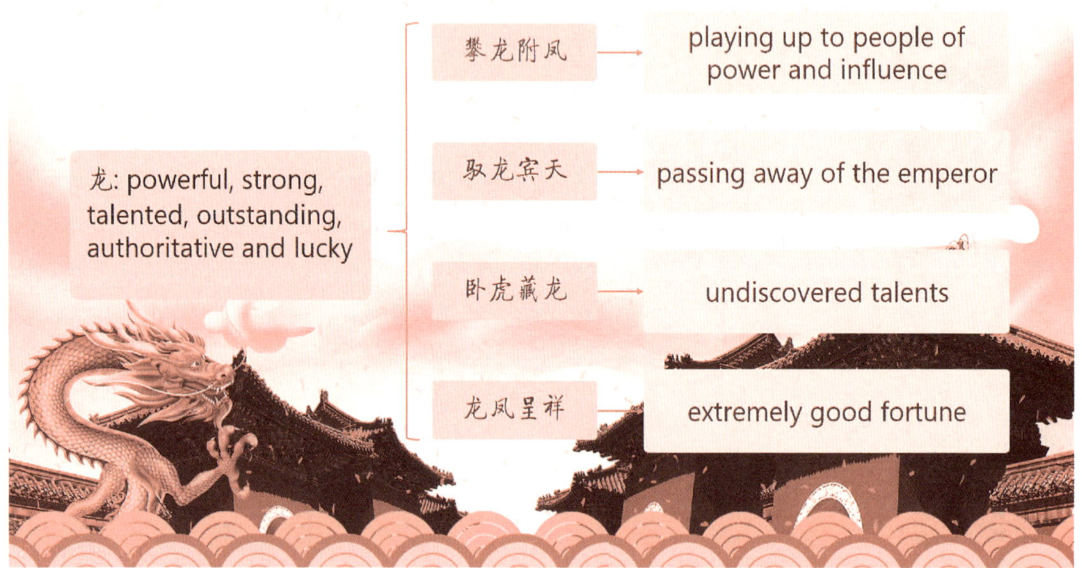

（2）文化知识延伸与翻译

中国是龙的故乡，中华民族是龙的传人，中华民族历来信龙、尊龙、祭龙，并把美好的理想和愿望寄予龙，相信龙会给人们带来好运，赐予幸福。龙是神灵和权威的象征，龙的观念、龙的形象已经渗透到社会的各个方面。	China is the home of dragons. Ethnic Chinese people are the **descendants** of Chinese dragons. Chinese people have always believed in, worshipped and offered sacrifices to dragons. They often place their beautiful ideals on, or make wishes to, dragons and believe that they will bring them good luck and happiness. The dragon is a symbol of **deity** and authority. The concept and image of the dragon have **penetrated** every aspect of Chinese society.
在中华民族的历史长河中，作为中国独特文化现象之一的龙，出现在政治、经济、文化、艺术、建筑等各个领域。从秦砖汉瓦到木雕石刻，从古寺塔林到钟鼎华	In Chinese history, the dragon, as part of China's unique cultural phenomena, appears in such various fields as politics, economy, culture, art, and architecture. Chinese dragon culture appears everywhere, from the

（续表）

表，从皇室宫殿到民间生活用品，从绘画剪纸到民间传说，到处都体现着中国龙文化。从节日风俗到娱乐风俗以及各种喜庆活动，象征吉祥的龙灯往往会出现在人们面前。龙的图像在许多工艺品、建筑物及其他器物上也大量出现，各种字体的“龙”字书法作品也在许多场合展现出来。龙象征吉祥，代表理想，代表力量。	bricks in the Qin Dynasty or the tiles in the Han Dynasty to wood or stone carvings, from ancient temples or forest of pagodas to **vessels** or bells or **ornamental** columns, from the royal palace to folk living articles, and from paintings or paper-cuts to folk legends. From festivals, entertainment to ceremonious activities, the dragon lantern, which is the symbol of **auspiciousness**, often appears in front of people. The dragon's image also appears in many arts, crafts, buildings, and other utensils. Various forms of the Chinese character, “龙”, which means dragon, are seen in calligraphy works in many occasions. The dragon is a symbol of auspiciousness, which represents ideal and strength.
在一些重大庆典中，往往也有龙的形象出现，如舞龙、赛龙舟等。龙在中国政治、文学、艺术、习俗及宗教信仰中都有着极其重要的作用。	The image of the dragon can be seen as well in such grand celebrations as dragon performances and dragon boat races. The dragon therefore plays a very important role in Chinese politics, literature, art, customs, and religious belief.

词汇

descendant [dɪ'sendənt] *n.* 后裔；子孙

deity ['deɪətɪ] *n.* 神；神性

penetrate ['penətreɪt] *v.* 渗透；穿透

vessel ['vesl] *n.* 器皿；船，舰；脉管，血管

ornamental [ˌɔːnə'mentl] *adj.* 装饰的

auspiciousness [ɔː'spɪʃəsnɪs] *n.* 吉兆；兴盛

3.3.5　讨论问题

（1）你能举出一些例子说明龙在中国政治、文学、艺术、习俗及宗教信仰中的重要作用吗？

（2）“龙”这一词在中西方的形象和联想意义相去甚远，我们在翻译时怎么样才能做到忠于原文，求得译文和原文在意思、功能、褒贬色彩方面的对等呢？

（3）汉译英的过程中我们为什么要删减汉语中的一些范畴词呢？你能自己举出一些例子吗？

3.4 梅兰竹菊(删减技巧总结)

本节我们将介绍“四君子”——梅花、兰花、竹子、菊花,并总结和复习前面两课讲到的删减法。为了让更多外国友人了解我们中国深厚的文化底蕴,了解“花中四君子”的傲、幽、坚、淡,我们需要掌握一些翻译技巧。

3.4.1 例句讲解

我们将通过翻译下面这段关于梅兰竹菊的短文来总结和巩固汉译英中的减译法。

“梅兰竹菊”,是指“梅花、兰花、竹子、菊花”四种植物,它们常被中国人誉为“花中四君子”。① 它们是中国传统水墨画中常见的题材,属于中国艺术中的花鸟画范畴。梅兰竹菊的品质分别是“傲、幽、坚、淡”,② 除此之外,它们还有“自强不息、清华其外、澹泊其中、不作媚世之态”等共同的品格特点。③ 梅花因在隆冬时节开花而闻名,它的淡香在一年中最冷的时候散发出来,很难被忽视。④ 像梅花一样,兰花的香气永远不会那样的浓烈,象征着谦逊和高贵的品格。在传统中国文化中,竹子象征着生命力与长寿。⑤ 菊花在深秋时节绽放,预示着冬天的来临,象征着抵御一切逆境的美德。因此,梅兰竹菊从古代起,就已成为中国人感物言志的精神象征,它们也是中国历代大量咏物诗歌和文人绘画中最常见的题材。

① 它们是中国传统水墨画中常见的题材,属于中国艺术中的花鸟画范畴。

在“花鸟画范畴”短语中,前面的实词“花鸟画”已经清楚地陈述了信息,后面的词语“范畴”本身属于范畴词,没有太大实际意义。因此,在翻译过程中“范畴”一词宜省略,否则会造成译文冗长。本句译文如下:

They are common subjects in traditional ink and wash paintings, belonging to the **bird-and-flower painting** in Chinese art.

② 除此之外,它们还有“自强不息、清华其外、澹泊其中、不作媚世之态”等共同的品格特点。

如前所述,汉语表达特别讲究平衡对称。若将汉语中的对称结构搬到英语中就会显得多余,所以在翻译汉语意思相近的四字词组时,只需翻译其中的一个同义

或近义词组，或进行概括化翻译。这里"自强"和"不息"意思略微相近，取其中一个即可。另外，本句话的主语是"它们"，后面的品格特点指的就是它们皆有的，"共同的"一词的语义已经暗含在上下文中，此处省略后译文更简洁。删减后译文如下：

In addition, they enjoy **humane characteristics** like "**self-reliance**, elegance in look but lightness in taste, and never bowing before power" .

③ 梅花因在隆冬时节开花而闻名。

在这句话里，"隆冬"就是指的冬天最冷的一段时间，已经把意思表达清楚了，后面的虚词"时节"只是为了汉语表达结构的完整而存在，属于范畴词，没有实际意义，因此在翻译过程中，应该省略不译。

The plum blossom is renowned for bursting into a riot of blossoms **in the dead of winter**.

④ 像梅花一样，兰花的香气永远不会那样的浓烈，象征着谦逊和高贵的品格。

Like plum blossom, orchid's fragrance is never overpowering, symbolizing **humility and nobility**.

在本例中，"谦逊"和"高贵"两个词语本身就指代品格，为了行文结构的需要，汉语中经常会和"品格"连用，这里"品格"就属于范畴词。如果照搬翻译成英语，从语法角度讲句子是没有错误的，但是译文就变得冗长烦琐。

⑤ 菊花在深秋时节绽放，预示着冬天的来临……

The chrysanthemum blooms **in the late autumn** and foretells the coming of winter ...

翻译例句⑤时应像例句③一样删减范畴词"时节"。

3.4.2 双语对照

梅兰竹菊
Plum Blossom, Orchid, Bamboo and Chrysanthemum

“梅、兰、竹、菊”，是指“梅花、兰花、竹子、菊花”四种植物，它们常被中国人誉为“花中四君子”。它们是中国传统水墨画中常见的题材，属于中国艺术中的花鸟画范畴。梅兰竹菊的品质分别是“傲、幽、坚、淡”，除此之外，它们还有“自强不息、清华其外、澹泊其中、不作媚世之态”等共同的品格特点。梅花因在隆冬时节开花而闻名，它的淡香在一年中最冷的时候散发出来，很难被忽视。

像梅花一样，兰花的香气永远不会那样的浓烈，象征着谦逊和高贵的品格。在传统中国文化中，竹子象征着生命力与长寿。菊花在深秋时节绽放，预示着冬天的来临，象征着抵御一切逆境的美德。因此，梅兰竹菊从古代起，就已成为中国人感物言志的精神象征，它们也是中国历代大量咏物诗歌和文人绘画中最常见的题材。

“Mei Lan Zhu Ju” refers to the four plants of “Plum blossom, Orchid, Bamboo and Chrysanthemum”. They are often known among Chinese as the “Four Gentlemen among Flowers”. They are common subjects in traditional ink and wash paintings, belonging to the **bird-and-flower painting** in Chinese art. The quality of the plum blossom, orchid, bamboo, and chrysanthemum is respectively that of “being proud, quiet, firm and light”. In addition, they enjoy **humane characteristics** like “**self-reliance**, elegance in look but lightness in taste, and never bowing before power”. The plum blossom is renowned for bursting into a riot of blossoms **in the dead of winter**. Its subtle fragrance spills forth at one of the coldest times of the year, making it difficult to go unnoticed.

Like plum blossom, Orchid’s fragrance is never overpowering, symbolizing **humility and nobility**. In traditional Chinese culture, bamboo is a metaphor of vitality and longevity. The chrysanthemum blooms **in the late autumn** and foretells the coming of winter, which symbolizes the virtue to withstand all adversities. Therefore, since ancient times, the Plum blossom, Orchid, Bamboo and Chrysanthemum have become spiritual symbols for the Chinese to express their sentiments and ideals. Large numbers of such plant-themed poems and literary paintings are found throughout different dynasties in Chinese history.

3.4.3 译技总结

重复在汉语中是很常见的，作为一种修辞手段，能起到强调的作用，同时在构词上起到平衡对称的作用，语音上读起来也朗朗上口，如“繁荣昌盛”“无忧无虑”“合情合理”“一生一世”等。为了行文需要，汉语中也经常使用范畴词，如“态度”“方面”“情况”“工作”“状况”等，它们用来表示行为、现象、属性等概念所属的范畴，本身没有太多实际意义。但是在将汉语翻译成英语时，汉语中的范畴词和重复使用的词语常需省略，以使译文简洁明了，符合英语的表达习惯。

我们需要注意的是，省略或删减不是把原文中的思想内容随意删去，只是删去一些

可有可无的，或者有了反嫌累赘，抑或违背译入语习惯的词，不能随意改变原文的意义。正如刘勰所云："善删者字去而意留，善敷者辞殊而义显。"（《文心雕龙·熔裁篇》）

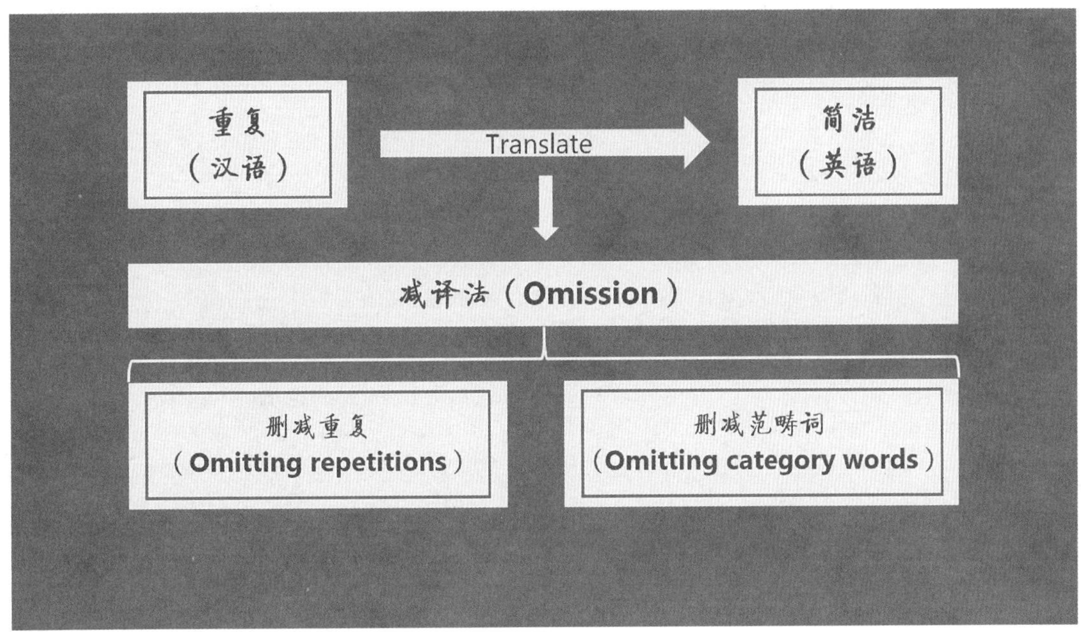

3.4.4　文化表达

(1) 文化基本知识与表达

百花争艳	flowers bloom in competition of splendor
茉莉花	jasmine
牡丹	peony
百合花	lily
月季花	Chinese rose
荷花	lotus
桂花	sweet-scented osmanthus
樱花	sakura
玫瑰花	rose
杜鹃花	azalea
山茶花	camellia
郁金香	tulip

（2）延伸阅读与翻译拓展

除了十大名花，自古以来，中国人赋予了许多花木深刻的精神意义。植物因其自身的特点，可以象征长寿、财富、繁荣等。比如，桃象征长生，竹象征韧性，石榴象征多子，葡萄象征充裕等。	Apart from the top ten famous flowers, quite a lot of plants have deep symbolic meanings over the long history of China. Due to their individual properties, certain plants can symbolize longevity, wealth, and **prosperity**. For example, the peach is the symbol of immortality, the bamboo is the symbol of **resilience**, the pomegranate is the symbol of **fertility**, the grape is the symbol of **abundance** and so on.
橘 橘谐音“吉”，所以象征吉利。春节上门拜年时除了送红包还要带上一篮橘子，这是传统习俗。	Mandarin Orange The pronunciation for “orange” in Chinese is similar to that of “auspicious”. Therefore, the orange symbolizes good luck. Tradition has it that you must bring a basket of mandarin oranges together with a red packet of gift money when visiting relatives or friends during the Chinese New Year celebrations.
桃 在中国文化中，桃最能代表长寿，因而有“仙桃”“寿桃”之美称。据古籍载，桃已有千年栽培历史，为历代皇室贡品。桃木常被古代中国人视为避邪之物。	Peach For longevity, the peach is the most symbolic of any tree or fruit in Chinese culture. Hence, it has the name of “immortal peach” and “longevity peach”. According to ancient books, the peach has a cultivation history of over 1,000 years in China, and was a **tribute** to the imperial families of past dynasties. It is also believed in ancient China that the peach wood could keep demons at bay.
梧桐 梧桐树在中国的文学作品中时常见到。传说中，梧为雄，桐为雌，梧桐同长同老、同生同死。于是，梧桐便成为伉俪深情的象征。我国有“梧桐相待老，鸳鸯合双死”之说。	Chinese **Parasol Tree**/Wutong Wutong, the Chinese parasol tree, figures prominently in literature. Ancient myth has it that “wu” is male and “tong” is female. “Wu” and “tong” grow in the same tree to live and die together. Therefore, it is an emblem of strong affection between husband and wife. As a Chinese saying goes, “wu and tong treat each other; **mandarin ducks** die together.”
松柏 松常与柏并称，且都四季常青，历严冬而不衰。中国人将其耐寒而又常青的自然特性理解为一种抗击环境变化而保持自身不变的社会品格，有坚强不屈的精神。因此，古人把松柏看作强壮、长生、自律和坚定的象征，它也成了画家笔下经常出现的主题。	Pine and Cypress Pine is often mentioned together with cypress. Both trees remain green and stand upright despite the severe cold in winter. Chinese people favor pine tree for its quality of cold resistance and being evergreen. This natural property of pine is regarded as being of moral character — being firm and unyielding. Pine, a favorite tree of Chinese painters, symbolizes **browniness** and **longevity**, and **epitomizes** self-discipline and **steadfastness**.

词汇

prosperity [prɒ'sperəti] *n.* 繁荣；成功

resilience [rɪ'zɪlɪəns] *n.* 恢复力；弹力

fertility [fə'tɪləti] *n.* 多产；肥沃

abundance [ə'bʌndəns] *n.* 充裕；丰富

tribute ['trɪbju:t] *n.* 礼物；贡物

parasol tree 梧桐树

mandarin duck 鸳鸯

brawniness ['brɔ:nɪnəs] *n.* 顽强，坚强

longevity [lɒn'dʒevətɪ] *n.* 长寿；长命

epitomize [ɪ'pɪtəmaɪz] *v.* 概括；成为……的典型

steadfastness ['stedfɑ:stnəs] *n.* 坚定不移

3.4.5 讨论问题

（1）荷花——花中仙子，在中国民间传说和象征中，荷花寓意和平、纯洁、真诚和完美。你还知道哪些在中国文化中具有较强象征意义的植物？

（2）汉译英的过程中我们为什么要删减汉语中的一些范畴词和重复的词语呢？你能举出一些例子吗？

3.5 单元练习

1. 从两个备选项中选出对汉语原句翻译得较好的一个选项。

① 黄河流经九个省区，在中国北方蜿蜒流动。

A. The Yellow River flows through nine provinces, meandering in northern China.

B. The Yellow River flows through nine provinces, meandering and flowing in northern China.

② 喜马拉雅山脉的长度超过了2 450千米，是中国另一种意义上的长城。

A. The length of the Himalayas is over 2 450 kilometres and they are the Great Wall of China in another sense.

B. Over 3,000 kilometres, the Himalayas are China's real Great Wall.

③ "黄"这个字描述的是河水浑浊的颜色。

A. The word "yellow" describes the muddy water of the river.

B. The word "yellow" describes the color of the muddy water of the river.

④ 中国古代的文人墨客认为梅花具有不畏强暴、傲然不屈的精神。

A. In ancient China, men of literature and writing viewed the plum blossom as being fearless of violence and unyielding.

B. In ancient China, men of literature and writing viewed the spirit of the plum blossom as being fearless of violence and unyielding.

⑤ 在过去几十年里，政府采取了各种措施防止灾害发生。

A. In the past few decades, the government has taken various measures to prevent disasters from happening.

B. In the past few decades, the government has taken various measures to prevent disasters.

2. 翻译下面的句子，注意运用本单元所学的翻译技巧。

① 兰花（orchid）在中国文化中象征着正直和高贵的品格。

____

② 区内有珍贵的动植物资源。

____

③ 倘若没有坚韧不拔的精神，你肯定要失败。

____

3.6 单元测验

1. 从两个备选项中选出对汉语原句翻译得较好的一个选项。(5×5分=25分)

① 舞龙始于汉代，至今不衰。这表明中国文化光辉灿烂，具有强大的生命力。

A. The Dragon Dance, first seen in the Han Dynasty, is still popular to this day. This shows the great vitality of the splendid Chinese culture.

B. The Dragon Dance, first seen in the Han Dynasty, is still popular to this day. This shows the great vitality of the splendid and brilliant Chinese culture.

② 在出土的五千年以前的文物中，人们发现了“玉猪龙”和“玉雕龙”。它们的形象比今天的龙简单许多。

A. Among the unearthed cultural relics which have the history of more than five thousand years are Jade Pig Dragon and Jade Dragon. They are much simpler than the dragon today.

B. Among the unearthed cultural relics which have the history of more than five thousand years are Jade pig dragon and Jade dragon. Their images are much simpler than the image of today's dragons.

③ 大自然中的花草树木与一个国家的传统文化、民族心理和民族精神有着千丝万缕的联系。

A. Plants have relations with the traditional culture, national psychology, and national spirit like a thousand of silk and ten thousand of threads.

B. Plants have countless ties with the traditional culture, national psychology, and national spirit.

④ 梅花不畏严寒，代表了勇气、希望和新生的品质。

A. With the characteristic of cold resistance, plum blossom stands for courage, hope and new life.

B. With the characteristic of cold resistance, plum blossom stands for the qualities of courage, hope and new life.

⑤ 这个物种处于不利地位。

A. This species is at a disadvantage.

B. This species is at a disadvantageous position.

2. 翻译下面的句子，注意运用本单元所学的翻译技巧。（3×10分=30分）

① 龙只是一种传说中虚构的动物形象。

____

② 河北地处华北地区的腹心地带，东临渤海，西倚太行，北偎燕山。

____

③ 中国气候复杂多样，既有多种多样的温度带，又有各式各样的干湿地区。

____

3. 将下面短文翻译成英语，注意运用本单元所学的翻译技巧，增补必要信息以帮助目的语读者理解。（45分）

大熊猫在海拔不同的高度觅食竹子。春夏秋冬，从海拔1 600米到3 600米，大熊猫都能随着季节交替找到适合自己口味的脆嫩清香的竹笋或枝叶。看大熊猫吃竹子是一件十分有趣的事。你看它迈着绅士步子，东瞧瞧，西嗅嗅，选择最好的竹从，调整好最舒适的姿势，用“手”将竹竿扳弯，从中间咬断，握在手中，就像小孩儿吃甘蔗（sugar cane）一样。

饮食服饰

Food, Drinks and Costume

4.1 背景介绍

Lead-in Questions

(1) What are the three essential factors by which Chinese cuisines are judged?

(2) How do you understand the saying "Garments (服装) have always been the truest reflection of social and historical scenes"?

China's long history, vast **territory** and extensive contact with other nations and cultures have given birth to the **distinctive** Chinese **culinary** art. With several thousand years of creative and **accumulative** efforts, the Chinese cuisines have become increasingly popular among more and more overseas **gourmets**, **virtually** functioning as an **envoy** of friendship in China's cultural exchanges with foreign countries.

Modern China enjoys a worldwide reputation as the "kingdom of cuisine". The **exquisite** Chinese culinary art, regarded **indisputably** as one of the world's finest culinary traditions, has **prevailed** all over the world. The nearly endless variety of natural **ingredients** and cooking methods employed in Chinese cuisine stand out unequaled in the world, which may very well account for the universal popularity of Chinese restaurants and Chinese cuisine overseas.

Generally speaking, there are three essential factors by which Chinese cooking is judged, namely "color, **aroma** and taste". "Color" refers to the **layout** and design of the dishes. "Aroma" implies not only the smell of the dish, but also the freshness of the materials and the **blending** of **seasonings**. "Taste" involves proper seasoning and fine slicing techniques. These three essential factors are achieved by careful coordination of a series of delicate activities: selecting ingredients, mixing flavors, timing and cooking, adjustment of the heat and laying out the food on the plate.

As with cuisine, clothing also enjoys a **time-honored** position in Chinese culture, because the country has a world reputation of being producers of exquisite silk. China was the first country in the world to cultivate **silkworms** and develop silk **weaving**. In ancient **feudal** society, people's rank and social status could easily be figured out from their daily dress, especially between ordinary people and the upper-class. Among the upper dominating classes, only the Emperor was assigned the color yellow and the dragon **emblem** on traditional Chinese **imperial** dress as an exclusive affirmation of their power. As for the ministers, generals, councilors and their wives, their uniforms were also restrictively regulated for how many lions or **cranes** could be **embroidered** on.

There is no "typical" Chinese clothing. If any style of clothing **epitomizes** "Chinese", it would be the cheongsam①, or *qipao*, which has evolved from ancient clothing of the Manchu ethnic minority②. Cheongsam is popular because it fits the Chinese female figure well, has simple lines and looks elegant. It is suitable for wearing all year round for both the young and old. And it can either be long or short.

Cheongsam is recognized around the world and has inspired many foreign adaptations because of its simple yet exotic lines. It is popularly worn in northern China as the wedding dress, traditionally in red. Cheongsam is usually embroidered with **elaborate** gold and silver designs. Brides in southern China wear *qipao* or two-piece dresses named *qungua* or *kwa*③, which are elaborately adorned with gold dragon and **phoenix** patterns. Dragon and phoenix *kwa* (*longfeng kwa*) is a traditional wedding dress favored by Chinese brides nowadays.

词汇

territory ['terətri] *n.* 领土；地域

distinctive [dɪ'stɪŋktɪv] *adj.* 独特的，有特色的；与众不同的

culinary ['kʌlɪnəri] *adj.* 烹饪的；烹饪用的

accumulative [ə'kjuːmjʊlətɪv] *adj.* 累计的；累积的

gourmet ['gʊəmeɪ] *n.* 美食家

virtually ['vɜːtʃʊəli] *adv.* 事实上；几乎；实质上

envoy ['envɒi] *n.* 使者；全权公使

exquisite [ɪk'skwɪzɪt] *adj.* 精致的；高雅的

indisputably [ˌɪndɪ'spjuːtəbli] *adv.* 无可争辩地

prevail [prɪ'veɪl] *v.* 盛行，流行

ingredient [ɪn'griːdɪənt] *n.* 原料

aroma [ə'rəʊmə] *n.* 芳香；香味

layout ['leɪaʊt] *n.* 布局；设计

blending ['blendɪŋ] *n.* 混合；调配

seasoning ['siːzənɪŋ] *n.* 调味品；佐料

time-honored ['taɪmˌɒnəd] *adj.* 历史悠久的；因古老而受到尊重的

silkworm ['sɪlkwɜːm] *n.* 蚕；桑蚕

weaving ['wiːvɪŋ] *n.* 编织；纺织物

feudal ['fjuːdl] *adj.* 封建制度的

emblem ['embləm] *v.* 象征

imperial [ɪm'pɪərɪəl] *adj.* 帝国的；皇帝的

crane [kreɪn] *n.* 鹤

embroider [ɪm'brɒɪdə] *v.* 装饰；镶边

epitomize [ɪ'pɪtəmaɪz] *v.* 成为……的典型

elaborate [ɪ'læbərət] *adj.* 精心制作的

phoenix ['fiːnɪks] *n.* 凤凰

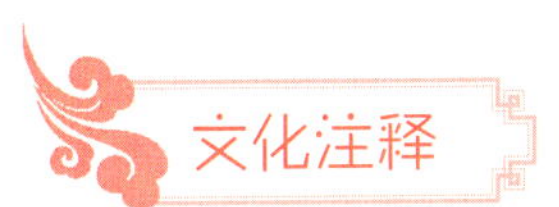

文化注释

① Cheongsam 旗袍（中国和世界华人女性的传统服装之一，曾被誉为中国女性国服。）

② Manchu ethnic minority 满族

③ Qungua or Kwa 裙褂（新娘出嫁的传统礼服，图案以龙、凤为主，传统上为手工制造。）

4.2 旗袍（词类转换Ⅰ）

当谈到中国人的日常生活必需时，我们首先想到的是衣、食、住、行，衣服位居其首。在不同的朝代、地区和民族，中国服饰的风格总是千变万化。下面要谈论的是一种典型的中国传统女性服饰。

该服饰是展现中国女性独有魅力的服装之一，在重要的场合，如国事访问、外事接待、外交事务等身着它，可以充分展现女性独特的东方魅力。

这就是旗袍（cheongsam/*qipao*）。cheongsam是英语词典中的外来语，源于广东话“长衫”的发音，后逐渐成为“旗袍”在英语中的名称。我们也可以使用*qipao*一词，它

是根据现代汉语拼音音译而成。

本节在学习旗袍简短故事的基础上还将介绍一种新的翻译技巧，即转换。转换是汉译英中常见的一种方法。它是以一种灵活的方式对词类、表达方式、句型、文化形象等进行适当转换。从本单元开始我们将讲解四种转换技巧（见下图），本节将集中讨论词类转换的一种，即将动词转换为名词和介词。

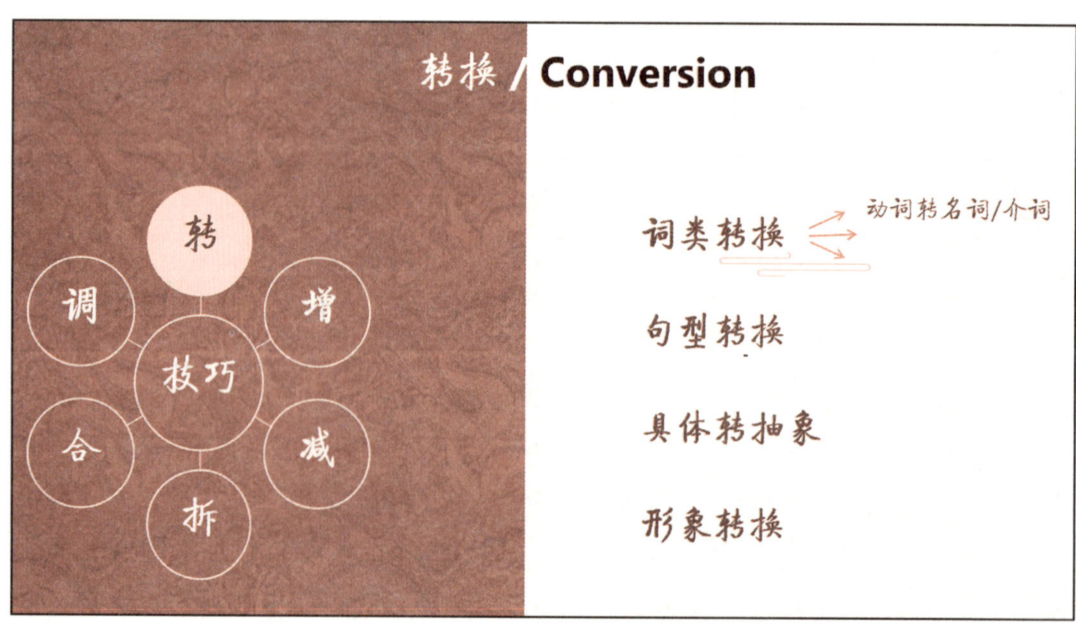

4.2.1 例句讲解

请阅读这段关于旗袍的简短介绍。

① 旗袍由上海人创造，开始流行于20世纪20年代。② 它融合满族妇女的传统袍服、中国南方服饰及西洋晚礼服的样式于一体。紧身、窄袖、立领、盘扣、开叉，③ 加上烫发和高跟鞋，旗袍充分显示了女性的曲线美与端庄。它的美含蓄细腻，活泼不张狂。

① 旗袍由上海人创造，开始流行于20世纪20年代。

第一句中三个汉语动词"创造""开始""流行"聚集在一起。但我们知道一个英语句子通常只包含一个主要谓语动词。我们可将前半句中的"创造"保留作为主句谓语动词，并将"旗袍由上海人创造"部分译作主句。后半句可以译成并列分句，或译成定语从句嵌入主句。但关键是处理好"开始"和"流行"两个连续动词。表示某事流行，我们可用一个常用英语短语"enjoy ... popularity"。"popularity"一词前面还可加形容词作修饰语，例如，"enjoy a growing popularity"表示"日益流行"，"enjoy great popularity"表示"广泛流行"。所以，在翻译"开始流行"时可将"开始"转换为形容词修饰"popularity"，得到"enjoy initial popularity"这一表达。据此，全句翻译如下：

The cheongsam, which **enjoyed initial popularity** in the 1920s, **was first designed** by people in Shanghai.

在翻译这个句子时，原汉语动词"流行"被转换为英语名词"popularity"，动词"开始"被转换为形容词，整句译文地道流畅。

② 它融合满族妇女的传统袍服、中国南方服饰及西洋晚礼服的样式于一体。

该句中"融合"是一个动词，意思是使结合。如果我们按原文结构将"融合……为一体"翻译成"combine A, B, and C into one entity"，但宾语过长而割裂了该词组，可以考虑把"combine"一词转化为名词形式，将全句译为：

It is a **combination** of the styles of Manchu women's traditional gowns, the clothing in southern China and European evening dresses.

③ 加上烫发和高跟鞋，旗袍充分显示了女性的曲线美与端庄。

第三个句子包含两个动词"加上"和"显示"。首先，我们可以把动词"显示"翻译成“display”，作为英语句子中的谓语动词。然后，另一个动词“加上”就需要转换。这里可以把它转换为介词“with”，将第一个小句整体转化为状语成分，全句翻译如下：

With permed hair and high-heeled shoes, the cheongsam fully **displays** a woman's graceful curves and dignified manner.

4.2.2 双语对照

美丽的旗袍/Beautiful Cheongsam	
旗袍由上海人**创造**，**开始流行**于20世纪20年代。它**融合**满族妇女的传统袍服、中国南方服饰及西洋晚礼服的样式于一体。紧身、窄袖、立领、盘扣、开叉，**加上**烫发和高跟鞋，旗袍充分**显示**了女性的曲线美与端庄。它的美含蓄细腻，活泼而不张狂。	The cheongsam, which **enjoyed initial popularity** in the 1920s, **was first designed** by people in Shanghai. It is a **combination** of the styles of Manchu women's traditional gowns, the clothing in southern China and European evening dresses. It is a close-fitting dress with narrower cuffs, stand-up collar, coiled buttons, and slits. **With** permed hair and high-heeled shoes, the cheongsam fully **displays** a woman's graceful curves and dignified manner. Its beauty is implicit and delicate, vibrant yet reserved.

4.2.3 译技总结

通过上面短文的汉英对比，我们能清楚地看出一些汉语动词在翻译过程中被转换成英语的名词或介词。但是为什么译者会进行这种转换呢？根据对英语词汇的总体调

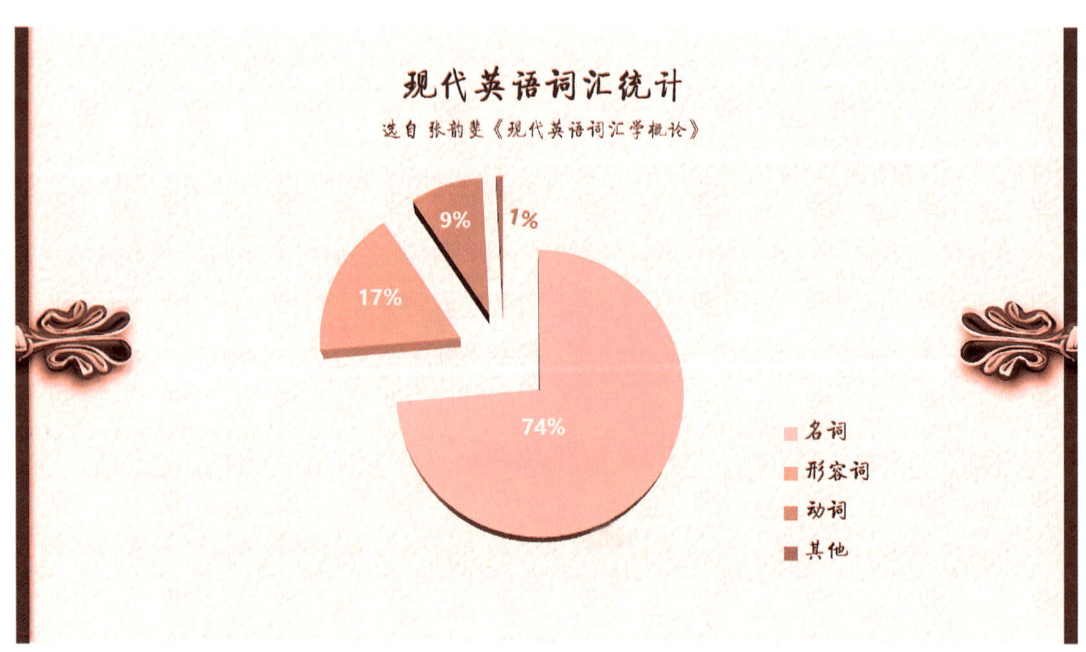

查，现代英语中近四分之三的词汇都是名词，可以说英语更像是以名词为主体的静态型语言。

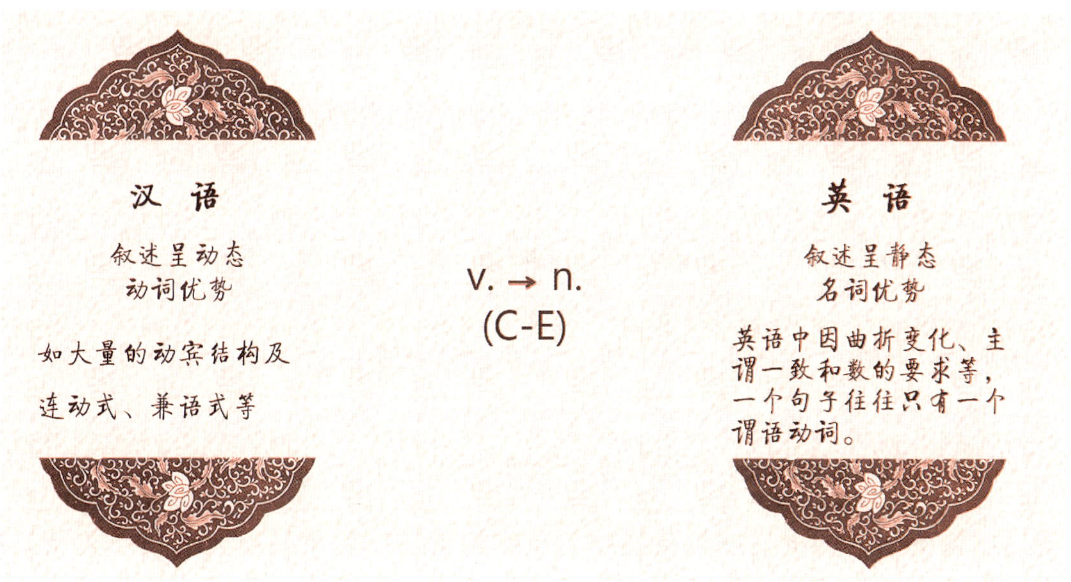

大量比较研究发现汉语更像是一种动态语言，动词在一个汉语单句中经常被连续使用；而英语则是一种偏静态的语言，大量使用名词或名词性短语。因此，翻译时将动词转换为名词是汉译英的一种常见做法。我们再来看一些例子：

④ 旗袍在融合了满族妇女服饰和西方服饰的元素后，最终形成了一种新型女装样式。

As a result of the **incorporation** of Western clothing elements into Manchu women's clothing, *qipao* eventually emerged as a new type of female garment.

⑤ 它充分考虑东方女子身材的特点，突出了女子身材的曲线美。

It takes full **consideration** of the characteristics of Chinese women's figures to best display their grace and dignity.

此外，由于介词和名词之间的紧密联系以及英语频繁使用介词的特点，将汉语动词转换为英语介词也是一种常见的做法。转换后译文能更好地体现英语的行文风格，更加简洁自然。

请看下面的例子：

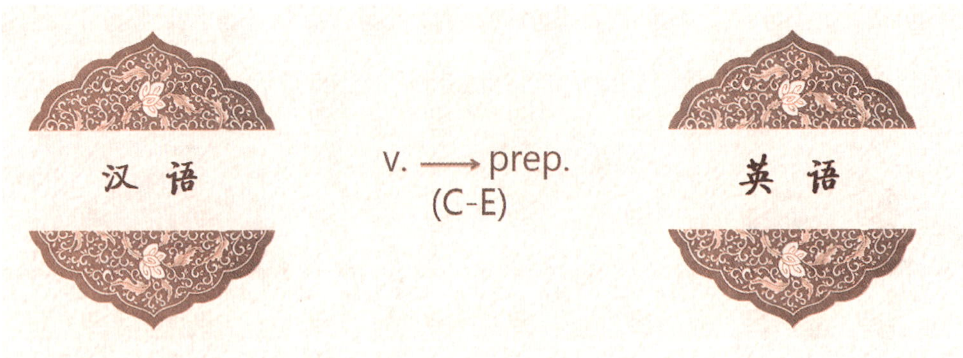

介词功用：多位于名词或名词短语前，表示句子成分间的关系。

英语介词：相对活跃，且常带动作含义。

⑥ 旗袍是一种雅致的中国服装，源于中国的满族。

Qipao, as an exquisite Chinese dress, originates from China's Manchu nationality.

⑦ 她们让世界各地的观众欣赏到身穿旗袍的中国女性的美。

They have provided a chance for world audiences to appreciate the charm of Chinese women in cheongsam.

那么，何时使用两种转换呢？以下表格总结了常见情况。

汉译英 动转名/介常见类别	例　句
一句话出现多个汉语动词	• 例1、例3、例4、例5、例6、例7等
汉语动词已有对应的英语派生名词	• 例2、例4、例5 • 看到我们的喷气式飞机，听见隆隆的机声，令我特别神往。 The sight and sound of our jet planes filled me with special longing.
汉语中表人物性格与行为的词(-er, -or)	• 她老是说谎。 She is a great liar. • 他总喝很多酒。 He is a heavy drinker.
汉语标题、书名中的动词	• 窥探生物 Animal Camera • 企鹅群里有特务 Penguins: Spy in the Huddle • 寻找神话和英雄 In Search of Myths and Heroes

4.2.4 文化表达

（1）文化基本知识与表达

众所周知，旗袍是中国风服饰的代表。“中国风”也被称为“Chinoiserie”，是一个源自法语的外来词。当谈到中国风服饰时，我们不仅有旗袍，还有其他服装，比如中国古代的汉服、民国时期的文明学生装、中山装、少数民族的精美服饰，还有当代的唐装。

当代唐装并不是指唐朝流行的服饰。对比下面两张图片，其区别显而易见，当代唐装实际上是汉服的一种样式。

汉服是汉族的传统服饰。在古代，汉人设计了两种基本样式的服装：衣裳和上下连属。第二种以“深衣”为典型代表，是一种全长的、衣和裳连为一体的服装。深衣对后来众多的中国服装款式都产生了深远的影响。

深衣
Shenyi
辛追深衣（马王堆汉墓帛画）
Shenyi on the paintings on silk in tombs of Han Dynasty in Mawangdui

近年来，汉服重回大众视野，逐渐成为一种“新”的流行服饰。我们经常会在重要的场合看到它，也偶尔会在大街上看到它。中国的年轻人，特别是青少年，甚至发起了一项名为“汉服复兴运动”(Movement of Reviving Han Chinese Clothing)的活动，以弘

扬和发展我们的传统文化。

（2）文化知识与表达拓展

旗袍（cheongsam）是独具中国特色的女性服饰，在高端时尚的国际世界中日益流行。它上身容易，穿着舒适，而且特别适合中国女性的身材。旗袍衣领高，领部闭合，根据季节和品味不同，旗袍有短袖、中袖和长袖可供选择。旗袍右侧系扣，胸部宽松，腰部合身。它的好处在于可以使用多种材质，并以不同长度制作，因此在休闲和正式场合都可穿着。无论身处何种场合，旗袍都给人带来一种简洁而安静的魅力，显得优雅而整洁。

The cheongsam is a female dress with distinctive Chinese features and enjoys a growing popularity in the international world of high-end fashion. Easy to slip on and comfortable to wear, the cheongsam fits well the female Chinese figure. Its neck is high, **collar** closed, and its **sleeves** may be short, long or of medium length, depending on seasons and tastes. The dress is **buttoned** on the right side, with a loose **chest** and a fitting **waist**. The beauty of the cheongsam is that, made of different materials and to varying lengths, it can be worn either on casual or formal occasions. In either case, it creates an impression of simple and quiet charm, elegance, and **neatness**.

词汇

collar ['kɒlə(r)] *n.* 衣领

sleeve [sliːv] *n.* 袖子

button ['bʌtn] *v.* 在……上装纽扣

chest [tʃest] *n.* 胸部

waist [weɪst] *n.* 腰；腰部

neatness ['niːtnəs] *n.* 干净；整洁

4.2.5 讨论问题

(1)你认为哪种风格的服装最能代表中国传统服饰文化?

(2)为什么要将汉语中的动词译为英语名词呢?你能举出一些例子吗?

4.3 川菜(词类转换Ⅱ)

本节将讨论川菜并继续讨论翻译中的词类转换。

《三国志》有云:“礼之初,始之饮食。”《礼记》有云:“国以民为本,民以食为天。”可见食物对百姓和国家的发展至关重要。中国菜美味、营养又诱人,中国餐馆遍布世界各地。中国菜是中国灿烂文化的一面。在所有的菜系里,川菜脱颖而出,颇受欢迎。

4.3.1 例句讲解

本节将学习用英语介绍川菜,为此我们需要使用一些翻译技巧,如学习词类的转换方法。请看下面的短文,我们选择了一些句子作为讲解。

①号称天府之国的四川,也是饮食的天国。在四川,几乎走进任何一家小饭馆,都可吃到一顿味道鲜美而又价格便宜的饭菜。②四川菜使用的原料并不特别,但它的调味品却很别致。③四川菜口味偏辣,但那并不是它的特点,湖南菜、贵州菜也辣。

四川菜是辣中带麻，麻才是川菜独有的风味。四川有被称为“三椒”的花椒、辣椒、胡椒配料，④ 还有风味独特的豆瓣酱，又有一套独特的制作方法，这才使川菜风靡天下。川菜中最有名的有四川火锅、宫保鸡丁、麻婆豆腐等。⑤ 在寒冷的冬天里，吃火锅是一件惬意十足的事情。

① 号称天府之国的四川，也是饮食的天国。

在这句话里，“饮食的”是一个形容词短语，用来修饰“天国”。“饮食”我们可用“cuisine”，“天国”我们可用“paradise”，但两个都是名词。如果我们将“饮食的天国”直接翻译成“cuisine storehouse”，在英语里显得难以理解。这里我们可以利用“of”结构来翻译“……的”，也就是将“饮食的”转化为介词词组，置于“storehouse”之后，作后置修饰语。词类转化后本句译文如下：

Sichuan, known as nature’s storehouse, is also a paradise **of cuisine**.

② 四川菜使用的原料并不特别，但它的调味品却很别致。

此句中“四川菜使用的”是一个较长形容词性短语，可以考虑将其转变为介词词组“for Sichuan cuisine”并后置，用作“ingredients”的后置限定语。

The ingredients **for Sichuan cuisine** are simple but the spices used are quite different.

③ 四川菜口味偏辣，但那并不是它的特点，湖南菜、贵州菜也辣。

第3例中，译者采取了较为灵活的方法。“四川菜口味偏辣”中的“辣”是形容词作谓语，译者将此形容词转换为名词短语“being hot and spicy”作英语句子的主语。译者又将汉语名词“特点”转换为英语动词“distinguish”，作为英语译文的谓语。经历这些转换后，原文的三个并列短句转换成了只有一个主谓动词、层级分明的英文长句。这样的译文从句式结构上看更符合译入语风格。整句翻译如下：

Yet just **being hot and spicy** does not necessarily **distinguish** it from other hot and spicy cuisines such as those from Hunan and Guizhou cuisines.

④ 还有风味独特的豆瓣酱，又有一套独特的制作功夫，这才使川菜风靡天下。

本例中“风靡”是汉语使动句中的动词，使动句是汉语常用的一种特殊结构，一般难以直接英译。"风靡"一词让我们容易联想到英语中"popular"或"famous"等形容词，"风靡天下"可以这样翻译"be famous and popular across the world"。在将动词转化为形容词短语后，整句话翻译如下：

Using fermented bean sauce and a set of unique **cooking** methods, Sichuan Cuisine is now **famous and popular** across the world.

⑤ 在寒冷的冬天里，吃火锅是**一件惬意十足的事情**。

如果我们严格按照汉语进行字对字的翻译，那么译文将是：In the cold winter, eating Hot Pot is a very delightful thing. 这样的译文虽然语法上没有错，意思也能被理解，但是用词用句风格俨然有汉语的深深烙印。值得指出的是，"sth. is a very delightful thing"显得啰唆，其核心含义是"sth. is delightful"，因而此处可以省掉"a"和"thing"两个无重要意义的词语。在经过其他变化后我们得到以下译文：

It is **very delightful** to eat Hot Pot in the cold winter.

在翻译此句过程中我们实际上将名词性短语"一件惬意十足的事情"转换为形容词短语"very delightful"。经过这样的词性转变译文更加简洁地道。

4.3.2 双语对照

川菜/Sichuan Cuisine	
号称天府之国的四川，也是**饮食的**天国。在四川，几乎走进任何一家小饭馆，都可吃到一顿味道鲜美而又价格便宜的饭菜。**四川菜使用的**原料并不特别，但它的调味品却很别致。四川菜口味偏**辣**，但那并不是它的**特点**，湖南菜、贵州菜也辣。 四川菜是辣中带麻，麻才是川菜独有的风味。四川有被称为"三椒"的花椒、辣椒、胡椒配料，还有风味独特的豆瓣酱，又有一套独特的**制作**方法，这才使川菜**风靡**天下。川菜中最有名的有四川火锅、宫保鸡丁、麻婆豆腐等。在寒冷的冬天里，吃火锅是**一件惬意十足的事情**。	Sichuan, known as nature's storehouse, is also a storehouse **of cuisine**. Here each and every restaurant provides delicious yet economical culinary fare. The ingredients **for Sichuan cuisine** are simple but the spices used are quite different. Sichuan cuisine is famous for its spicy and hot food. Yet just **being hot and spicy** does not necessarily **distinguish** it from other hot and spicy cuisines such as those from Hunan and Guizhou cuisines. What is really special about Sichuan cuisine is the use of Sichuan pepper, the taste of which leaves a feeling of numbness on one's tongue. Besides this unique spice, Sichuan dishes are usually prepared with other spices like chili pepper. Using fermented bean sauce and a set of unique **cooking** methods, Sichuan cuisine is now **famous and popular** across the world. The most famous Sichuan dishes are Sichuan Hot Pot, Kung Pao Chicken and Mapo Tofu, etc. It is **very delightful** to eat Hot Pot in the cold winter.

4.3.3 译技总结

通过上面原文本和目的语文本的比较，我们可以清楚地看到一些单词的词性在翻译过程中进行了转换。由于汉英两种语言的差别，英译汉或汉译英时不能够照搬原文词类，而应根据具体需要进行适当转换。在上述段落中译者将形容词转换为介词或名词，将名词转换为动词或形容词，以及将动词转换为形容词。当然因为语法、修辞和风格的需要，汉译英中还有其他一些词类需要转换。

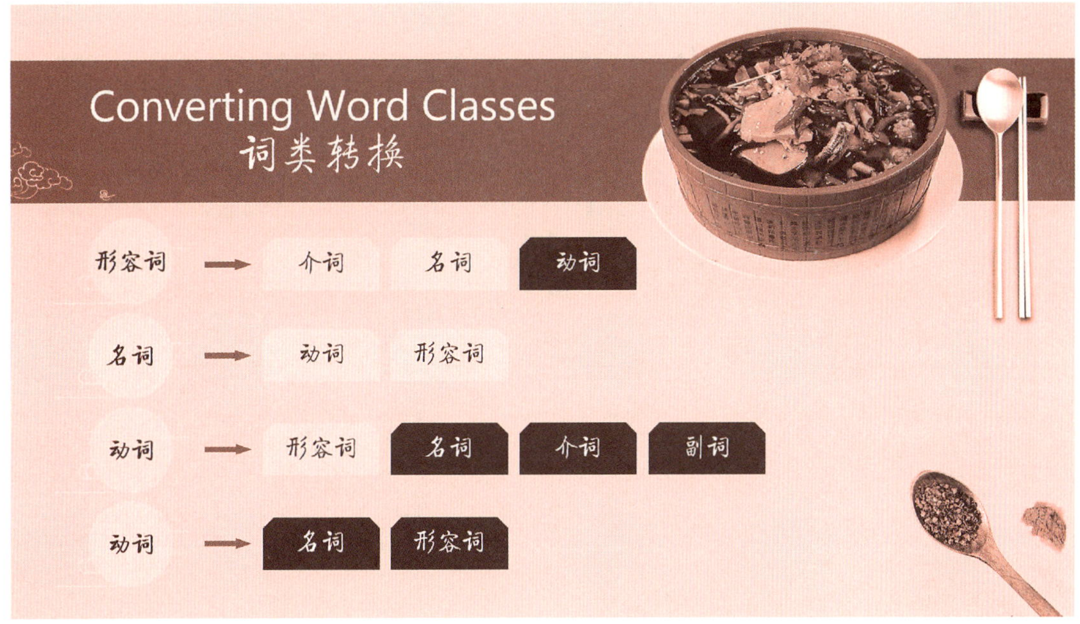

例如，我们可以将形容词转换为名词，动词转换为副词，副词转换为名词或者形容词。

⑥ 他的新菜十分成功。

His new dish is a great success.

⑦ 烹饪节目还在进行着。

The cooking show is still on.

⑧ 他兴奋地接受了她的邀请。

He accepted her invitation with excitement.

⑨ 你能准确地把这个菜名翻译出来吗?

Can you give an accurate translation of the name of the dish?

4.3.4 文化表达

(1)文化基本知识与表达

中国菜的特点是其特殊的佐料、别具一格的烹饪技巧、多样化的烹饪食材和独特的风味。

中国菜因色、香、味俱全而享有盛誉。

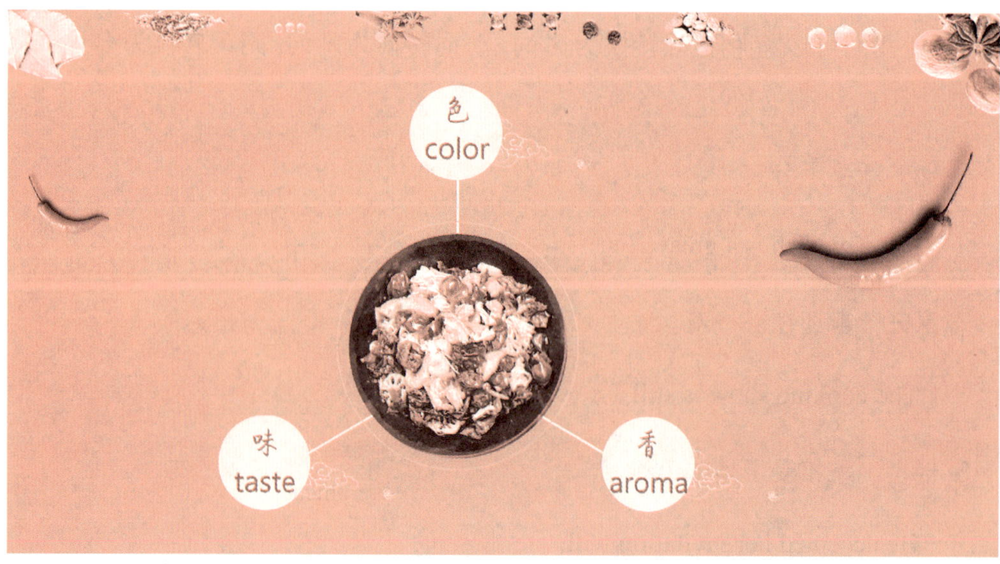

由于中国幅员辽阔、物产丰富、气候多变、生活习惯多样等因素，来自不同地方的食物风味差异很大，因此形成了各地区种类丰富、特色各异的美食。其中主要的有鲁菜、川菜、苏菜和粤菜，它们被统称为中国四大菜系。

几乎每个菜系都有自己的招牌菜。鲁菜有一特色菜叫一品豆腐(Steamed Tofu Stuffed with Vegetables)，即蔬菜馅的豆腐。它是将蔬菜巧妙地塞入蒸好的豆腐中。川菜中有一名菜叫宫保鸡丁(Kungpao Chicken)。它以四川总督丁宝桢的名字命名，丁宝桢被授予“太子少保”的称号，也被称为“宫保”。在苏菜中，所有中国人都知道的一道名菜是东坡肉(Dongpo Pork)。这道菜以北宋伟大词人苏东坡的名字命名，其在杭州任知州时创造了这道名菜。广东省简称粤，位于中国南部，粤菜以其独创性和精致的烹饪过程而闻名。其著名的白切鸡(Plain Chicken)受到了全国人民的喜爱。

中国人喜欢各种风格的美食，我们对饮食的热爱使我们的母语有了丰富多彩的表达。简单的“吃”字凭借众多扩展的含义，可能已经成为汉语中最复杂的词语之一。

吃亏	to be taken advantage of
吃耳光	to be slapped in the face
吃子弹	to be hit by a bullet
吃赌饭	to make a living in a gambling trade
吃皇粮	to get one’s salary from the government

（2）文化知识与表达拓展

川菜是中国八大菜系之一，以火辣著称。但认为川菜只专注于火辣是一种常见的误解。邓扶霞说："有人认为川菜只有火辣，这是一种刻板印象。当然，四川人喜欢使用辣椒和花椒——让你的唇齿发麻——但这只是一个方面。川菜有复杂的、多层次的味道。川菜真正有趣的地方在于它有多种味道。我在那里学习厨艺的时候，我们学到了23种复杂的味道。这就像法国的经典酱汁，只是甜、酸、辣、麻的比例各不相同。"尽管川菜是中国最受欢迎的地方菜系之一，但直到20年前，川菜才真正开始在西方流行起来。

Sichuan cuisine is one of the eight major cuisines of China and is famous for its **fiery** dishes, but it is a common **misconception** that the cuisine focuses only on spiciness. Fuchsia Dunlop says, "There's the **stereotype** that it is all just fiery and hot, and of course Sichuanese love using chilies and Sichuan **pepper** (*huajiao*) — with its lip **tingling** sensation — but that's just one part of the story. Sichuan cuisine is of complex **multilayered** flavors. The really interesting thing about Sichuan cuisine is its diversity of flavors. When I was studying to be a chef there, we learned 23 complex flavors. It is like French classic sauces, but with different balances of sweet, sour, spicy and tingly." While Sichuan cuisine is one of the most popular regional cuisines in China, it only really caught on in the West 20 years ago.

词汇

fiery ['faɪərɪ] *adj.* 燃烧般的

misconception [ˌmɪskən'sepʃn] *n.* 误解

stereotype ['sterɪətaɪp] *n.* 刻板形象

pepper ['pepə(r)] *n.* 胡椒

tingling ['tɪŋglɪŋ] *n.* 麻刺感

multilayered [ˌmʌltɪ'leɪəd] *adj.* 多层的

4.3.5 讨论问题

（1）你能否用英语介绍一两道川菜中的名菜？

（2）你能给出两三个与本节相关的词类转化的例子吗？

4.4 茶文化（句型转换）

本节将介绍中国茶文化以及翻译技巧中的句型转换。茶起源于中国古代，在中国人民日常生活中起着重要的作用。如古语有云："早晨开门七件事：柴、米、油、盐、酱、醋、茶。"

茶是中国古代文人眼中的宝贝，它被列入文人雅士所钟爱的"八雅"之物，即琴、棋、书、画、诗、酒、花、茶。

茶在中国与世界文化交流中举足轻重。17世纪到20世纪初期，继丝绸之路后再兴起了一条万里茶道，以中国武夷为起点，以俄罗斯圣彼得堡为终点，全长共14 000公里，是一条贯穿南北、融通中外的茶叶、货物贸易之路。

4.4.1 例句讲解

请阅读以下有关茶的短文，并了解如何通过转换某些句子结构将其正确地翻译成英语。我们将重点探讨标号的三个句子。

"你要茶还是要咖啡？"是用餐人常被问到的问题。许多西方人会选咖啡，而中国人会选茶。① 相传，中国的一位帝王于五千年前发现了茶，并用来治病。② 在明清期间，茶馆遍布全国。③ 饮茶在6世纪传到日本，但直到17、18世纪才传到欧美。如今，茶是世界上最流行的饮料(beverage)之一。茶是中国的民族饮品，也是中国传统文化的重要组成部分。

① 相传，中国的一位帝王于五千年前发现了茶，并用来治病。

要翻译汉语"相传"一词，我们最好使用英语的被动结构，因为我们不知道是谁确切地说了这一点。我们可以使用英语常用的被动句型"It is said that"或"It is reported that"。翻译此句时我们将汉语的主动结构转换成了英语的被动结构。

It is said that 5,000 years ago, an emperor in China discovered tea and used it to cure diseases.

② 在明清（the Ming and Qing Dynasties）期间，茶馆遍布全国。

在第二句中，"茶馆"是没有生命的物体，不能像人类一样执行动作。所以，在这里"遍布全国"我们可以理解为在全国各地都可以看见，因而最好使用英语中的被动结构"be found/seen"来翻译句子。经过主动转被动后，全句翻译如下：

In the Ming and Qing Dynasties, tea houses could be found all over the country.

③ 饮茶在6世纪传到日本，但直到17、18世纪才传到欧美。

在第三个例子中，"饮茶"（tea-drinking）一词处于主语位置，动词"传到"（introduce）在谓语中使用了两次。但是饮茶是被人们传到国外的，而不是茶自己传到国外。因此，英译时最好将两个汉语小句转换成英语被动句。

汉语句子"直到……才"的后半部分是一个肯定结构。为了将其翻译成地道的英语，我们最好遵循英语惯用法，使用否定句结构"not ... until"来更好地重现汉语句子的含义。此示例展示了翻译中正反转换的翻译技巧。整个句子在使用两种转化技巧后翻译如下：

Tea-drinking was introduced to Japan in the sixth century, but was not introduced to Europe and America until the 17th and 18th centuries.

4.4.2　双语对照

茶/Tea	
"你要茶还是要咖啡？"是用餐人常被问到的问题。许多西方人会选咖啡，而中国人会选茶。相传，中国的一位帝王于五千年前发现了茶，并用来治病。在明清期间，茶馆遍布全国。饮茶在6世纪传到日本，但直到17、18世纪才传到欧美。如今，茶是世界上最流行的饮料（beverage）之一。茶是中国的民族饮品，也是中国传统文化的重要组成部分。	"Tea or coffee?" Diners are frequently asked this question. Many Westerners may choose coffee, while the Chinese may prefer tea. It is said that 5,000 years ago, an emperor in China discovered tea and used it to cure diseases. In the Ming and Qing Dynasties, tea houses could be found all over the country. Tea-drinking was introduced to Japan in the sixth century, but was not introduced to Europe and America until the 17th and 18th centuries. Since then, tea has become one of the most popular beverages in the world. It is the national drink of China and an important part of traditional Chinese culture.

4.4.3 译技总结

在前一节短文的翻译过程中，我们将三个汉语主动结构转换为英语被动结构，还将一个汉语肯定句转换为英语否定句。因为两种语言的差异，我们经常需要将汉语主动句结构转换为英语被动语态，并在肯定句和否定句之间进行转换。现将这两种常见的句型转化技巧总结如下。

第一种是主被动转换。汉语和英语都有主动和被动句子结构。但是与英语相比，汉语使用被动句结构的频率要低得多，故而译者经常需要将汉语主动句转换为英语被动句。下图是对汉译英主、被动句转换几种典型情形的归纳。

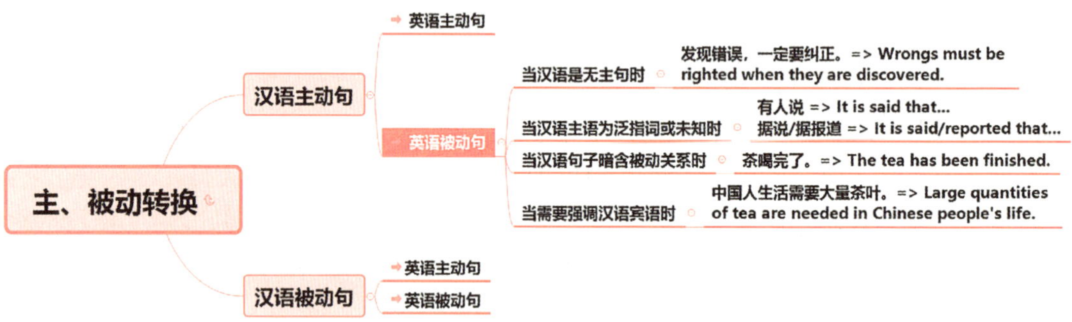

第二种是正反转换。翻译时我们常对肯定句和否定句进行转换，或是因为更好地遵循译入语表达习惯，或是因为要特意强调某部分，或是为了让译文更准确、简洁地表达原文意思。

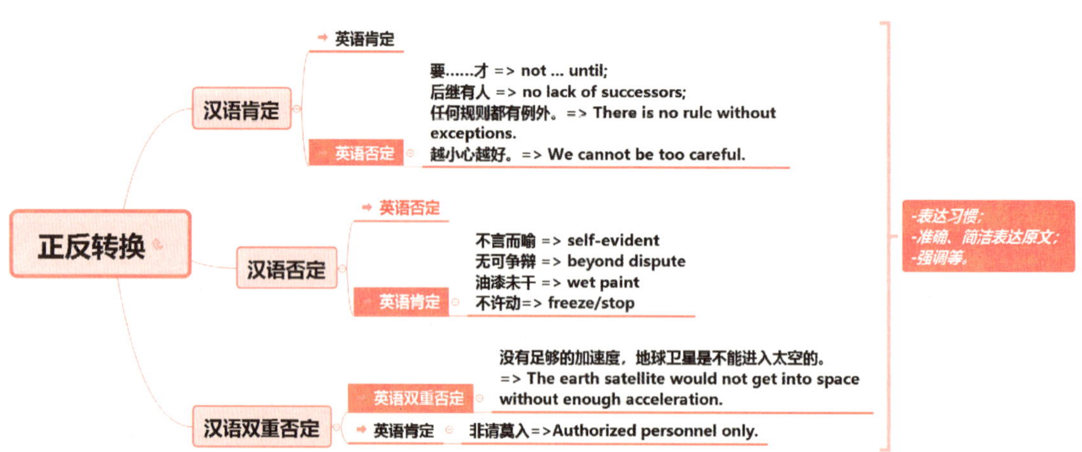

4.4.4　文化表达

(1)文化基本知识与表达

根据茶的发酵程度，中国茶大致可分为六种。完全未经发酵的是绿茶，发酵茶包含白茶、黄茶、乌龙茶、红茶和黑茶，其中黑茶具有最高的发酵度。

Types of Tea in Terms of the Degree of Fermentation

饮茶时有一套完整的工具。除了茶杯，还有其他辅助工具：茶筒、茶则、茶匙、茶夹、茶针和茶漏，这六种工具被称为“茶道六君子”。

除了茶叶的类型和饮茶工具，饮茶的步骤也很重要。在冲泡茶之前，我们需要置茶和洗茶。我们在品茗之前可以观赏茶的香气、颜色、形状等。

饮茶不仅有益于健康，还具有许多社会功能，比如表达尊重（paying respect）、表示感激（expressing gratitude）和表达歉意（making apologies）。这些功能体现了中国茶道的核心精神"和"，这种精神为佛、儒、道三家共有。

（2）文化知识与表达拓展

中国是世界上最大的茶叶生产国之一。茶在中国有悠久的历史。相传，神农非常善于耕种。一天，他在户外煮水时有些叶子落入水中，水随即变黄。神农尝了尝。他发现泡过这种叶子的水味道更佳。 一条古道使茶在中国各地广为流传，这条路便是茶马古道。茶马古道有两条主要路线。一条始于四川省，另一条始于云南省。两条道路都止于西藏。	China is the biggest tea producers in the world. Tea has a long history in China. According to old stories, there was an emperor named Shennong who was good at farming. One day, when he was boiling water outdoors, some leaves fell in and turned the water yellow. Shennong drank the yellowed water and discovered that it tasted much better. One ancient road makes tea popular all over China and it is called the Ancient Tea-horse Road. It has two main routes: one begins in Sichuan province and the other in Yunnan province, and both of them end in Tibet.

4.4.5 讨论问题

（1）茶马古道和万里茶道有什么异同？

（2）茶和咖啡有什么共同点和区别？

（3）你能结合具体的汉译英例子谈谈主被动句型转换的优点吗？

4.5 单元练习

1. 从两个备选项中选出对汉语原句翻译得较好的一个选项。

① 旗袍是一种具有中国特色的女装。

A. The cheongsam is a female dress with distinctive Chinese features.

B. The cheongsam is a female dress has distinctive Chinese features.

② 湘菜以辛辣味浓为特点。

A. Hunan cuisine has the thick and pungent flavor feature.

B. Hunan cuisine is characteristic of thick and pungent flavor.

③ 那位著名小说家酷爱川菜。

A. That well-known novelist is a great lover of Sichuan cuisine.

B. That well-known novelist loves Sichuan cuisine ardently.

④ 丝绸时髦了，人造纤维过时了。

A. Silk is in and synthetic fibers are out.

B. Silk has become voguish, synthetic fibers have become outdated.

⑤ 辣椒是川菜中必需的。

A. Chilies are absolute necessary in Sichuan cuisine.

B. Chilies are an absolute necessity in Sichuan cuisine.

2. 翻译下面的句子，注意运用本单元所学的翻译技巧。

① 烹饪节目还在进行。

____

② 有人说早在五千年前中国就有了茶树（tea-shrub）。

____

③ 旗袍是一种雅致的（exquisite）中国服装，源于中国的满族（Manchu nationality）。

____

4.6 单元测验

1. 单项选择。从两个备选项中选出对汉语原句翻译得较好的一个选项。（5×5分=25分）

① 中国是一个文化历史悠久的（time-honored）国度。

A. China is a country with a time-honored civilization.

B. China is a country which has a time-honored civilization.

② 旗袍在中国民族服装中独领风骚，久盛而不衰。

A. The cheongsam developed its own trend, which has not declined.

B. The cheongsam developed its own trend, which has been long lasting.

③ 在清代，旗袍是皇室女性穿的宽松长袍。

A. In the Qing Dynasty, the cheongsam was a loose robe which was dressed by the royal women.

B. In the Qing Dynasty, the cheongsam was a loose robe for the royal women.

④ 无论中国人走到哪里，都不会改掉喝茶的习惯。

A. Wherever Chinese go, the custom of drinking tea follows.

B. No matter where Chinese people go, they will not give up the custom of drinking tea.

⑤ 旗袍充分考虑东方女子身材的特点，突出了女子气质的优雅高贵。

A. The cheongsam takes full consideration of the characteristics of Chinese women's figures to best display their grace and dignity.

B. The cheongsam considers the characteristics of Chinese women's figures fully to best display their grace and dignity.

2. 翻译下面的句子，注意运用本单元所学的翻译技巧。(3×10分=30分)

① 她的新菜十分成功。

____

② 你能准确地译出这些茶具的名称吗？

____

③ 他老是说谎。

____

3. 将下面短文翻译成英语，注意运用本单元所学的翻译技巧，增补必要信息以帮助目的语读者理解。(45分)

茅台酒(Moutai)产生于距今2 000多年前的汉代(the Han Dynasty)。茅台酒以色清透明(clear and transparent)、口感柔绵(smooth)、清冽甘爽(fresh and cool)、回香持久(long-lasting)等特点而扬名天下。如今茅台享有“国酒”称号。

____

____

古今建筑
Ancient and Modern Chinese Architecture

5.1 背景介绍

Lead-in Questions

(1) Can you introduce one famous Chinese architectural miracle to an English-speaking friend?

(2) What are the general features of traditional Chinese architecture?

Traditional Chinese Architecture: The Beauty of Balance and Symmetry

Chinese architecture enjoys a long history and great achievements and **boasts** many architectural **miracles** such as the Great Wall. In the process of its development, superior architectural techniques and artistic design were combined to make unique Chinese architecture one of the three greatest architectural systems①.

Ancient Chinese architecture is an independent art featuring wooden structures. It consists of various roof **molding**, **upturned eaves** and wings, **brackets**② with paintings, **vermilion pillars** and golden roofs, **ornamental** gates and gardening. All of these embody the **maturity** and artistic appeal of Chinese architecture.

The combination of units of space in traditional Chinese architecture follows the principles of balance and **symmetry**. The main structure is the **axis**, and the secondary structures are positioned as two wings on each side to form the main rooms and yard. The

construction of **residences**, official buildings, temples, and palaces follows these basic principles. The **distribution** of **interior** space③ reflects Chinese social and ethical values. For instance, in traditional residential buildings, members of a family are assigned living quarters based on the family **hierarchy**. The master of the house occupies the main room, and the elder members of the master's family live in the **compound** in the back. The younger members of the family live in the wings to the left and right; and those with **seniority** on the left and the others on the right.

As with many other elements of the Chinese culture, traditional Chinese architecture has been **interwoven** with modern technology. Although many traditional buildings still exist, almost all new buildings are built in Western style. It is not uncommon to see **skyscrapers** in large cities in China.

词汇

boast [bəʊst] *v.* 以有……而自豪

miracle ['mɪrəkl] *n.* 奇迹

molding ['məʊldɪŋ] *n.* 成型；造型

upturned [ˌʌp'tɜːnd] *adj.* 朝上的；向上翘的

eave [iːv] *n.* 屋檐

bracket ['brækɪt] *n.* 斗拱

vermilion [və'mɪlɪən] *adj.* 朱红色的

pillar ['pɪlə(r)] *n.* 柱子

ornamental [ˌɔːnə'mentl] *adj.* 装饰的；装饰性的

maturity [mə'tʃʊərəti] *n.* 成熟

symmetry ['sɪmətri] *n.* 对称(性)

axis ['æksɪs] *n.* 轴线

residence ['rezɪdəns] *n.* 住宅；住处

distribution [ˌdɪstrɪ'bjuːʃn] *n.* 分配

interior [ɪn'tɪrɪə(r)] *adj.* 内部的；里面的

hierarchy ['haɪərɑːki] *n.* 等级制度

compound ['kɒmpaʊnd] *n.* 混合物；有围栏的场地

seniority [ˌsiːnɪ'ɒrəti] *n.* 年长；资历较高的人

interweave [ˌɪntə'wiːv] *v.* (使)交织

skyscraper ['skaɪskreɪpə(r)] *n.* 摩天楼

文化注释

① the three greatest architectural systems 三大建筑体系(中国建筑、欧洲建筑和伊斯兰建筑被认为是世界三大建筑体系，又因中国建筑和欧洲建筑延续时代最长、流域最

广,成就也就更为辉煌。)

② bracket 斗拱(中国建筑特有的一种结构。在立柱和横梁交接处,从柱顶上加的一层层探出成弓形的承重结构叫拱,拱与拱之间垫的方形木块叫斗,合称斗拱。)

③ the distribution of interior space 内部空间的分配(内部空间的分配反映出中国的社会观和伦理观。在传统的住宅建筑中,一家之主居主屋,长辈居住在后面建筑,家里年轻成员则居住在左右两翼,资历较高的居左侧,其他人则住在右侧。)

5.2 长城(具体转抽象)

中国建筑具有悠久的历史与光辉的成就。从秦朝气势恢宏的兵马俑、明朝举世闻名的长城、明清富丽堂皇的故宫,到闪耀璀璨的东方明珠、别具一格的鸟巢场馆、大气磅礴的港珠澳大桥,无不吸引着中国和世界的目光。本单元我们将介绍中国古今名建筑,并继续学习转换这一常用翻译技巧。

一谈到中国的奇观,我们大多数人都会首先想到长城。长城已有两千多年的历史,从空中鸟瞰宛如一条巨龙,从西向东蜿蜒6 700公里。长城最初是抵抗外侵的壁垒,如今成为名胜古迹,吸引着世界各地游客。俗话说,“不到长城非好汉”,长城已经成为文学和艺术的永恒主题,象征着中国人爱国、勤奋、睿智的民族精神。本单元第一节将聚焦我国第一大建筑奇观,并学习具体转抽象这一翻译技巧。

5.2.1 例句讲解

请先阅读下面这篇介绍长城的短文。

长城是世界上最伟大的奇迹之一,1987年被列为联合国教科文组织世界文化遗产。① 它宛如一条巨龙,蜿蜒曲折,穿越草地、沙漠和高山,自西向东绵延8 851.8公里(明长城)。② 经过两千多年的沧桑,长城部分城墙已经被毁或湮灭。③ 但是,由于它建筑雄伟、历史悠久,长城现今依然是世界上最具吸引力的景点之一。长城始建于春秋战国时期的燕、赵、秦等国,用作防御工事。秦始皇将各段城墙连接起来,抵御北方部落的侵袭。④ 从那时起,长城就成为中华民族的一道丰碑,此后历朝历代都在不断扩建和修缮。⑤ 长城承载着博大精深的中国文化,体现了中国人民的智慧和顽强。

① 它宛如一条巨龙,蜿蜒曲折,穿越草地、沙漠和高山,自西向东绵延8 851.8公里(明长城)。

本句将长城比喻为巨龙，用“蜿蜒曲折”和“绵延”二词将长城形象化。“蜿”指的是蛇的凹形，“蜒”指软体动物蛞蝓，“蜿蜒”是形容蛇或龙爬行的样子。“蜿蜒曲折”指道路迂回曲折的样子，“绵延”有丝绵展开的意思。

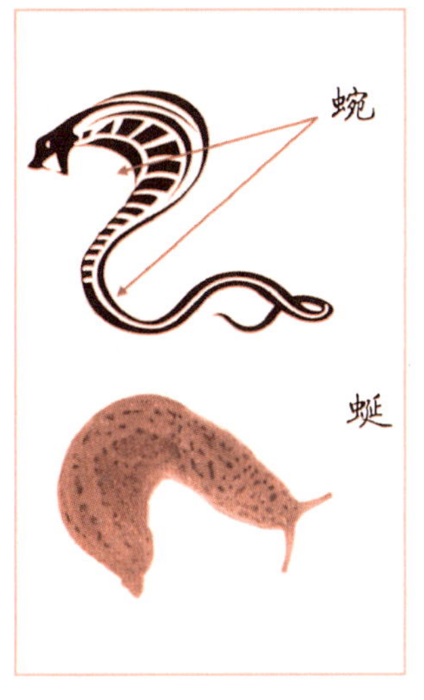

英译时很难在英语中找到如汉语原词那样形象贴切的词，因此只能丢弃具体形象，进行抽象化处理，将“蜿蜒曲折”译为动词“wind (to have many bends and twists)”，将“绵延”译为“stretching (to spread over an area of land)”。

Like a giant dragon, the Great Wall **winds** its way across grasslands, deserts, and mountains, **stretching** approximately 8,851.8 kilometers (the Ming Walls) from west to east of China.

② 经过两千多年的**沧桑**，长城部分城墙已经被毁或湮灭。

“沧桑”是一个生动形象的词，来自成语“沧海桑田”，意为大海变成桑田，桑田变成大海，比喻世事变化很大。在英语中，我们无法找到一个具有相同历史典故和文化寓意的词，因此我们只能将“沧桑”一词抽象化，用“history”去表达岁月变化、历史变迁之意。

With a **history** of more than 2,000 years, some of the sections are now in ruins or have disappeared.

③ 但是，由于它建筑雄伟、历史悠久，长城现今依然是世界上最具吸引力的**景点**之一。

“景点”通常译为表意具体的“scenic spot”，但在本句中为了突出长城最具吸引力(the most appealing),我们可以用“attraction”这一表意抽象但更具美感的词语与“appealing”搭配。比起“appealing scenic spot”,用“appealing attraction”更能展现出长城的魅力,更能吸引一批批怀着向往之心的游客。

However, it is still one of the most appealing **attractions** all around the world owing to its grandeur and history.

④ 从那时起,长城就成为中华民族的一道丰碑,此后历朝历代都在不断**扩建**和**修缮**。

我们将“扩建和修缮”两个动词转化为抽象名词的形式,以求译文语法正确与行文连贯。

Since then, the Great Wall has served as a monument of the Chinese nation. It went through constant **extensions** and **renovations** in later dynasties.

⑤ 长城承载着**博大精深**的中国文化,体现了中国人民的智慧和顽强。

“博大精深”意为广博高深,“博”“大”“精”“深”四个单字分别代表四方面的具体含义,即种类多、范围广、精辟、有深度,这四方面具体含义语义相近,有重复,如果进行字对字的翻译(如broad, extensive, profound, and deep),译文烦冗累赘。我们可以把这个成语处理为单一含义,译为“a considerable part of”。

The Great Wall carries **a considerable part of** Chinese culture and demonstrates the wisdom and tenacity of the Chinese people.

5.2.2 双语对照

长城/The Great Wall	
长城是世界上最伟大的奇迹之一,1987年被列为联合国教科文组织世界文化遗产。它宛如一条巨龙,**蜿蜒曲折**,穿越草地、沙漠和高山,自西向东**绵延**8 851.8公里(明长城)。经过两千多年的**沧桑**,长城部分城墙已经被毁或湮灭。但是,由于它建筑雄伟、历史悠久,长城现今依然是世界上最具吸引	The Great Wall, one of the greatest wonders of the world, was listed as a UNESCO World Cultural Heritage Site in 1987. Like a giant dragon, the Great Wall **winds** its way across grasslands, deserts, and mountains, **stretching** approximately 8,851.8 kilometers (the Ming Walls) from west to east of China. With a **history** of more than 2,000 years, some of the sections are now in ruins or have disappeared. However, it is still one of the most appealing **attractions** all around the world owing to its grandeur and history. The Great Wall was originally built in

（续表）

长城/The Great Wall	
力的景点之一。长城始建于春秋战国时期的燕、赵、秦等国，用作防御工事。秦始皇将各段城墙连接起来，抵御北方部落的侵袭。从那时起，长城就成为中华民族的一道丰碑，此后历朝历代都在不断扩建和修缮。长城承载着博大精深的中国文化，体现了中国人民的智慧和顽强。	the Spring and Autumn Period and the Warring States Period as a defensive project by states including Yan, Zhao, and Qin. Emperor Qinshihuang succeeded in his effort in having the walls joined to fend off the invasions from tribes in the north. Since then, the Great Wall has served as a monument of the Chinese nation. It went through constant **extensions** and **renovations** in later dynasties. The Great Wall carries **a considerable part** of Chinese culture and demonstrates the wisdom and tenacity of the Chinese people.

5.2.3　译技总结

通过上面双语短文的对比可以发现"蜿蜒曲折""绵延""沧桑"这些形象的词语运用拟人的手法，呈现给读者生动的画面，但在英译时无法字对字地将这些字词直译出来，因为在英语国家，这些文化形象本身就是缺失或寓意不同。翻译时可首先将这些词语概括化、抽象化，保留原文基本含义，确保其可读性。为使译文语法正确与行文连贯，有时我们需要将一些具象词转换为抽象名词，有时还需将具有丰富或深厚含义的词简化，以使译文清晰简洁。

因为中西思维文化各方面的差异，整体上汉语更为具象生动，而英语更为抽象概括。为了达到忠实与通顺的效果，原文中许多有着具体形象或意义的短语在英译时，需要抽象化与概括化。从下表可以看出汉语成语多生动具体，英译时需将其概括化、抽象化。

Specification →	Abstraction
势如破竹	with irresistible force
手忙脚乱	in a frantic rush
三六九等	ranks and grades
唇枪舌战	to engage in a battle of words
单枪匹马	all by oneself
五光十色	multi-colored

5.2.4 文化表达

(1) 文化基本知识与表达

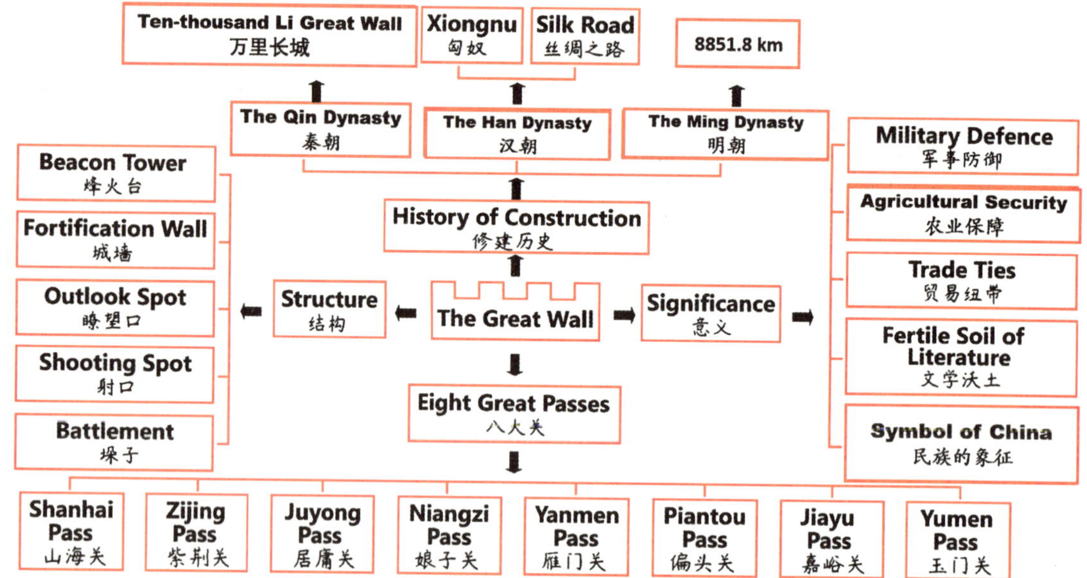

长城修建的历史与八大关

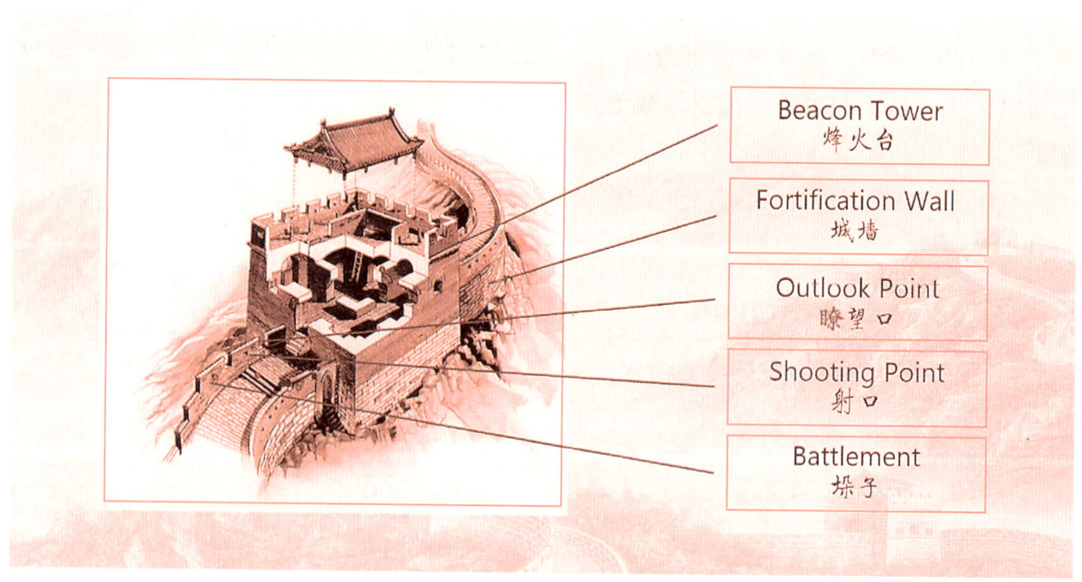

长城的建筑结构

（2）文化知识与表达拓展

中国有一句家喻户晓的民间俗语："不到长城非好汉！"这句话现在也成了来中国旅游的外国旅游者人人皆知的名言。被誉为世界建筑史奇迹的万里长城，在北京北部山区绵延600余公里，像一座天然屏障，保护着古代中原国家的首都不会受到少数民族的侵扰。这个始建于2 000余年前的伟大的工程，在北京留下了其最壮观、最精华的部分。作为拱卫京师的军事要冲，北京地区的八达岭、慕田峪、司马台长城在永乐年间重修，现在是北京最有吸引力的旅游名胜。	There is a popular saying in China: "He who has not been to the Great Wall is not a true man." The idiom is also well-known to foreign tourists as a proverb. Famed as a miracle in the world architecture history, the Great Wall stretches about 600 kilometers long in the northern suburb of Beijing, and served as a natural defense with its **fortifications** to defend against the invasion into the capital of the central country from northern ethnic minorities. This great historical project constructed 2,000 years ago retains the most grandiose and essential sections in Beijing region, where sections at Badaling, Mutianyu, and Simatai, rebuilt in the period of Yongle (1402~1424 AD) in the Ming Dynasty, are the most attractive historical sites for tourists.
八达岭长城是长城最著名的地段，位于北京西北延庆县关沟北口，是扼守京北的咽喉要道。长城起伏蜿蜒，如苍龙凌空飞舞，雄伟壮观。	The Great Wall at Badaling is the most famous section of the Great Wall. It locates at Guangou of Yanqing county of the northern part of Beijing and is a strategic pass to protect Beijing. It winds up and down like a black dragon dancing magnificently in the sky.
如果说八达岭长城的特色是雄伟，那么，慕田峪长城的特色就是秀丽。慕田峪位于北京东北郊的怀柔区，这一带植被繁茂，春花秋叶、夏荫冬雪。长城四季景色不同，极具观赏价值。慕田峪长城的建筑很独特，城墙多为双面垛口，敌楼密集，便于防御。特别是箭扣一带，长城往往矗立在绝壁之上，给人"无限风光在险峰"之感。	If we were to describe the Great Wall at Badaling in a single word, it would be magnificent, and Mutianyu would be elegant. Mutianyu section is located in Huairou District in the north-eastern suburb of Beijing, where the mountains are densely covered by various plants and full of flowers in spring and fallen leaves in autumn, as well as tree shades in summer and snow in winter. All the year round, here offers varied sceneries worthy of viewing. The architecture of Mutianyu has its distinctive style. Most parts of the wall have two parapets at either side with **crenels** and **watchtowers** densely distributed for defense. In particular, near Jian Kou, the walls were built along steep ridges, giving us the feeling that "the best scenery often appears at dangerous cliff peaks".
司马台长城蜿蜒于北京东北郊区密云县境内的崇山峻岭之上，以险峻著称。这一带城墙及敌楼的形式变化多端，被专家认为是"中国长城之最"。	The Great Wall at Simatai section meanders along the lofty mountains and high ranges in Miyun county in the north-eastern suburb of Beijing and is known for its steepness and dangerousness. The walls and watchtowers are of various forms and are admired by some experts as the best section of the Chinese Great Wall.

词汇

fortification [ˌfɔːtɪfɪˈkeɪʃn] *n.* 防御工事

watchtower [ˈwɒtʃtaʊə(r)] *n.* 瞭望塔

crenel [ˈkrenl] *n.* 垛口

5.2.5 讨论问题

（1）长城是在极其艰难的条件下历经上千年修建而成的，它对中国社会的发展有什么作用？

（2）你能用英语谈谈对“不到长城非好汉”这句话的理解吗？

（3）为什么在翻译时我们需要将具体的词转化为抽象的词呢？请解释原因并举例说明。

5.3 故宫（形象转换）

中国有这么一个地方，精美绝伦，是中世纪的伟大杰作之一，也是世界上最大的木质结构建筑群，这就是故宫。本节我们将聚焦故宫并学习翻译中的形象转换。

5.3.1 例句讲解

请先阅读下面这篇介绍故宫的短文。

北京故宫也叫紫禁城，是世界上现存最大、最完整的古建筑群。故宫建筑分为“外朝”与“内廷”两大部分。①“外朝”为太和、中和、保和殿，三大殿前后排列在同一个庞大的“工”字型汉白玉石殿基上。“内廷”为乾清宫、交泰殿、坤宁宫。② 故宫是中国古代建筑的扛鼎之作，1987年已被联合国教科文组织评定为世界文化遗产。

① “外朝”为太和、中和、保和殿，三大殿前后排列在同一个庞大的**“工”字型**汉白玉石殿基上。

如果将“工”字直译为“work”，这与原文所传达的意思大相径庭。因此，我们可将“工”字型转换为英语读者更为熟悉的形象——字母“H”，它有着和“工”同样的形象，只是方位颠倒了而已。这样翻译既保留了原文所传达的意义，又利于西方读者理解原文。经过形象转换后译文如下：

The outer court consists of the Hall of Supreme Harmony, the Hall of Complete Harmony, and the Hall of Preserving Harmony. The Three Big Halls are built on a spacious **H-shaped** marble terrace.

② 故宫是中国古代建筑的扛鼎之作……

“鼎”是中国古人用以烹煮和盛贮的重要器具，也是祭祀用的一种礼器，被后世认为是最能代表至高无上权力的青铜器物。“扛鼎之作”意为最重要、最有影响力的作品。因为“鼎”在英语中无相同的形象与词汇，很难实现完全对等的翻译。我们可根据“鼎”的含义将其翻译为“the pinnacle”（建筑物小尖顶，顶点，顶峰），把中国文化特色词转换为西方读者熟知的形象，最大程度、最便捷地传达原文的意思。

The Imperial Palace is the **pinnacle** of ancient Chinese architecture.

5.3.2　双语对照

故宫/The Imperial Palace	
北京故宫也叫紫禁城，是世界上现存最大、最完整的古建筑群。故宫建筑分为“外朝”与“内廷”两大部分。“外朝”为太和、中和、保和殿，三大殿前后排列在同一个庞大的“工”字型汉白玉石殿基上。“内廷”为乾清宫、交泰殿、坤宁宫。故宫是中国古代建筑的扛鼎之作，1987年已被联合国教科文组织评定为世界文化遗产。	The Imperial Palace, also called the Forbidden City, is the largest and most complete imperial palace and ancient building complex in the world. The Imperial Palace is made up of the outer court and the inner court. The outer court consists of the Hall of Supreme Harmony, the Hall of Complete Harmony, and the Hall of Preserving Harmony. The Three Big Halls are built on a spacious **H-shaped** marble terrace. The Hall of Heavenly Purity, the Hall of Union and the Hall of Earthly Tranquility comprise the inner palace. The Imperial Palace is the **pinnacle** of ancient Chinese architecture. In 1987, the United Nations' Educational, Scientific and Cultural Organization recognized the Imperial Palace as the World Cultural Heritage.

5.3.3　译技总结

中英文是两种完全不同的语言系统，翻译时常会遇见词汇空缺、形象空缺的现象，译者应找到相似的形象进行替换、转换或增补，以此提高译文的可理解性。例如：

掌上明珠（意为极钟爱的人）　→　the apple of one's eye
力大如牛（比喻力量、力气很大）　→　as strong as a horse

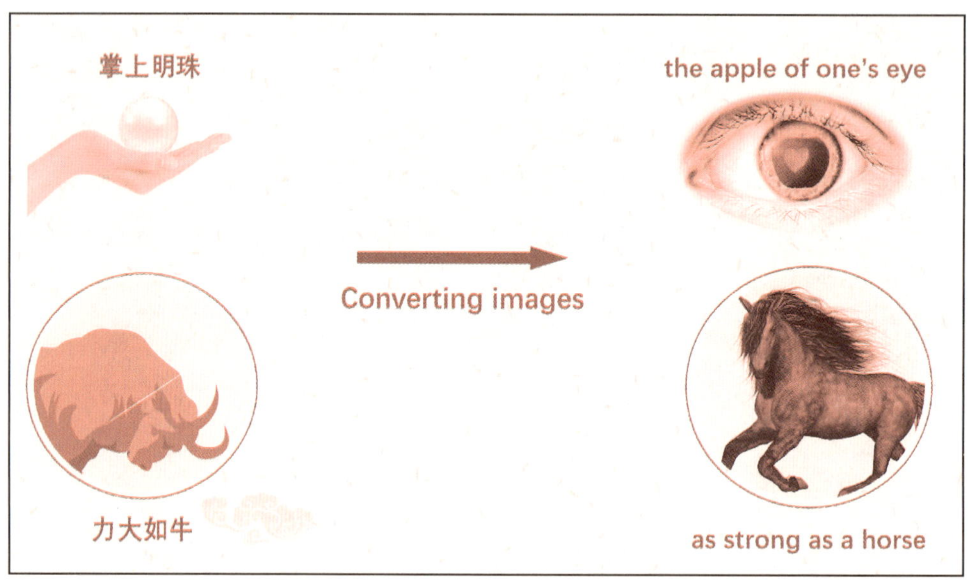

5.3.4 文化表达

(1) 文化基本知识与表达

- 故宫建筑

斗拱	The Chinese Brackets
金柱	Six Golden Pillars with Dragon Carvings
琉璃瓦	Brilliant Glazed Roof Tiles

- 故宫色彩

- The Roof — Yellow represents earth, the central element (the emperor was the center of the country).
- The Wall — Red represents happiness, good fortune, and wealth.

- 故宫英语表达扩展

① The Meridian Gate (Wu Men)
② "Painting and Calligraphy Gallery": Hall of Martial Valor (Wuying Dian)
③ "Ceramics Gallery": Hall of Literary Brilliance (Wenhua Dian)
④ Gate of Supreme Harmony (Taihe Men)
⑤ Hall of Supreme Harmony (Taihe Dian)
⑥ Hall of Central Harmony (Zhonghe Dian)
⑦ Hall of Preserving Harmony (Baohe Dian)
⑧ Palace of Heavenly Purity (Qianqing Gong)
⑨ Hall of Union (Jiaotai Dian)
⑩ Palace of Earthly Tranquility (Kunning Gong)
⑪ Hall of Mental Cultivation (Yangxin Dian)
⑫ Area of Six Western Palaces
⑬ Imperial Garden (Yu Huayuan)
⑭ Area of Six Eastern Palaces
⑮ "Hall of Clocks": Hall for Ancestral Worship (Fengxian Dian)
⑯ "The Treasure Gallery, Gallery of Qing Imperial Opera": Area of Palace of Tranquil Longevity (Ningshou Gong)
⑰ Gate of Divine Prowess (Shenwu Men)

（2）文化知识与表达拓展

故宫，又称紫禁城，是中国现存规模最大、保存最完整的古建筑群。它是中国最后两个封建王朝的皇宫。从明至清，共有24位皇帝在这里居住和生活过。历经500多年的朝代更替，世事变迁，这座城中之城辉煌依旧，壮丽依旧。紫禁城以其规划严谨的整体布局，巍峨

The Palace Museum, also known as the Forbidden City, is the largest and the best-preserved palace complex extant in China. As it was the imperial palace of China's last two feudal dynasties, the Ming and the Qing, altogether 24 emperors lived and ruled here during its 500-year span. After the passing of time and with **vicissitudes** of dynasties, the palace is still as splendid and magnificent as before. With its carefully-designed layout, splendid structure and decoration, clear and rigid

（续表）

壮丽的宫殿建筑，主次分明的等级制度，灵活多变的空间组合形式，最完美地体现了中国传统文化的博大精深，是中国宫殿建筑艺术的最高成就和总结。	**hierarchy**, and flexible spatial composition, the Palace Museum embodies the extensiveness and profundity of traditional Chinese art, and represents the highest achievements that China was able to make in architectural engineering and art.
中国古代建筑之宏伟，不以单体建筑的壮丽而彰显，而以群体组合的完善而著称。在紫禁城72万平方米的空间内，有近千座建筑、100多座院落。每个院落都是封闭的内向空间，自成体系。它们以南北中轴线为中心，以多层次、多方位的院落分区和一系列富于韵律变化的空间，被井然有序地组合成一个有机的整体，最集中、最完整地体现了中国宫殿建筑的传统和精髓。巍峨的宫殿，庄严肃穆，疏朗的广庭，韵律天成，飞檐斗拱宛若神工，无一不别具匠心。城中层层方庭相接，对称严谨，主次分明，并以形制不同的门墙，划分出风格迥异的空间。用重重宫门隔断视线，以这种“隔则深、畅则浅”布局方式，加强了宫院的纵深感，以体现皇帝九重宫阙的神秘莫测。	The **grandeur** of Chinese ancient architectures is not only reflected in the magnificence of a single structure, but also in the harmony achieved by the whole complex. In the 720,000-square-meter Forbidden City, there are almost a thousand buildings and more than a hundred courtyards. Each courtyard is a closed and independent **spatial** system. Taking the north-south central axis as the center, these systems of different styles and levels in the hierarchy are organized into an organic whole in great harmony, fully reflecting the essence and tradition of Chinese **palatial** architecture. The magnificent and grand palaces and halls, wide and open courtyards and compounds, pavilions and corridors designed with great creativity, and roofs and eaves are all decorated with **prodigious** craftsmanship. Units of architecture complex in the City are strictly connected in a symmetrical way in accordance with the level of feudal hierarchy. Spatial units of various styles were divided by walls and gates of different shapes. What is more, layers of city walls are so laid out that they prevent people from looking inside, which adds to the depth of the palaces, as well as the mystery of the imperial palaces.

词汇

vicissitude [vɪ'sɪsɪtjuːd] *n.* 变迁；盛衰

hierarchy ['haɪərɑːki] *n.* 等级制度

grandeur ['ɡrændʒə(r),'ɡrændjə(r)] *n.* 高贵；威严

spatial ['speɪʃl] *adj.* 空间的

palatial [pə'leɪʃl] *adj.* 宏伟的；壮丽的

prodigious [prə'dɪdʒəs] *adj.* 巨大的

5.3.5 讨论问题

（1）你能结合具体例子谈谈为什么使用形象转换这一翻译技巧吗？

（2）你能用英语介绍故宫建筑的特色吗？

5.4 港珠澳大桥(转换技巧总结)

本节我们先来赏析一首南宋名诗:

过零丁洋

南宋·文天祥

辛苦遭逢起一经,干戈寥落四周星。
山河破碎风飘絮,身世浮沉雨打萍。
惶恐滩头说惶恐,零丁洋里叹零丁。
人生自古谁无死?留取丹心照汗青。

这首诗是南宋时期的民族英雄文天祥被敌人俘获时所写。在诗中他既叹国运,又叹自己,将家国之恨、艰危困厄渲染到极致。诗中所描述的零丁洋是七百年前文天祥被俘的地方,是一个北起虎门、南达港澳的巨大河口湾。如今这里伫立着世界上最长的跨海大桥——港珠澳大桥。

本节我们将领略港珠澳大桥的魅力,同时复习前两个单元所学的翻译技巧"转"。在四、五单元中我们共学了四种类型的"转",分别是词类转换、句型转换、具体转抽象及形象转换。以下这篇文段的翻译将展示这些技巧的综合使用。

5.4.1 例句讲解

① 港珠澳大桥于2009年12月15日开始建造,2017年7月7日全面贯通。② 大桥东连香港,西接珠海、澳门,集桥梁、沉管隧道、人工岛为一体。③ 它长55公里,是世界最长的跨海大桥。④ 从空中俯瞰,那逶迤的桥身如长龙。⑤ 桥身上还建设了"中国结""海豚""风帆"三座造型独特的斜拉桥。⑥ 当我们注目于这座壮观的跨海大桥时,我们会看到中国上千年的桥梁建造史与现代技术的结合,中华民族的汗水与智慧正在熠熠闪光。

① 港珠澳大桥于2009年12月15日开始建造,2017年7月7日全面贯通。

根据我们之前所学,英语表述呈静态,习惯多用名词和介词;而汉语表述呈动态,习惯多用动词。在本句中我们可先将汉语动词"建造"译为名词形式"construction"。

后半句“全面贯通”的真实含义是指港珠澳大桥全面贯通，但桥本身不能发出这一动作。该汉语句子形式上虽是主动结构，但暗含被动语意，英译时最好转化为被动语态。

The construction of the Hong Kong-Zhuhai-Macao Bridge (HZMB) began on December 15, 2009, and it was fully completed on July 7, 2017.

由此可见，翻译时常需将词类、句型进行转化，使译文更符合英语语法习惯。

② 大桥东连香港，西接珠海、澳门，集桥梁、沉管隧道、人工岛为一体。

本句是常见的汉语流水句，由三个小句组成。这三个小句分别由三个动词“连”“接”“集”作谓语，在翻译时我们最好保留其中一个作为主要谓语动词。这里我们暂且将表达句子最主要意思的第三小句的动词词组“集……为一体”作为英语整句的主要谓语动词，将句子译成“combinc ... into one entity”，但是原句中的主语“大桥”自身能否发出“combine”这一动作？还是“大桥”本身被修成了一个集合体（a combination of sth.）？经过分析我们最好还是把动词转化为名词，这样翻译原文整句的主要结构“The HZMB is a combination of sth.”。

我们再来思考怎么翻译前两个小句。因为“连”“接”在本句中意思相同，所以我们将这两个动词合译为“link”；同时，因为我们前面已经确定一个主要谓语结构，现在可以把“link”变为分词形式“linking”，形容词化后作“大桥”的后置修饰语。这样经过词性转换后的译文在句式结构上层级分明，主次清晰，译文简洁。

The HZMB, linking Hong Kong to the East, and Zhuhai and Macao to the West, is a combination of bridges, immersed tunnels, and artificial islands.

③ 它长55公里，是世界最长的跨海大桥。

本句中有两个动词“长”和“是”。我们将“长”转化为名词“length”置于“with”引导的介词词组中，从而避免了在英语一句话中出现两个谓语动词又没有关联词连接的情况。

With a total length of 55 kilometers, it is the world’s longest sea crossing.

④ 从空中俯瞰，那逶迤的桥身如长龙。

本句中的“桥身”是从空中被俯瞰之意，汉语的“从空中俯瞰”形式上虽然是主动，

却暗含被动之意。"逶迤"也是本句翻译的难点，"逶"指"winding（蜿蜒的）"，"迤"指的"snake（蛇）"，所以"逶迤"原意为"be winding just like a snake"，但在此句中后面又有"桥身如长龙"的表述，故翻译"逶迤"时我们需要简化其含义，丢掉蛇的具体形象，将"逶迤"抽象为"winding"。在经过主动转被动、具体转抽象后，整句话翻译如下：

Seen from the air, the winding bridge looks like a long dragon.

⑤ 桥身上还建设了"中国结""海豚""风帆"三座造型独特的斜拉桥。

在本句中"海豚"和"风帆"都可直译为"Dolphin"和"Sail"，但"中国结"不能直译为"Chinese Knot"。因为"knot"指用绳索等打的结，还暗含有麻烦、难题这样不好的含义。在本句中"结"是指大桥将原本遥远的地方连接在一起，因此我们将其形象进行转化，译为"connection"，表达联通之意，更具褒义色彩。

On the way, there are three specially modeled cable-stayed bridges named "China Connection", "Dolphin" and "Sail".

⑥ 当我们注目于这座壮观的跨海大桥时，我们会看到中国上千年的桥梁建造史与现代技术的结合，中华民族的汗水与智慧正在熠熠闪光。

在本句中有几个翻译难点。一是"汗水"，"汗水"是形象化的词，根据词义，我们可将其抽象化地翻译为"diligence"；二是"熠熠闪光"，"熠熠"指光彩闪耀的样子（a bright and shining look），"闪光"指闪烁闪耀（glitter），二者语意重叠繁复，翻译时宜简化，概括性地译为"glitter"即可。三是为使整体句式工整对仗，最好将"glitter"由动词转化为名词，以此来构成"we can see a combination of ... and the glitter of ..."的句式结构。

When we look at this magnificent sea crossing, we can see a combination of the millennia-long history of bridge building in China and modern technology, and the glitter of the Chinese people's diligence and wisdom.

可以看出，进行形象转化不仅可以更准确地表达作者原意，也能增强译文可读性，便于目的语读者理解，达到准确交流的目的。

5.4.2 双语对照

港珠澳大桥 The Hong Kong-Zhuhai-Macao Bridge	
港珠澳大桥于2009年12月15日开始建造，2017年7月7日全面贯通。大桥东连香港，西接珠海、澳门，集桥梁、沉管隧道、人工岛为一体。它长55公里，是世界最长的跨海大桥。从空中俯瞰，那逶迤的桥身如长龙。桥身上还建设了“中国结”“海豚”“风帆”三座造型独特的斜拉桥。当我们注目于这座壮观的跨海大桥时，我们会看到中国上千年的桥梁建造史与现代技术的结合，中华民族的汗水与智慧正在熠熠闪光。	The construction of the Hong Kong-Zhuhai-Macao Bridge (HZMB) began on December 15, 2009, and it was fully completed on July 7, 2017. The HZMB, linking Hong Kong to the East, and Zhuhai and Macao to the West, is a combination of bridges, immersed tunnels, and artificial islands. With a total length of 55 kilometers, it is the world's longest sea crossing. Seen from the air, the winding bridge looks like a long dragon. On the way, there are three specially modeled cable-stayed bridges named "China Connection", "Dolphin" and "Sail". When we look at this magnificent sea crossing, we can see a combination of the millennia-long history of bridge building in China and modern technology, and the glitter of the Chinese people's diligence and wisdom.

5.4.3 译技总结

至此我们已经学习了多种转换技巧，包括词类转换、句型转换、具体转抽象、形象转换（见下表）。进行这些转换往往是因为两种语言句式结构有差异，使用偏好有区别。使用这些转换的最终目的是使译文更加忠实、准确地传递原文意思，使译文清晰、简洁、流畅，更贴近英语的语言特点和表达习惯，更容易被读者理解和接受。

类　型	英 汉 差 异
词类转换 Word-class conversion	汉语表述呈动态，习惯多用动词；英语表述呈静态，习惯多用名词和介词，词义更灵活，词的含义范围更广泛。
句型转换 Sentence-structure conversion	汉语句子常用无主句，有主句也倾向于选择人称主语；英语句子倾向于选择物称主语，而当物作主语时，常会用到被动语态。
具体转抽象 Specification-to-abstraction conversion	汉语偏好具体化的表达方法；英语更多使用抽象的表达方法。
形象转换 Image conversion	用目的语读者所熟知的形象替换原文中难以理解的形象。

5.4.4 文化表达

（1）文化基本知识与表达

中国传统建筑包含以下几个方面：

① 讲究平衡对称之美——中轴线（the central axis）。

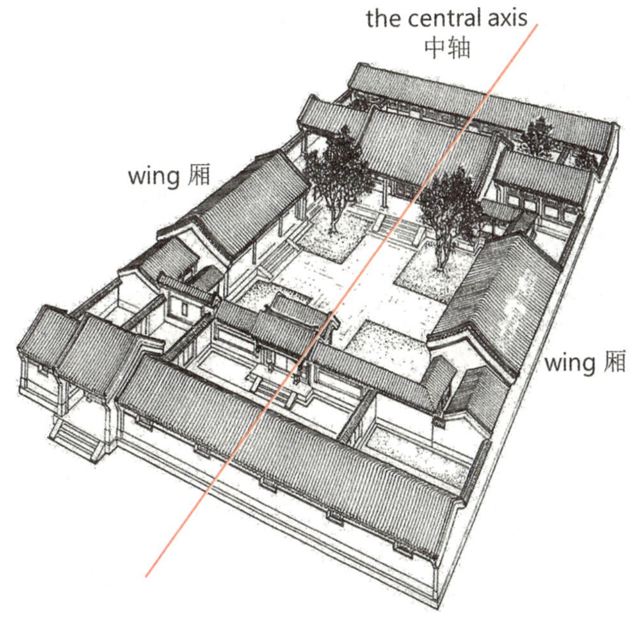

如四合院（*Siheyuan*/quadrangle）和故宫（the Imperial Palace/Forbidden City）。

② 以木质结构（the timber-framed structures）为主。

如山西应县木塔/释迦塔（Shanxi Yingxian Wood Tower/Buddha Tower）。

③ 崇尚天人合一的思想(the unity of man and heaven)。

乐山大佛
Leshan Giant Buddha

苏州园林
The Classical Gardens of Suzhou

(2)文化知识与表达拓展

港珠澳大桥是一个全长55公里的桥岛隧综合跨海工程,也是目前世界上最长的跨海大桥。大桥包含一段6.7公里的海底隧道,是我国第一条外海沉管隧道,也是目前世界上最长的公路沉管隧道。它通过东西两个海中人工岛与桥梁部分连接。	The Hong Kong-Zhuhai-Macao Bridge (HZMB) is a 55-kilometer long bridge-island-tunnel complex across the Pearl River **Estuary**. It is the world's longest sea crossing at present. The bridge consists of a 6.7-km undersea tunnel, which is the country's first **offshore** immersed tunnel and the world's longest immersed tunnel for road traffic. It is connected to the bridge through two offshore artificial islands at the east and west.
建隧道是为了给珠江口将来的航运发展预留可通行30万吨邮轮的航道。由于航道位置靠近香港国际机场,满足相应航道宽度的斜拉桥的桥塔会超过机场附近的空域限高,因此只能走海下,建隧道。	The tunnel is built to reserve room for a planned shipping channel for passenger liners with a **displacement** of 300,000 tons. As the planned location is close to the Hong Kong International Airport, where there is height limitation in the airspace, a tunnel must be built subsea instead of a bridge with tall towers.
大桥总投资额约1 200亿人民币,其中三地投资共建的主桥部分,长29.6公里,占其中的480.68亿元。剩余部分为各地政府投资兴建的口岸和连接线。这一比例是三方政府根据大桥建成后各自可获得的经济效益占比拟定的。	The gross investment of HZMB is about 120 billion yuan (US$17.4 billion), of which the 29.6-km Main Bridge invested by three local governments is about 48.1 billion yuan. The rest are investments by individual governments on their ports and road links to the Main Bridge. The cost **allocation** among the three governments shown above is settled by the assessment of economic benefits they can get after the bridge is completed.

（续表）

更重要的是，两地的货运有了直接的陆上通道，这对于两岸物流业、会展业、食品行业等需要快速交通支援的行业，将有非常显著的促进作用。	The most important benefit is that the bridge will provide the east and west of the Pearl River Estuary with direct road connections, which can enormously facilitate the industries that rely on fast transportation, such as logistics, exhibition and food service.

词汇

estuary ['estʃʊeri] *n.* 河口；江口

offshore [ˌɒf'ʃɔ:(r)] *adj.* 近海的

displacement [dɪs'pleɪsmənt] *n.* 排水量；位移

allocation [ˌælə'keɪʃn] *n.* 分配

logistics [lə'dʒɪstɪks] *n.* 后勤；物流

5.4.5　讨论问题

（1）你能用英语谈谈我国古代赵州桥和现代港珠澳大桥修建的意义吗？

（2）请结合实例谈谈翻译转换技巧和汉英两种语言之间的哪些差异有关。

5.5　单元练习

1. 单项选择。从两个备选项中选出对汉语原句翻译得较好的一个选项。

① 颐和园内的人工景观与自然山峦、宁静的湖水和谐地融为一体。

A. The artificial landscape in the Summer Palace melted harmoniously with natural hills and peaceful lakes as a whole.

B. The artificial landscape in the Summer Palace is harmoniously combined with natural hills and peaceful lakes.

② 长城既是历史文化古迹，也是独一无二的自然景观。

A. The Great Wall is a cultural relic and a unique natural landscape.

B. The Great Wall is cultural relic and the only landscape without the second one.

③ 虽然解决了桥梁构造设计的难题，实际建造中仍然面临许多困难。

A. Although we have overcome the problem of the design for the structure of the bridge, we still confront many difficulties concerning its actual construction.

B. Although the problem of the design for the structure of the bridge has been overcome, we are still confronted with many difficulties concerning its actual construction.

④ 最终，工程师们克服了一个又一个难题，港珠澳大桥于2017年7月7日实现了全面贯通。

A. Finally, engineers overcame the difficulties one by one, and the Hong Kong-Zhuhai-Macao Bridge opened on July 7, 2017.

B. Finally, after innumerable difficulties had been overcome, the Hong Kong-Zhuhai-Macao Bridge was fully opened on July 7, 2017.

⑤ 多数紫禁城的宫殿都是木结构，黄琉璃瓦（glazed tile）顶，青白石底座，看上去庄严肃穆，金碧辉煌。

A. Most of the buildings in the Forbidden City were built with wood, roofed with yellow glazed tiles, and built on blue-and-white stone foundations, looking solemn and brilliant.

B. Most of the buildings in the Forbidden City were built with wood, and people used yellow glazed tiles as the roofs, blue-and-white stones as foundations, so it looked solemn and glittered gold and jade.

2. 句子翻译。翻译下面的句子，注意运用本单元所学的翻译技巧。

① 对于大多数去北京的外国访客来说，万里长城是必不可少的参观游览项目。

____

② 港珠澳大桥（the Hong Kong-Zhuhai-Macao Bridge）位于珠江（the Pearl River）出海口（estuary），横跨伶仃洋（the Lingding Channel），全长55公里。

____

③ 当沉管（immersed tunnels）最终严丝合缝地沉放到预定位置（designated position）时，有的人立刻累得一屁股坐到地上，七倒八歪地睡着了。

____

5.6 单元测验

1. 单项选择。从两个备选项中选出对汉语原句翻译得较好的一个选项。（5×5分=25分）

① 中国河流地域众多，情况复杂多变，古人因地制宜、就地取材，方能巧夺天工。

A. China has a multiplicity of complicated rivers and landforms, and the ancients took local conditions into account and used local resources to ensure a perfect addition to Nature.

B. China has a multiplicity of complicated rivers and landforms, and the ancients take effective measures according to local conditions and used local resources to ensure the superb craftsmanship excelling nature.

② 人民大会堂坐西面东，平面略呈“山”字形。

A. From west to east, the curve of Great Hall of the People is like the letter “W” .

B. From west to east, the curve of Great Hall of the People is like “山” .

③ 留园的各区之间由一条长廊蜿蜒相连。

A. A winding corridor links every hall of the Lingering Garden.

B. A corridor winds, links every hall of the Lingering Garden.

④ 颐和园是清代皇家园林，建于1765年。

A. The Summer Palace was a royal garden of the Qing Dynasty and constructed in 1765.

B. The Summer Palace, a royal garden of the Qing Dynasty, was constructed in 1765.

⑤ 昏暗中隐约见到四周天然石壁，把人带回神秘莫测的远古时代。

A. The natural stone walls can only be dimly seen as if the mysterious ancient times have appeared again.

B. People see the natural stone walls as if the mysterious ancient times have appeared again.

2. 句子翻译。翻译下面的句子，注意运用本单元所学的翻译技巧。(3×10分=30分)

① 人民大会堂（Great Hall of the People）平面呈“口”字型，中央的庭院内，植以花卉树木。

____

② 三星堆博物馆（Sanxingdui Museum）延续了古蜀人的超然神力，也体现了当代审美情趣。

____

③ 河北武当山延绵400公里，拥有世界上最宏伟的宗教建筑群。

3. 将下面短文翻译成英语，注意运用本单元所学的翻译技巧，增补必要信息以帮助目的语读者理解。（45分）

佛像（Buddha）开凿于公元713年，是海通法师（Monk Haitong）为减杀水势、普度众生修凿的。海通法师圆寂后工程停止，多年后又由四川两位节度使（Jiedushi, regional military governors）续建，至公元803年完工，历时90年。

第6单元

中国文学

Chinese Literature

6.1 背景介绍

Lead-in Questions

(1) Can you give a brief introduction to the Four Classical Novels in English?

(2) What influences do you think the Four Classical Novels have on Chinese people?

The Four Classical Novels — Everlasting Classics

During the Ming and Qing Dynasties narrative creation **flourished**. It was in this period that the four great Chinese classical novels were written, namely, *Romance of the Three Kingdoms*①, *Water Margin*②, *Journey to the West*③ and *A Dream of Red Mansions*④.

Luo Guanzhong⑤, the author of *Romance of the Three Kingdoms*, based his novel on both **folk tales** and historical records of the conflicts between the kingdoms of Wei, Shu and Wu (220 ~ 265 AD), established by Cao Cao, Liu Bei and Sun Quan respectively. Written in the early Ming Dynasty, it is the first historical novel in China.

Water Margin was written by Shi Nai'an,⑥ almost at the same time as *Romance of the Three Kingdoms*. It is based on folk tales about a band of "**rebels**" led by Song Jiang at the close of the Northern Song Dynasty. There are 108 heroes and heroines in the novel, which is a **savage satire** on official **corruption** and **feudal oppression**.

Journey to the West was written by Wu Cheng'en⑦ in the Ming Dynasty. It is based on the true story of a Tang Dynasty monk who made a **perilous** overland trip to India and brought back the Buddhist scriptures. In the novel, the monk is protected by Sun Wukong, the "Monkey King", a figure from folk legend.

A Dream of Red Mansions, also named *The Story of the Stone*, is composed of 120 chapters, of which the first 80 were written by Cao Xueqin⑧ and the remaining 40 by Gao E.⑨ With the **tragic** love story of Jia Baoyu and Lin Daiyu as the main theme, the novel describes the decline of four feudal **noble** families. The novel is a treasure house of information about the way **aristocratic** families lived in the Qing Dynasty.

词汇

flourish ['flʌrɪʃ] *v.* 茁壮成长；处于旺盛时期

folk [fəʊk] *adj.* 民间的

tale [teɪl] *n.* 故事

rebel ['rebl] *n.* 反抗权威者

savage ['sævɪdʒ] *adj.* 狂怒的

satire ['sætaɪə(r)] *n.* 讽刺文学；讽刺作品

corruption [kə'rʌpʃn] *n.* 贪污；腐败

feudal ['fju:dl] *adj.* 封建制度的

oppression [ə'preʃn] *n.* 镇压

perilous ['perələs] *adj.* 危险的；冒险的

tragic ['trædʒɪk] *adj.* 悲剧的

noble ['nəʊbl] *adj.* 贵族的

aristocratic [ˌærɪstə'krætɪk] *adj.* 贵族的

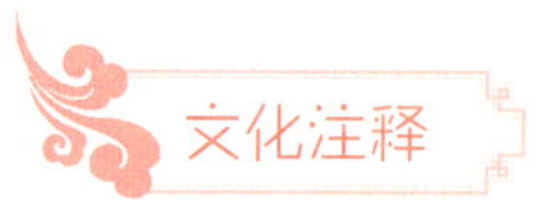

文化注释

① *Romance of the Three Kingdoms*《三国演义》(中国古典四大名著之一，也是中国第一部长篇章回体历史演义小说，作者是元末明初的小说家罗贯中。)

② *Water Margin*《水浒传》(中国古典四大名著之一，是一部以北宋末年宋江起义为主要故事背景、类型上属于英雄传奇的章回体长篇小说。)

③ *Journey to the West*《西游记》(中国四大名著之一，讲述的是孙悟空、猪八戒、沙僧辅保大唐高僧玄奘去西天取经的故事。师徒四人一路抢滩涉险，降妖伏怪，历经八十一难，取回真经，终修正果。)

④ *A Dream of Red Mansions*《红楼梦》(中国古代章回体长篇小说，被列为中国古典四大名著之首，是一部具有世界影响力的人情小说，举世公认的中国古典小说巅峰之作，中国封建社会的百科全书，传统文化的集大成者。)

⑤ Luo Guanzhong 罗贯中(名本，字贯中，号湖海散人，元末明初小说家，《三国志通

俗演义》的作者。)

⑥ Shi Nai'an 施耐庵(原名彦端,字肇瑞,号子安,别号耐庵,《水浒传》的作者。)

⑦ Wu Cheng'en 吴承恩(字汝忠,号射阳山人,汉族,我国四大名著之一《西游记》的作者、明代小说家,淮安府山阳县河下人。)

⑧ Cao Xueqin 曹雪芹(名沾,字梦阮,号雪芹,中国古典名著《红楼梦》的作者。)

⑨ Gao E 高鹗(字云士,号秋甫,中国古典名著《红楼梦》出版史、传播史上首个刻印本、全璧本——程高本的两位主要编辑者、整理者和出版者之一。)

6.2 三国演义(调整层级)

在本单元,我们将介绍中国古典文学,同时继续学习调整法中的调整语序与层级。

中国文学博大精深,源远流长。历朝历代都有着独特的文学体裁,大气的唐诗,婉转的宋词,明丽的元曲,丰富的明清小说,都是世界文学宝库中令人瞩目的瑰宝。

中国四大名著是中国文学史中的经典作品,被誉为中国文学史上的巅峰之作,是中国乃至世界共同的文化瑰宝,影响深远。《水浒传》描写了北宋末年,奸臣当道,各阶层人士被逼上梁山起义的故事。《三国演义》是中国第一部长篇章回体小说,描写了东汉末年的群雄割据混战及魏、蜀、吴三国的政治军事斗争。《西游记》是我国第一部浪漫主义章回体小说,讲述了唐僧、孙悟空、猪八戒、沙僧西行取经,历经九九八十一难,最终到达西天见到如来佛祖,五圣成真的故事。《红楼梦》被誉为我国古典小说的巅峰之作和中国古代社会的百科全书。本节将聚焦《三国演义》。让我们先看《三国演义》的开篇词:

> 滚滚长江东逝水,浪花淘尽英雄。是非成败转头空,青山依旧在,几度夕阳红。白发渔樵江渚上,惯看秋月春风。一壶浊酒喜相逢,古今多少事,都付笑谈中。(明·杨慎)

如果想要真正读懂这首诗,就必须了解其背后的故事。

6.2.1 例句讲解

请仔细阅读下面关于《三国演义》的概要介绍:

> 罗贯中所处的时代是一个民族矛盾和阶级矛盾异常尖锐复杂的时代。① 青年罗贯中参加了张士诚领导的起义军,为义军运筹帷幄,是一个有政治抱负的人。

②《三国演义》是他后期的作品。③ 这部古典文学名著描述了从东汉中平元年(184年)的黄巾起义,到西晋武帝太康元年(280年)统一中国的将近一个世纪中,魏、蜀、吴三国间的政治和军事斗争历史。④ 他依据陈寿《三国志》提供的历史线索和历史人物,博采裴松之对《三国志》补缺、备异、惩妄、论辩所保存的大量宝贵史料,汲取了民间传说的丰富营养,并在此基础上结合自己参加元末农民起义军的生活经历,发挥个人的卓绝艺术才能,纵横捭阖,巧妙驾驭,形象生动地描述了近一百年中浩瀚繁复的历史事件。

① 青年罗贯中参加了张士诚领导的起义军,为义军运筹帷幄,是一个有政治抱负的人。

原句由三个并列短动句组成,翻译时可以按照原文句式结构译成含三个并列分句的英语句子。然而,我们也可以调整独立小句“是一个有政治抱负的人”的语言层级,将其变为名词短语作主语同位语。

An ambitious youngster, Luo Guanzhong joined the uprising army led by Zhang Shicheng and served as a strategist.

经过调整,译文层级分明、句意紧凑,更好地体现了英语句式风格。英语名词短语在语义上概括性很强,将分句等层级下推变为名词短语是汉译英中的重要技巧。

②《三国演义》是他后期的作品。

在本句中,“后期的”用来修饰“作品”,但翻译时很难找一个对等的英语词来进行表达,在这种情况下,我们可以求助于高一级的语言单位——短语。因此,我们可以将词语“后期的”向上推移语言层级,翻译为过去分词短语“written during his later literary career”并后置。

Romance of the Three Kingdoms was a novel **written during his later literary career**.

③ 这部古典文学名著描述了从东汉中平元年(184年)的黄巾起义,到西晋武帝太康元年(280年)统一中国的将近一个世纪中,魏、蜀、吴三国间的政治和军事斗争历史。

本句的主干结构为“这部古典文学名著描述了……三国间的政治和军事斗争历史”。“从东汉……将近一个世纪中”为较长的时间状语,里面还包含有较长修饰语的两个名词结构“……的黄巾起义”和“……统一中国的”。该状语较长、较复杂,包含信息

较多，翻译时宜将其单独成句，将其由状语上推一个层级，成为一个独立句子，使译文表述更加清晰，易于理解。

This great classic chronicles the century-long political and military struggle among the three kingdoms Wei, Shu and Wu. It spans the period from 184 AD **when the Yellow Turbans Uprising broke out** to 280 AD **when Emperor Wu of Western Jin reunited China**.

④ 他**依据**陈寿《三国志》提供的历史线索和历史人物，**博采**裴松之对《三国志》补缺、备异、惩妄、论辩所保存的大量宝贵史料，**汲取**了民间传说的丰富营养，并在此基础上**结合**自己参加元末农民起义军的生活经历，**发挥个人的卓绝艺术才能，纵横捭阖，巧妙驾驭，形象生动地**描述了近一百年中浩瀚繁复的历史事件。

面对较长句子首先应梳理句子结构。不难看出本句中用了大量动词引导汉语流水句（依次铺排的短动句），如"依据""博采""汲取""结合""发挥""描述"。首先可以将具有相同意义的"依据"和"博采"引导的两个分句下移合并为一个过去分词短语"Based on *the Records of Three Kingdoms* by Chen Shou as well as Pei Songzhi's corrections and additions to it"。

接着我们可将"汲取"和"结合"这两个分句下移为现在分词短语"drawing on"。为避免机械翻译，我们将名词短语"民间传说的丰富营养"上移为从句"what local folklore has to offer"，作"drawing on"的宾语。最后可根据句义将原文中"发挥个人的卓绝艺术才能，纵横捭阖，巧妙驾驭，形象生动地……"这四个意义相似的小分句合并，语言层级下移为副词"skillfully"，让译文更加清晰简洁。

Based on *the Records of Three Kingdoms* by Chen Shou as well as Pei Songzhi's corrections and additions to it, Luo Guanzhong, **drawing on what local folklore has to offer** and his own experience in the uprising army, **skillfully** presents a panoramic view of the turbulent period of almost a hundred years.

6.2.2 双语对照

三国演义/Romance of the Three Kingdoms	
罗贯中所处的时代是一个民族矛盾和阶级矛盾异常尖锐复杂的时代。青年罗	The period during which Luo Guanzhong lived was marked by sharp ethnic and class conflicts. **An**

（续表）

三国演义/Romance of the Three Kingdoms	
贯中参加了张士诚领导的起义军，为义军运筹帷幄，是一个有政治抱负的人。《三国演义》是他后期的作品。这部古典文学名著描述了从东汉中平元年（184年）的黄巾起义，到西晋武帝太康元年（280年）统一中国的将近一个世纪中，魏、蜀、吴三国间的政治和军事斗争历史。他依据陈寿《三国志》提供的历史线索和历史人物，博采裴松之对《三国志》补缺、备异、惩妄、论辩所保存的大量宝贵史料，汲取了民间传说的丰富营养，并在此基础上结合自己参加元末农民起义军的生活经历，发挥个人的卓绝艺术才能，纵横捭阖，巧妙驾驭，形象生动地描述了近一百年中浩瀚繁复的历史事件。	ambitious youngster, Luo Guanzhong joined the uprising army led by Zhang Shicheng and served as a strategist. *Romance of the Three Kingdoms* was a novel written during his later literary career. This great classic chronicles the century-long political and military struggle among the three kingdoms Wei, Shu and Wu. It spans the period from 184 AD when the Yellow Turbans Uprising broke out to 280 AD when Emperor Wu of Western Jin reunited China. Based on *The Records of Three Kingdoms* by Chen Shou as well as Pei Songzhi's corrections and additions to it, Luo Guanzhong, drawing on what local folklore has to offer and his own experience in the uprising army, skillfully presents a panoramic view of the turbulent period of almost a hundred years.

6.2.3 译技总结

在汉译英时我们需要调整和移动语言层级，对词、短语、分句（偏句）、句子、句群进行上移或下移，以达到译文的语法正确、自然流畅、简约清晰、重点突出。

汉译英语言层级推移

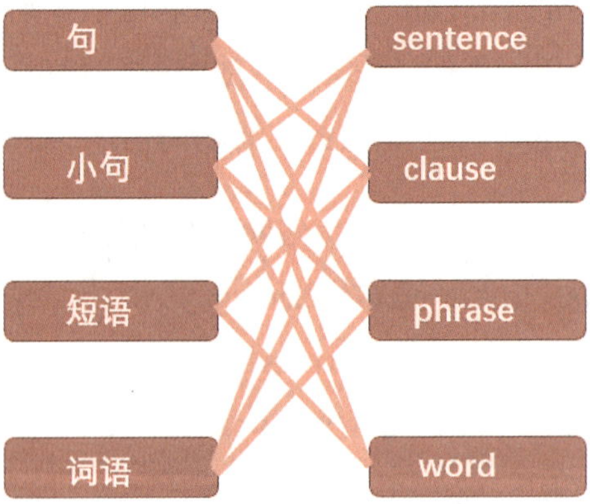

句　　sentence

小句　　clause

短语　　phrase

词语　　word

6.2.4 文化表达

（1）文化基本知识与表达

当我们谈到《三国演义》时，总会想到叱咤风云的英雄、令人叫绝的计谋和波澜壮阔的战争场面。那么第一个让你想到的英雄是谁呢？

英雄

① Zhuge Liang(诸葛亮)— the top-level hero with great wisdom

pay three visits to the cottage(三顾茅庐)

② Guan Yu(关羽)— a hero of great loyalty

③ Zhang Fei(张飞)— a hero of great bravery

three heroes, Liu Bei, Guan Yu and Zhang Fei; peach garden sworn brothers(桃园结义)

计谋

① to borrow arrows with thatched boats(草船借箭)

② to let the enemy leave in order to catch him later(欲擒故纵)

③ the ruse of inflicting an injury on oneself to win the confidence of the enemy(苦肉计)

④ honey-trap(美人计)

⑤ to take away the firewood from under the cauldron(釜底抽薪)

战争

① The Battle of Chibi(赤壁之战)

② The Battle of Guandu(官渡之战)

③ The Battle of Yiling(夷陵之战)

谚语

① There is life for those who are with me, death for those against.(顺我者生,逆我者亡。)

② I would rather betray the world than let the world betray me.(宁教我负天下人,休教天下人负我。)

③ O God, since thou made Zhou Yu, why did thou also create Zhuge Liang?(既生瑜,何生亮。)

④ Man proposes, God disposes. We cannot wrest events to our will.(谋事在人,成事在天。不可强也!)

⑤ The clever bird chooses the branch whereon to perch; the wise servant selects the master to serve.(良禽择木而栖,贤臣择主而事。)

⑥ How can swallows and sparrows understand the flight of the crane and the wild goose?(燕雀安知鸿鹄之志哉?)

⑦ Indeed, Lv Bu was the man among humans, as Red-Hare was the horse among horses.(人中吕布,马中赤兔。)

⑧ To achieve this end, I would use the last remnant of my strength and could die content.（鞠躬尽瘁，死而后已。）

⑨ All are in your wish, but wind from the east.（万事俱备，只欠东风。）

（2）文化知识延伸与翻译

三顾茅庐/Three Visits to the Thatched Cottage	
刘备、关羽、张飞自桃园结义后，虽整天东奔西跑，但因缺少谋士，总觉得恢复汉朝天下无望。后来得徐庶帮助，连打胜仗。徐庶为救母无奈去了曹营。临走推荐了诸葛亮。	After they had become **sworn brothers** at Taoyuan, Liu Bei, Guan Yu, and Zhang Fei made concerted efforts to restore the Han Dynasty. However, they felt that it would be impossible to do it without the help of a smart adviser. The Liu-Guan-Zhang alliance later won one battle after another thanks to the advice of Xu Shu. But before long, Xu had to **surrender** to the opposing camp of Cao Cao in order to save the life of his mother who was abducted by the Cao troops. Before he left, Xu Shu recommended Zhuge Liang to the brothers.
一日，刘备带关羽、张飞来到隆中卧龙冈，想请诸葛亮出山。小僮说："先生今早出去了。"刘备让僮子转告先生说他来访，然后拉马闷闷不乐地回去了。又过了数日，刘备探得诸葛亮已回家，便同关、张二次来访。僮子说："先生正在草堂看书。"刘备求见后得知不是诸葛亮，而是其弟诸葛钧。于是留下一封信，表达敬慕之情。兄弟三人又冒雪回去了。	Accompanied by Guan Yu and Zhang Fei, Liu Bei went to Wolonggang in Longzhong in the hope of inviting Zhuge Liang to be their military adviser, but Zhuge's servant said: "The Mentor left in the morning." Liu Bei asked the servant to forward to Zhuge Liang his message that the brothers had come to visit him. After that, Liu rode his horse away, returning home **sullenly**. A few days later when he learned that Zhuge Liang was at home, Liu Bei went for another visit along with Guan Yu and Zhang Fei. The servant said: "The Mentor is reading books at his thatched cottage." Liu requested to see him. When they learned that the one reading books at the thatched cottage was not Zhuge Liang himself but his brother Zhuge Jun, the Liu-Guan-Zhang brothers left a letter to express their admiration and then braved heavy snows to return home.
回到新野不久，刘备想再次去请诸葛亮。关羽劝说："可能诸葛亮没本事，怕见我们。"张飞则说："你们别去了，我用绳子捆来。"刘备忙讲了当年文王访姜子牙的故事。兄弟三人又第三次来到卧龙冈。他们一到，小僮忙说："先生在睡觉。"刘备一直等到诸葛亮睡醒后更衣相见。刘备不辞劳苦，三顾茅庐，终于请出诸葛亮出山辅佐，共图大业。	Not long after they returned to their **barracks** at Xinye, Liu Bei wanted to visit Zhuge Liang's thatched cottage once more. However, Guan Yu **dissuaded** Liu from going by saying that perhaps Zhuge Liang was not as smart as expected and that he was simply dodging the visiting brothers. Zhang Fei said: "You don't need to go. I'll tie him up and force him to come and see you instead." Liu Bei lost no time in telling his brothers the story of King Wen who was bent on visiting one of his **subjects** called Jiang Ziya. Liu, Guan and Zhang, therefore, paid a third visit to Wolonggang. They had no sooner arrived than the servant said: "The Mentor is sleeping." Liu Bei waited until Zhuge Liang was awake and dressed. Finally, Zhuge Liang consented to see the brothers. Liu Bei paid three visits to the thatched cottage without complaint. He finally succeeded in inviting Zhuge Liang to be his military adviser and to help the brothers in their cause.

词汇

sworn brothers 结拜兄弟

surrender [sə'rendə(r)] *v.* 投降

sullenly ['sʌlənli] *adv.* 阴沉地；不高兴地

barrack ['bærək] *n.* 营房；兵舍

dissuade [dɪ'sweɪd] *v.* 劝阻；劝止

subject ['sʌbdʒɪkt] *n.* 臣民

6.2.5　讨论问题

（1）汉语流水句英译时通常应该怎么样翻译？

（2）怎么样用英语介绍《三国演义》中刘备、张飞、关羽、诸葛亮、曹操等主要人物的特点？

6.3　红楼梦（调整语序和层级）

《红楼梦》被誉为中国四大名著之首，是中国古典文学的巅峰之作、中国封建文化的百科全书、传统文化的集大成者。本节我们将一起来探讨《红楼梦》中的爱恨纠葛、悲欢离合，同时复习“调”这一类翻译技巧。

6.3.1　例句讲解

《红楼梦》是一个悲剧性的爱情故事。① 它描述了一个贵族大家庭的兴衰变化，揭露了封建统治阶级的奢靡、丑恶，展示出封建社会必然走向崩溃的历史命运。小说的男主人公贾宝玉生长在贵族之家，家族对他寄予厚望，但是他不爱读书，憎恨封建传统思想，厌恶束缚他的家庭，充满叛逆精神。② 少女林黛玉是寄居在荣国府中的女子，③ 她多愁善感而又才华横溢。她与宝玉两小无猜，后来成为生死相恋的情人，④ 但最终封建势力扼杀了他们的爱情。

① 它描述了一个贵族大家庭的兴衰变化，揭露了封建统治阶级的奢靡、丑恶，展示出封建社会必然走向崩溃的历史命运。

本句由三个短动句铺排构成，中间没有关联词连接，是典型的汉语流水句。我们可以严格按照原句句式进行翻译，只需在第二和第三小句间加上必要的关联词。另外一种方法是采用英语更喜好的树状句式结构进行翻译。

通过分析原文，三个小句形式上虽为并列关系，但发生有先后，隐晦的含有前为因后为果的关系，正是有了“一个贵族大家庭的兴衰变化”，才能“揭露封建统治阶级的奢靡、丑恶”和“展示出必然崩溃的命运”，而“封建统治阶级的奢靡、丑恶”也是“封建社会必然走向崩溃”的原因，且第三小句语意更为重要。经过分析我们可以将第一个分句下移为名词短语“the rise and fall of the family”作为句子的主语，然后把原文第三小句前移译为句子的谓语，而把第二小句层级下移译为介词短语并后置，作为表原因的修饰语。这样全句可翻译如下：

The rise and fall of the family reveals the inevitable decline of the feudal society **with the dissipated and corrupt ruling class**.

经过调整语言层级和前后位置后，译文变成了英语所偏好的树状结构，主干清晰，层级分明，译文也比原文凝练简洁（原文的三个动词“描述”“揭露”“展示”只保留了一个）。

② 少女林黛玉是**寄居在荣国府中的**女子……

“寄居在荣国府中”是用来修饰“女子”的前置定语，当前置偏正短语较长时，我们宜将其层级上推，译为定语从句并后置。

Lin Daiyu was a girl **who lived in the family as a relative**.

③ 她**多愁善感而又才华横溢**。

本句中“多愁善感（sentimental）”和“才华横溢（talented）”都是用来描述“她”的。当译成英语形容词作定语时，要按英文单词长短调整语序。

Lin Daiyu was a **talented sentimental** girl.

④ 但最终**封建势力**扼杀了**他们的爱情**。

汉语句子主语为“封建势力”，谓语为“扼杀”，宾语为“他们的爱情”。在翻译时为突出强调宾语部分，也为了用人称代词指代前句提及的人物以形成更好的句间衔接，可将汉语主动句译为英语被动句，将原文中的主语和宾语位置在译文中进行对调。

Eventually **their love** was strangled by **the feudal forces**.

6.3.2 双语对照

红楼梦 / A Dream of Red Mansions	
《红楼梦》是一个悲剧性的爱情故事。它描述了一个贵族大家庭的兴衰变化，揭露了封建统治阶级的奢靡、丑恶，展示出封建社会必然走向崩溃的历史命运。小说的男主人公贾宝玉生长在贵族之家，家族对他寄予厚望，但是他不爱读书，憎恨封建传统思想，厌恶束缚他的家庭，充满叛逆精神。少女林黛玉是寄居在荣国府中的女子，她多愁善感而又才华横溢。她与宝玉两小无猜，后来成为生死相恋的情人，但最终封建势力扼杀了他们的爱情。	*A Dream of Red Mansions* tells a tragic love story set in a large noble family. The rise and fall of the family reveals the inevitable decline of the feudal society with the dissipated and corrupt ruling class. Born to a wealthy and noble family, the hero Jia Baoyu has a lot to live up to. But his aversion to reading, defiance of outmoded conventions and resentment at the feudal family reveal his rebellious character. Lin Daiyu was a talented sentimental girl who lived in the family as a relative. Growing up together, Daiyu and Baoyu fell for each other, but eventually their love was strangled by the feudal forces.

6.3.3 译技总结

通过本单元的知识讲解，我们学习了在翻译时如何进行句子内部语序的横向调整和层级的纵向调整。

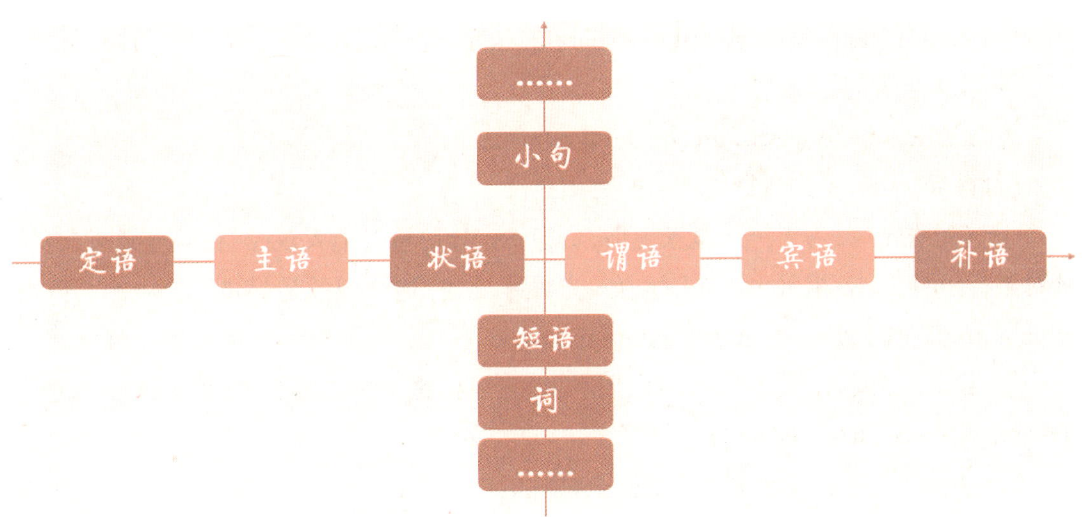

横向来看，我们根据汉英不同语言的语序偏好可调整句子成分之间的顺序，包括主、谓、宾、定、状、补之间的语序调整；纵向来看，我们可将词、短语、小句、句子、句群的层级进行上推或下移，推移的目的主要是为了准确达意、简化结构、锤炼语言，使译文主次分明，简洁自然。

6.3.4 文化表达

（1）文化基本知识与表达

《红楼梦》被誉为中国古典小说的巅峰之作，中国封建社会的百科全书，传统文化的集大成者。学术界因其异常出色的艺术成就和丰富深刻的思想底蕴而产生了专门研究它的学问——红学。下面我们从文学与文化的角度来谈谈《红楼梦》中的基本知识与英语表达。

首先，《红楼梦》的叙述形式是“章回体”，这是中国古典长篇小说的主要形式，其特点是将全书分为若干章节，称为“回”或“节”。每回用单句或两句对偶的文字作标题，称为“回目”，概括本回的故事内容。章回体小说（Zhangzhui-style novel）起源于宋元时期的“讲史话本”，古代四大名著都属于章回体小说。

《红楼梦》的语言因其具有独特个性、雅言共用、修辞之美等特点，具有极高的艺术价值。以下为三句描写女性角色的句子，你能否通过书中描述语言猜出具体人名？

① 两弯柳叶眉似愁非愁，一双含情目似喜非喜。

Her eyebrows were knitted and yet not frowning, her sparkling eyes held both joy and sorrow.

② 粉面含春威不露，丹唇未启笑先闻。

Her vermilion lips were parted in a sparkling smile.

③ 肌肤莹润，举止娴雅。

A beautiful, dainty girl of great natural refinements.

《红楼梦》反映了许多封建社会的文化礼仪：

① 元妃省亲时，为了符合皇家规格，贾家不仅斥巨资打造大观园，在迎接她时，她父亲对她行跪拜之礼，祖母也“按品大妆”方可拜见她，这体现的是封建社会中的君臣之礼（courtesy between the monarch and ministers）。

② 邢夫人为取悦丈夫贾赦，而让鸳鸯嫁给他，这反映的是夫为妻纲的夫妇之礼（courtesy between husband and wife）。

《红楼梦》作为中国封建社会百科全书式的作品，自然也是一部集中国服饰文化于一体的经典小说，从服装到饰品，从质地到工艺，从款式到色彩，华冠丽服（in splendid, brightly-colored livery），全方位展现了中华服饰文明成果。

（2）文化知识延伸与翻译

《红楼梦》中的成语英译：

① 香菱笑道：“好姑娘，趁着这个工夫，你教给我作诗罢。”宝钗笑道：“我说你‘得陇

望蜀’呢。”（第四十八回）

霍克斯译：

Bao-chai laughed. You’re like the famous general: “One conquest breeds appetite for another.”

杨宪益译：

“The more you get, the more you want!” chuckled Baochai.

乔利译：

“I say,” Pao-chai laughed, “You no sooner get the Lung state than you long for the Shu!”

② 黛玉纳罕道：“这些人个个皆敛声屏气，恭肃严整如此，这来者系谁，这样放诞无礼？”（第三回）

霍克斯译：

“Everyone else around here seems to go about with bated breath,” thought Dai-yu. “Who can this new arrival be? Who is so brash and unmannerly?”

杨宪益译：

Daiyu thought with surprise, “The people here are so respectful and solemn; they all seem to be holding their breath. Who can this be, so boisterous and pert?”

乔利译：

“Every one of all these people,” reflected Tai-yu, “holds her peace and suppresses the very breath of her mouth; and who, I wonder, is this coming in this reckless and rude manner?”

红楼梦诗词延伸阅读

作者题绝

满纸荒唐言，一把辛酸泪。
都云作者痴，谁解其中味？

Pages full of fantastic talk, **penned** with bitter tears.
All men call the author mad, none his message hears.

（杨宪益、戴乃迭译）

枉凝眉

一个是阆苑仙葩，一个是美玉无瑕。

若说没奇缘，今生偏又遇着他；
若说有奇缘，如何心事终虚化？
一个枉自嗟呀，一个空劳牵挂。
一个是水中月，一个是镜中花。
想眼中能有多少泪珠儿，
怎经得秋流到冬尽，春流到夏！

Vain Longing

One is an **immortal** flower of fairyland,
The other fair flawless jade,
And were it not **predestined,**
Why should they meet again in this existence?
Yet, if predestined,
Why does their love come to nothing?
One sighs to no purpose,
The other yearns in vain;
One is the moon reflected in the water,
The other but a flower in the mirror.
How many tears can **well** from her eyes?
Can they flow on from autumn till winter,
From spring till summer?

（杨宪益、戴乃迭译）

词汇

pen [pen] *v.* 写

immortal [ɪ'mɔːrtl] *adj.* 不朽的

predestined [ˌpriː'destɪnd] *adj.* 注定的

well [wel] *v.* 涌出

6.3.5 讨论问题

（1）你能谈谈翻译时句子间的层级转化的原因及方法吗？

（2）后世将《红楼梦》誉为中国封建社会的百科全书，你能谈谈你的看法吗？

6.4 单元练习

1. 单项选择。从两个备选项中选出对汉语原句翻译得较好的一个选项。

① 唐诗是中国珍贵的文化遗产，在中国文学和诗歌中占据重要地位。

A. The Tang poetry, a precious cultural heritage of China, occupied a significant place in the field of Chinese literature and poetry.

B. The Tang poetry is a precious cultural heritage of China, occupied a significant place in the field of Chinese literature and poetry.

② 贴春联是春节的一大传统习俗，也是中国人欢度新年春节的重要方式。

A. Pasting couplets is the Spring Festival's traditional custom, is also an important way for the Chinese people to celebrate the Spring Festival.

B. As a traditional custom during the Spring Festival, pasting couplets is also an important way for the Chinese people to celebrate the Spring Festival.

③ 这部小说以贾宝玉和林黛玉的爱情悲剧为线索，描写了封建官僚四大家族的衰落过程。

A. With the tragic love story of Jia Baoyu and Lin Daiyu as the main theme, the novel describes the decline of four feudal noble families.

B. The novel has Jia Baoyu and Lin Daiyu's tragic love story as its theme, describes the feudal noble families' decline.

④ 该小说讲述的是玄奘和尚在历经种种考验和磨难之后，成功到达西天取回真经的故事。

A. The story tells about the monk named Hsuan Tsang who went through many trials and much suffering, arrived at the "Western Regions", brought back the Buddhist sutras.

B. The story tells about the monk named Hsuan Tsang who successfully arrived at the "Western Regions" to bring back the Buddhist sutras after many trials and much suffering.

⑤ 小说共计120回，前80回的作者是曹雪芹，后40回由高鹗完成。

A. In the 120-chapter novel, the first 80 chapters were written by Cao Xueqin and the left 40 by Gao E.

B. The novel has 120 chapters altogether, the first 80 chapters were written by Cao Xueqin, the left 40 by Gao E.

2. 句子翻译。翻译下面的句子，注意运用本单元所学的翻译技巧。

① 春联(the Spring Festival couplet)是中国特有的一种文学形式，有着悠久的历史。

______

② 唐诗(Tang poetry)的题材非常广泛，从自然现象、政治动态(political dynamics)到社会风俗、个人感受，几乎包括生活的方方面面。

______

③ 春联(couplets)上的文字简洁、精巧，象征着人们对未来的巨大期盼，表达人们对新年的美好愿望。

______

6.5 单元测验

1. 从两个备选项中选出对汉语原句翻译得较好的一个选项。(5×5分=25分)

① 《四书五经》在中国古代封建社会是儒家文化的典范之作。

A. The Four Books and the Five Classics were the canonical works of the Confucian culture in the feudal society of ancient China.

B. The Four Books and the Five Classics in the feudal society of ancient China were the canonical works of the Confucian culture.

② 贾母因觉身上乏倦，便往稻香村来歇息。

A. The Lady Dowager, feeling rather tired, had a rest in Paddy-Sweet Cottage.

B. The Lady Dowager, feeling her body very tired, had a rest in Paddy-Sweet Cottage.

③ 凤姐忙笑道："老太太别高兴……使个巧法子，哄着我拿出四两银子来暗里补上，我还做梦呢！"

A. "Don't get carried away, Madam," warned Xifeng with a chuckle. "Then you'll play some clever trick to make me part with three or four times the amount

while I'm dreaming."

B. "Don't get carried away, Madam," warned Xifeng with a chuckle. "Then you'll play some clever trick to make me part unknowingly with three or four times the amount."

④《孙子兵法》被译成了几十种文字，成为各国军事家和国防教育的经典，也广为商界政界人士青睐。

A. Published in scores of languages, *The Art of War* is a classic for military strategists and national defense education and a preferred reading for politicians and businessmen.

B. *The Art of War* published in scores of languages, is a classic for military strategists and national defense education and a preferred reading for politicians and businessmen.

⑤ 鲁智深打死恶霸镇关西后，怕吃官司，逃往他地，先来到五台山出家。

A. Lu Zhishen killed the local tyrant Zhen Guanxi and he feared of being jailed, so he fled to Mount Wutai where he stayed in a temple as a monk.

B. For fear of being jailed after killing the local tyrant Zhen Guanxi, Lu Zhishen fled to Mount Wutai where he stayed in a temple as a monk.

2. 翻译下面的句子，注意运用本单元所学的翻译技巧。(3×10分=30分)

①《红楼梦》写成于18世纪，是中国著名的古典长篇小说。

____

② 中国军事安全思想的精华体现为一本享誉中国乃至全世界的古兵书——《孙子兵法》(*The Art of War*)。

____

③ 孟子(Mencius)提出"人性本善"的观点。

____

3. 将下面短文翻译成英语，注意运用本单元所学的翻译技巧，增补必要信息以帮助目的语读者理解。(45分)

中国的四大名著(the Four Great Classical Novels)指创作于明清时期的四部最伟大、最有影响力的小说。现在四部小说都已被改编成电影或电视剧(TV series)，受到很多观众的喜爱。四大名著都具有很高的艺术水平，是中华民族的宝贵遗产，也是中国文学史上的创举。

第 7 单元

戏剧杂技

Drama and Acrobatics

7.1 背景介绍

Lead-in Questions

(1) How much do you know about Chinese drama and acrobatics? Can you list some representative types?

(2) Do you know what the lion dance is? What are the cultural meanings behind the dragon dance?

Chinese Opera① is the traditional form of Chinese drama, which combines dialogue, music, **vocal** performance, dance, kung fu (*gongfu*), **acrobatics**, and so on. It is one of the three oldest **theatrical** art forms in the world, together with Greek Theatre② and Indian Sanskrit Opera③. The origin of it can be traced back to the singing, dancing and religious **rituals** in **primitive** times. But not until the late Song Dynasty (960~1279 AD) and the early Yuan Dynasty (1279~1368 AD) through a very long period of development and reforms did Chinese Opera form a mature and complete artistic system.

Among the hundreds of forms of opera throughout China, Beijing Opera④ has the greatest influence and is therefore regarded as a national opera. The roles in Beijing Opera are divided into four main types according to the sex, age, social status, and profession of the character: *sheng*⑤ (male roles), *dan*⑥ (female roles), *jing*⑦ (heroes and generals with painted faces) and *chou*⑧ (**clowns**). As well as these, there are some other **minor** types.

There are plenty of unique and popularized folk performing arts in China, such as dragon dance and lion dance. The dragon dance is widely popular among various ethnic groups throughout China. As early as in the Shang Dynasty, there were records about people gathering to **worship** the dragon and pray for rain. Poems and articles in later dynasties are rich in their descriptions of dragon dances. Even today, the dragon dance is still the most typical form of **entertainment** at festivals and celebrations. In China, there are over a hundred kinds of dragon dances whose performance is increasingly diverse and colorful. Displaying the Chinese spirit of being united and progressive, the dragon dance is China's **precious** cultural **heritage** and one of the symbols of Chinese culture.

The lion dance is a form of traditional dance in China, which can be often seen in important festivals and great events. With a history of over 1,000 years, lion dance can date back to the Three Kingdoms Period⑨. There are usually two performers in lion dance, one handling the lion's head and the other playing the body and the tail. They perform all kinds of lion's movements to the music played by **gongs** and drums. As the Chinese **migrate** abroad, the lion dance is famous all over the world, especially in Southeast Asian countries; however, each country and region has its own dancing style.

词汇

vocal ['vəʊkl] *adj.* 歌唱的

acrobatics [ˌækrə'bætɪks] *n.* 杂技

theatrical [θɪ'ætrɪkl] *adj.* 剧场的；戏剧的

ritual ['rɪtʃʊəl] *n.* 仪式

primitive ['prɪmətɪv] *adj.* 原始的；远古的

clown [klaʊn] *n.* 小丑

minor ['maɪnə(r)] *adj.* 次要的

worship ['wɜːʃɪp] *v.* 敬奉

entertainment [ˌentə'teɪnmənt] *n.* 娱乐

precious ['preʃəs] *adj.* 宝贵的

heritage ['herɪtɪdʒ] *n.* 遗产

gong [gɒŋ] *n.* 锣

migrate ['maɪgreɪt] *v.* 移动

文化注释

① Chinese Opera 中国戏曲（主要是由民间歌舞、说唱和滑稽戏三种不同艺术形式综合而成，与希腊悲剧和喜剧、印度梵剧并称为世界三大古老的戏剧文化。）

② Greek Theatre 希腊戏剧（分古希腊戏剧和近代希腊戏剧，其中古希腊戏剧细分为

悲剧、羊人剧、喜剧、摹拟剧等。)

③ Indian Sanskrit Opera 印度梵剧(印度古典戏剧,常取材于史诗传说、现实故事、宗教作品等。)

④ Beijing Opera 京剧(中国五大戏曲剧种之一,被视为中国国粹,中国戏曲三鼎甲"榜首"。)

⑤ Sheng 生(生角,中国戏曲表演主要行当之一,常指老生或青壮年男子。)

⑥ Dan 旦(旦角,戏曲中的女性形象,可分为青衣、花旦、刀马旦、武旦、老旦、花衫等。)

⑦ Jing 净(净角,俗称花脸。以面部化妆运用图案化的脸谱为标志,演唱风格粗壮浑厚,动作大开大合,顿挫鲜明。)

⑧ Chou 丑(丑角,一般扮演插科打诨比较滑稽的角色。文丑以做工为主,武丑以武打为主。)

⑨ the Three Kingdoms Period 三国时期

7.2 舞狮(合译法)

这个单元将介绍两个翻译技巧:合译与分译。同时我们将领略中国戏曲和民间表演的魅力。

在中国,一些动物具有独特的文化寓意。比如,龙代表至高无上的权力,乌龟似有通天道的灵性,鹤是美德和高洁的象征,喜鹊是喜事降临的吉兆。狮子虽源于外来文化,但在中国民间文化中也至关重要。

狮子是在中国西汉时期作为贡品由皇室引进的,但它为人熟知则是以狮子游戏的形式,这便是舞狮的前身。舞狮曾在唐朝作为宫廷燕乐的形式之一为皇家宴会助兴。后来舞狮逐渐在民间开始流行。民间舞狮活动在春节期间几乎天天举行。随着时间的推移,狮子在中国人民心中的形象从一种外来动物转变成了一种神兽,这其中,舞狮表演的影响不可忽视。本节我们将讨论舞狮文化,并学习合译的翻译技巧。

7.2.1 例句讲解

合译法多指将原文中两个或两个以上的词合译为一词,将两个或两个以上的简单句合译为一个长句,或将一个复合句在译文中用一个单句来表达。请看这篇题为舞狮的短文。让我们看看如何在翻译时合并单词、小句和句子。

① 舞狮是一种中国传统民间艺术，常由一人或两人身披狮型服装进行表演，以夸张的方式模仿狮子的各种动作。经过几千年的发展，舞狮已在各地形成了不同的表演风格。中国舞狮有北方武狮和南方文狮之分。② 武狮着重于武功，动作矫健，技巧性高，运用登高、跳跃、搏斗、争抢球、走跷跷板等高难度技巧；③ 文狮着重于表情，动作细腻诙谐，着意刻画狮子活泼好动、善于嬉戏的性格，如玩球、打滚、舔皮毛、抓耳朵等。④ 前者强大勇敢，后者则温顺有趣。

① 舞狮是一种中国传统民间艺术，常由一人或两人身披狮型服装进行表演，以夸张的方式模仿狮子的各种动作。

第一个汉语句子由三个相对独立短动句组成。他们有一个共同点，即这三个小句都描述了同样的事情：舞狮。我们可以保留第一部分“舞狮是一种中国传统民间艺术”作为主句，并将其翻译为“Lion dance is a traditional Chinese folk art.”然后以方式状语和后置修饰语的形式将剩下两部分整合到主句中。本句翻译如下：

Imitating various movements of lions in an exaggerated way, lion dance is a traditional Chinese folk art **performed by one or two persons in lion costumes**.

该例展示了如何将几个简短的、松散并列的独立小句组合成一个相对紧凑的英语句子。

② 武狮着重于武功，动作矫健，技巧性高，运用登高、跳跃、搏斗、争抢球、走跷跷板等高难度技巧……

第二个汉语句子也是由松散的几个部分连接而成的一个长句。但它们都围绕着同一个话题，即舞狮的武功。因此，我们可以将这些零散的部分合并成一个长而复杂的英语句子。首先，开头部分“武狮着重于武功”是主句，翻译成英文为“The wild lion dance attaches importance to the martial arts.”其次，可用介词短语作为方式状语，在表演中列出不同的特技。

The wild lion dance attaches importance to the martial arts **with nimble movement and high technique**, **by using high-difficulty feats like climbing, jumping, fighting, scrambling for the ball, and walking on the seesaw** ...

③ ……文狮着重于表情，动作细腻诙谐，着意刻画狮子活泼好动、善于嬉戏的性格，如玩球、打滚、舔皮毛、抓耳朵等。

第三句的结构与第二句极为相似。按照刚才使用的方法，我们将把这些零散的部分合并成一个长而复杂的英语句子。

> ... while the gentle lion dance focuses on facial expressions **with exquisite and humorous movements which strive to depict lions' dynamic and frolicsome character, such as playing with the ball, rolling about, licking its fur, and scratching its ears**.

第一部分为主句，其次是介词短语作为后置修饰语，然后在"with"结构中嵌入定语从句，以显示舞蹈动作的目的。"活泼好动"由两个汉语词语组成，可合译为一个单词"dynamic"。

④ 前者强大勇敢，后者则温顺有趣。

第四句包括两个简单小句，它们之间有一种隐藏的逻辑关系，即比较。翻译时最好加上一个连词"while"来把这两个汉语句子联系起来。

> The former is powerful and bold **while** the latter tame and funny.

7.2.2　双语对照

舞狮/Lion Dance	
舞狮是一种中国传统民间艺术，常由一人或两人身披狮型服装进行表演，以夸张的方式模仿狮子的各种动作。经过几千年的发展，舞狮已在各地形成了不同的表演风格。中国舞狮有北方武狮和南方文狮之分。武狮着重于武功，动作矫健，技巧性高，运用登高、跳跃、搏斗、争抢球、走跷跷板等高难度技巧；文狮着重于表情，动作细腻诙谐，着意刻画狮子活泼好动、善于嬉戏的性格，如玩球、打滚、舔皮毛、抓耳朵等。前者强大勇敢，后者则温顺有趣。	**Imitating various movements of lions in an exaggerated way**, lion dance is a traditional Chinese folk art **performed by one or two persons in lion costumes**. After thousands of years of development, diverse performing styles in different regions have been formed. The lion dance in China falls into the Northern lion dance (wild lion dance) and the Southern lion dance (gentle lion dance). The wild lion dance attaches importance to the martial arts **with nimble movement and high technique, by using high-difficulty feats like climbing, jumping, fighting, scrambling for the ball, and walking on the seesaw**; while the gentle lion dance focuses on facial expressions **with exquisite and humorous movements which strive to depict lions' dynamic and frolicsome character, such as playing with the ball, rolling about, licking its fur, and scratching its ears**. The former is powerful and bold **while** the latter tame and funny.

7.2.3 译技总结

汉英句型比较研究可以帮助我们找出合译的原因。汉语句子通常由短动句铺排而组成，相对较少使用连词；而英语句子往往长而复杂，从句相互嵌入，并常使用连词或介词作显性连接。因此，合译是汉译英时常用的技巧。

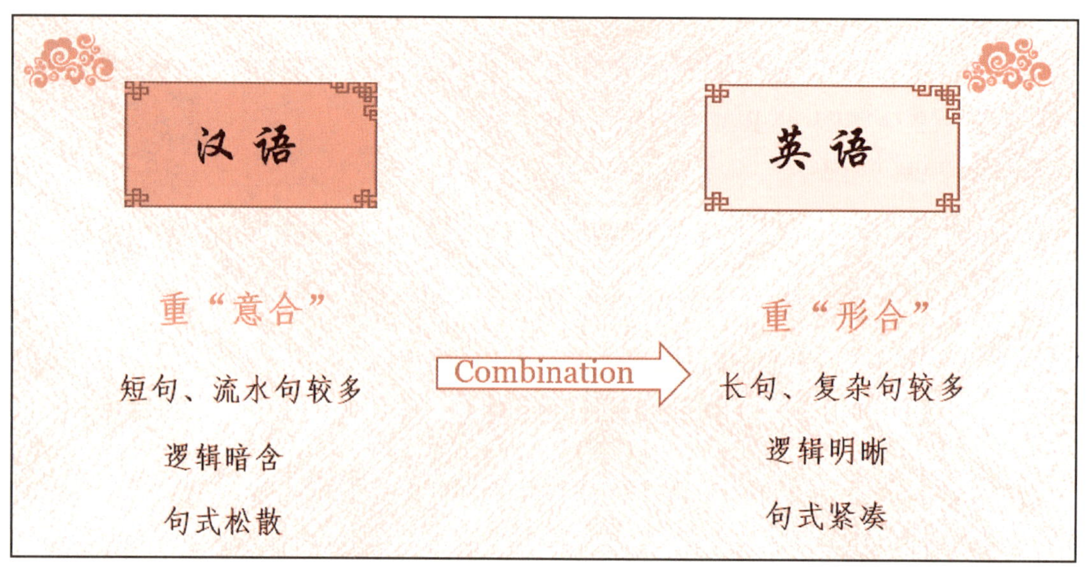

我们将常见汉译英合译情况总结如下：

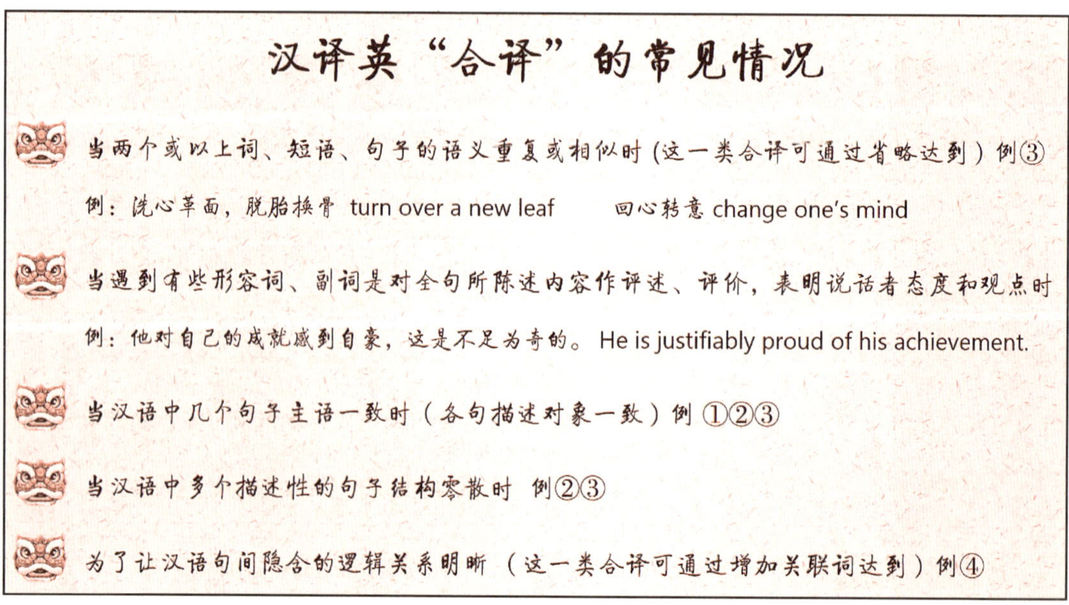

7.2.4　文化表达

(1)文化基本知识与表达

舞狮和舞龙是中国人在节庆时刻常见的民间娱乐活动。它们有共同点,也有区别。首先,从表演形式上看,舞狮通常由一名或两名表演者分别撑起狮头和狮尾,而舞龙则需要一队人合力用多根竹竿子将龙举起,使用的龙的长度从几米到百米不等。

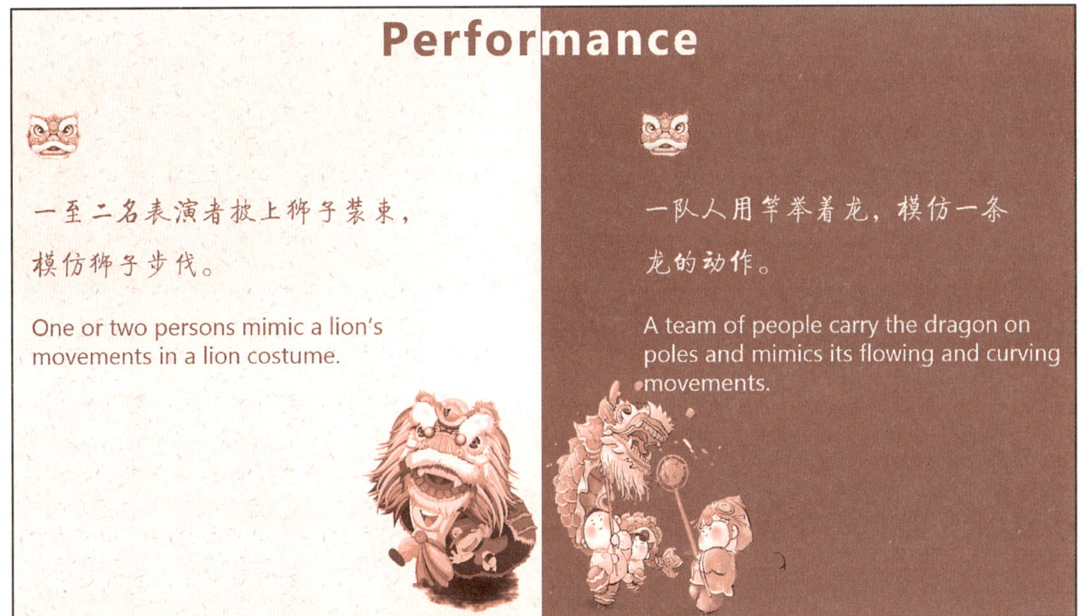

从材料上来讲,狮子道具通常是用木头或竹条编制成骨架,龙也常由竹条编制成,其他材料,如干草、树枝、莲花灯或长凳也可以使用。

从象征意义上来看,狮子象征勇敢和权力,而龙则代表财富、权力和高贵。传统上,舞狮被用来驱除邪恶,祈求好运;舞龙除了上述功用之外,还有求雨、祈丰收的目的。龙身越长预示着会带来越多的好运。

到目前为止,舞狮和舞龙都被视作典型的中国式民间表演。它们作为活跃节日气氛的方式常常在节日和庆典活动中出现。伴随着海外华人的宣传和影响,舞狮和舞龙在世界各地特别是在东南亚国家广受欢迎。

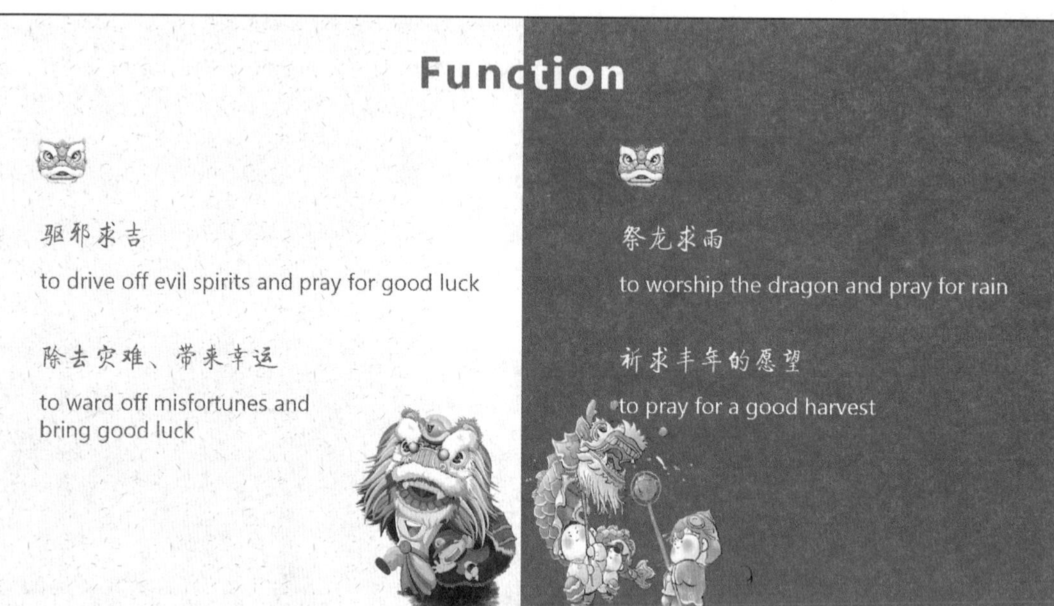

（2）文化知识延伸与翻译

舞狮是一种由一人或两人身披狮型服装进行表演的民间表演艺术。据记载，舞狮有两千多年的悠久历史，在唐朝时被引入皇室，成为皇室的娱乐项目。经过几千年的发展，舞狮已经在各地形成了不同的表演特色。	Lion dance is a folk performing art performed by one or two people in lion costumes. According to records, the dance, with a long history of more than 2,000 years, was introduced to the royal family as a form of entertainment during the Tang Dynasty. After several thousand years of development, diverse performing characteristics in different regions have been formed.
在狮子舞中，两位表演者同披一件狮子服，一个舞动头部，另一个舞动身体和尾巴。他们熟练配合，模仿狮子的各种动作。狮子是兽中之王，在中国的传统风俗中是一种可以去除灾难、带来幸运的吉祥物。所以，人们通常在春节和其他节日期间表演狮子舞。狮子舞也可能出现在其他重要场合，如商店开业和结婚典礼，往往吸引许多人观赏。	In the dance, two performers who share the same lion costume dance by moving the head, body and tail respectively. They cooperate skillfully to imitate various movements of a lion. As the king of animals, the lion is traditionally regarded as a **mascot** that **wards off misfortunes** and brings good fortune. Therefore, people usually have lion dances during the Spring Festival and other festivals or holidays. It can also be seen at many other important occasions such as opening ceremonies of new shops and wedding ceremonies, and attracts large audiences.

词汇

mascot ['mæskət] *n.* 吉祥物；福神

misfortune [ˌmɪs'fɔːtʃuːn] *n.* 不幸；灾祸

ward off 避开；挡住

7.2.5 讨论问题

（1）请你想想怎么用英语介绍舞狮、舞龙的社会文化功能？

（2）你能谈谈合译的常见使用情况和原因吗？

7.3 京剧（拆分法）

京剧是中国最具影响力和代表性的戏剧，于19世纪中叶完全成形。它吸收了许多其他地方戏中的精华，在很大程度上受北京方言和习俗的影响。京剧将传统音乐、舞蹈、诗歌、杂技和武术多种艺术形式有机融为一体。京剧有着大约200年的历史，发展了自己的音乐风格和表演技艺，并出现了许多杰出的艺术家。谭鑫培被称为京剧表演之王，是老生名角。梅兰芳被誉为伟大的戏曲艺术家，他常扮演女性角色，受到世界各地戏迷们的欢迎与尊敬。本节将聚焦京剧故事并学习翻译中的拆分法。

7.3.1 例句讲解

请仔细阅读下面这篇文章，并注意标号句子的翻译。

京剧是中国式戏剧的一种，兴起于19世纪中期，是中国文化艺术的瑰宝。

① 京剧在塑造人物方面有独特之处，即按照不同性别、年龄、身份、性格将人物划分为不同行当，代表形形色色的人物。京剧行当分为生、旦、净、丑四大类，每个行当都有自己的造型特征和表演体系。

外国人把京戏叫作Beijing Opera。② 其实京剧不是歌剧，歌剧只唱不说，事件的叙述和思想的表达都是由唱歌形式完成的，而京剧则讲究“唱、念、做、打”。

京剧表演中，演员与观众的互动也是京剧艺术的魅力之一。③ 过去京剧舞台多置于观众之中，台上唱戏，台下喝彩，台上台下一出戏，热闹非凡。现在京剧已成为中国的国粹和文化符号，直观地从一个侧面诠释了中国文化的博大精深。

① 京剧在塑造人物方面有独特之处，即按照不同性别、年龄、身份、性格将人物划分为不同行当，代表形形色色的人物。

在第一句中，“京剧在塑造人物方面有独特之处”是表明主要观点的小句，后面两个小句详细解释了第一个小句。换句话说，第一小句和第二、三小句形成总分关系。原来的汉语句子有点长，为了清楚地呈现它的总分关系，英译时最好把它分成两个单独的句子。

Beijing Opera is quite unique in role shaping. | It divides the roles into different categories according to their gender, age, identity, and character in order to represent various people.

② 其实京剧不是歌剧，歌剧只唱不说，事件的叙述和思想的表达都是由唱歌形式完成的，而京剧则讲究"唱、念、做、打"。

第二个例句的句间关系与第一个例子相似。第一个汉语小句"京剧不是歌剧"是一个概括性的陈述，它在后面小句中得到详细解释。为使译文清晰，最好把这样的汉语长句分成两个单独的英语句子。全句翻译如下：

In fact, Beijing Opera is different from opera. | The latter tells the story and expresses the thoughts by singing instead of speaking, while the former stresses *chang* (singing), *nian* (reciting), *zuo* (dancing), and *da* (martial arts performance).

③ 过去京剧舞台多置于观众之中，台上唱戏，台下喝彩，台上台下一出戏，热闹非凡。

第三个长句包含几个小句，这里的每个小句主语不同，表达了一个相对独立的意思。当主语发生变化时，最好把这样长的汉语句子切分成英语短句。这样我们就可以清楚地表示出汉语原文的多层含义。整句翻译如下：

In the past, the stage is often set within the audience. | The performers act on stage and the audience cheer up the stage, | forming a scene of bustle and excitement.

7.3.2 双语对照

京剧/Beijing Opera	
京剧是中国式戏剧的一种，兴起于19世纪中期，是中国文化艺术的瑰宝。 京剧在塑造人物方面有独特之处，即按照不同性别、年龄、身份、性格将人物划分为不同行当，代表形形色色的人物。京剧行当分为生、旦、净、丑四大类，每个行当都有自己的造型特征和表演体系。	Beijing Opera is a kind of Chinese opera which arose in the mid-19th century. It is widely regarded as one of the cultural treasures of China. Beijing Opera is quite unique in role shaping. | It divides the roles into different categories according to their gender, age, identity, and character in order to represent various people. Beijing Opera has four types of roles — *sheng*, *dan*, *jing*, and *chou*, each of which has its own modeling feature and acting system.

（续表）

京剧/Beijing Opera	
外国人把京戏叫作Beijing Opera。其实京剧不是歌剧，歌剧只唱不说，事件的叙述和思想的表达都是由唱歌形式完成的，而京剧则讲究“唱、念、做、打”。 京剧表演中，演员与观众的互动也是京剧艺术的魅力之一。过去京剧舞台多置于观众之中，台上唱戏，台下喝彩，台上台下一出戏，热闹非凡。现在京剧已成为中国的国粹和文化符号，直观地从一个侧面诠释了中国文化的博大精深。	Foreigners call Jingxi Beijing Opera. In fact, Beijing Opera is different from opera.|The latter tells the story and expresses thoughts by singing instead of speaking, while the former stresses *chang* (singing), *nian* (reciting), *zuo* (dancing), and *da* (martial arts performance). In Beijing Opera performance, the interaction between the performers and the audience is also one of the charms of this art. In the past, the stage is often set within the audience. | The performers act on stage and the audience cheer up the stage, | forming a scene of bustle and excitement. Today, Beijing Opera has become the quintessence and the sign of Chinese culture, directly reflecting its richness and profundity from one perspective.

7.3.3 译技总结

分译也叫拆分法，是把原文句子中的个别词、短语或从句分离出来，单独译出，自成短句，或使原文的一个句子分译成两个或两个以上的句子。

为什么长的汉语句子要被切成短的英语句子？一个长的汉语句子通常由一系列短动句组成，少有连接词来连接它们，但英语句子不可如此。翻译较长汉语句子的一个好办法是把它们分成几个简短英语句子，以便更清楚地呈现汉语句子原意。

为求译文语意明晰、结构正确，一般来说，以下较长的汉语句型可以拆分后再翻译：具有多层意义的长句，有概括句、阐述句的长句，带有疑问句、感叹句的长句，含有比方句的长句等。

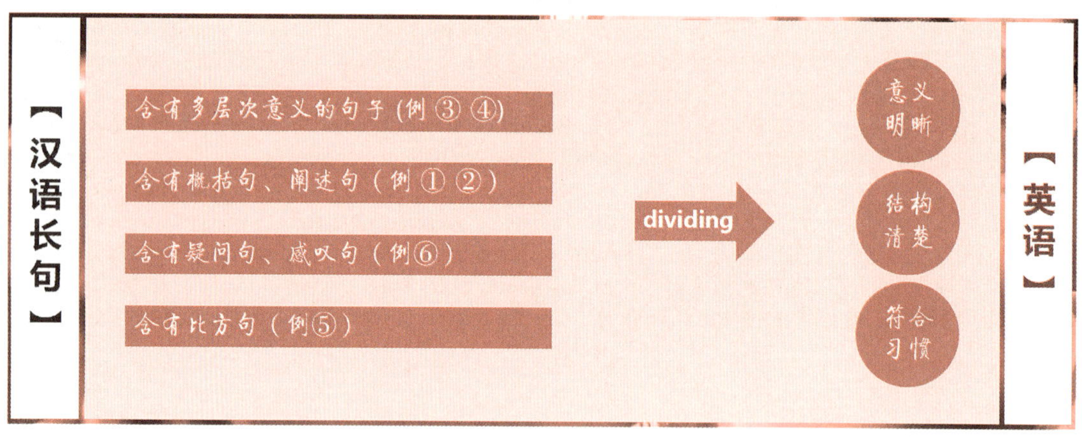

让我们再看三个例子。

④ 1828年，一些著名的湖北剧团进京，他们经常和安徽剧团同台演出，然后渐渐演变为京剧的主旋律。

第四句用三个分句告诉我们京剧的演变，每个分句都按时间顺序表达了一个独立的思想。第一、二分句主语相同，第三个分句的暗含主语实际包含了前两个分句的整个意思。我们可以在这里进行切分，添加一个词，如“combination”作主语。

In 1828, some famous Hubei troupes came to Beijing, and they often jointly performed on stage with Anhui troupes. Such combination gradually formed Beijing Opera's main melodies.

⑤ 此外，脸谱还常常带有图案来表述某个故事，比如后羿脸谱上有九个太阳，表明他曾经用箭射掉了九个太阳。

In addition, the facial makeup often comes with designs to tell some story. For instance, Hou Yi has nine suns painted on his face, indicating that he has ever shot nine suns from the sky.

第五句有三个小句，第二和第三小句通过举例来支持第一小句“脸谱还常常带有图案来表述某个故事”。由于整句较长，我们最好在此处将其拆分为两个英语句子，同时

也因为英语短语 “for example” 不能单独用来连接两个独立的小句。

⑥ 那可太好了，是什么戏？哪个剧团的？

第六个例子包含两个汉语句子，其中第一个句子又包含两个小句：一个陈述句和一个疑问句，且没有使用任何连接词。然而，在英语中逗号不能单独用于连接句子中的两个独立小句。因此，我们最好把这样一个汉语句子分成两个或两个以上的英语句子。

That's wonderful. What's it about? And which troupe will perform?

7.3.4　文化表达

（1）文化基本知识与表达

现在让我们了解更多关于京剧的知识。京剧在角色塑造上是相当独特的。它根据角色的性别、年龄、身份和性格，将角色分为四类：生、旦、净、丑。为了代表不同的人，每个角色都有自己的模型特征和表演体系。生是指男性人物，主要包括老生、小生和武生。旦代表女性人物，主要包括老旦、青衣、花旦和武旦。净是指具有鲜明个性和坚强人物的男性人物，如英雄、将军和上帝。丑是一个滑稽的角色，它是最有趣或消极的角色。

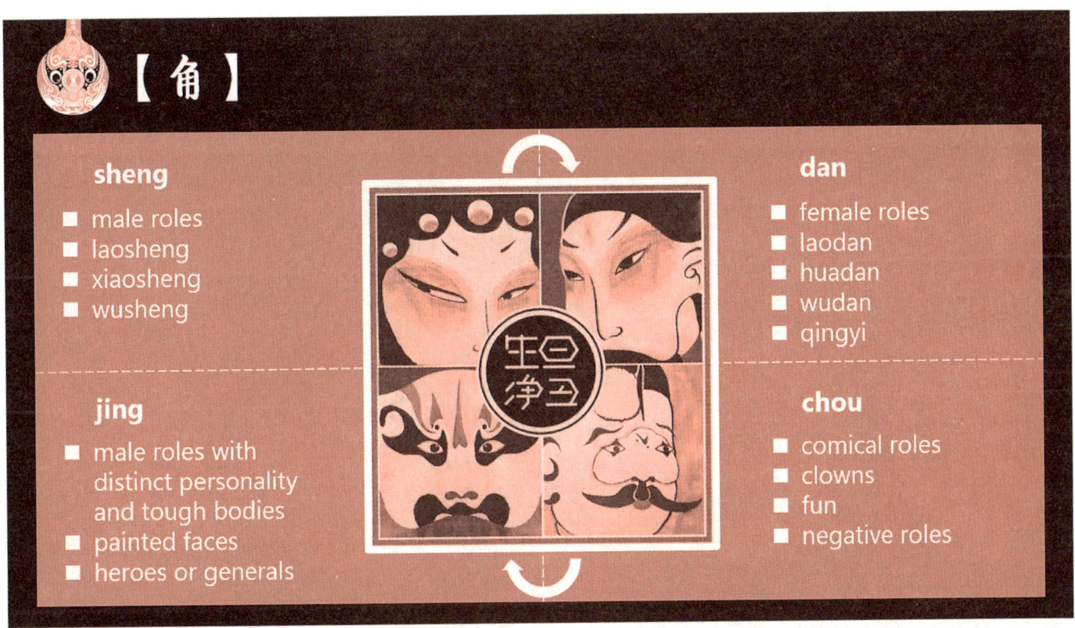

京剧是一门综合艺术。在京剧表演的舞台上，演员们需要有出色的技能。唱、念、做、打是京剧表演者必备的四要素。唱是指歌唱，念是指音乐性念白，做是指舞蹈化的

形体动作，打是指武打和翻跌技艺。

京剧中不同风格的服饰反映了不同人物的社会地位。贵族服装中有更多的装饰品，而穷人的服装往往是朴素和简单的。京剧的面部妆容具有中华民族特色。不同颜色和图案用来刻画不同年龄、性格、经历的人物。通常红色代表忠诚和正直，蓝色代表残忍和正直，黄色代表勇敢和易怒，白色代表背叛和怀疑，黑色代表正义和诚实。

北京人把观看戏剧也称为听戏。他们听戏的唱腔、看台中人的做和打。优美的歌唱和吟诵、优雅的动作和面部表情、五颜六色的京剧脸谱、精致繁复的戏服等都充满魅力，这就是京剧之美。

(2)文化知识延伸与翻译

京剧是中国的国粹。作为一门古老的艺术，京剧的服装、脸谱更易被人喜爱。不同的服装类型反映不同的人物身份特征。富贵者的服装缀满精美的刺绣，穷困者的服装则简单朴素，少有装饰。脸谱是京剧中塑造人物形象的重要手段，它是用不同的颜色在脸上勾画出来的。脸谱的颜色让人一看便知角色的善恶。比如，白色代表奸诈，黑色代表正直不阿，黄色是骁勇，蓝、绿色多用于绿林好汉，金、银色多用于神佛等。	Beijing Opera is the quintessence of the Chinese culture. As a traditional art form, its costumes and facial masks are more popular with people. Different styles of costumes reflect the status of different characters. There are more decorations in the costumes of nobles and rich men, while those of the poor tend to be simple and less **ornamental**. Facial masks reflect qualities of different characters by using different colors, which is an important way to portray characters. People can tell a hero from a villain by the colors of the masks. In general, white usually represents **treachery**, black righteousness, yellow bravery, blue and green **rebellious** fighters, while gold and silver represent **divinity** and Buddhism.

词汇

ornamental [ˌɔːnəˈmentl] *adj.* 装饰性的

rebellious [rɪˈbeljəs] *adj.* 反抗的；造反的

treachery [ˈtretʃəri] *n.* 背叛

divinity [dɪˈvɪnəti] *n.* 神

7.3.5 讨论问题

(1)京剧传统曲目中大多为激浊扬清、弘扬正气、褒扬美德的内容，如为官清廉、断案如神的包公戏，义薄云天、英雄如云的三国戏，除暴安良、善恶分明的水浒戏等。这些曲目歌颂真、善、美，批判假、恶、丑。你能用英语简单介绍一个经典曲目的基本内容给英语读者吗?

(2)你能结合典型译例谈谈使用拆分手段的好处吗?

7.4 川剧变脸(拆合技巧总结)

本节我们将聚焦川剧，总结拆分、合并两种翻译方法。请先阅读新浪网站上的一篇有趣的新闻。

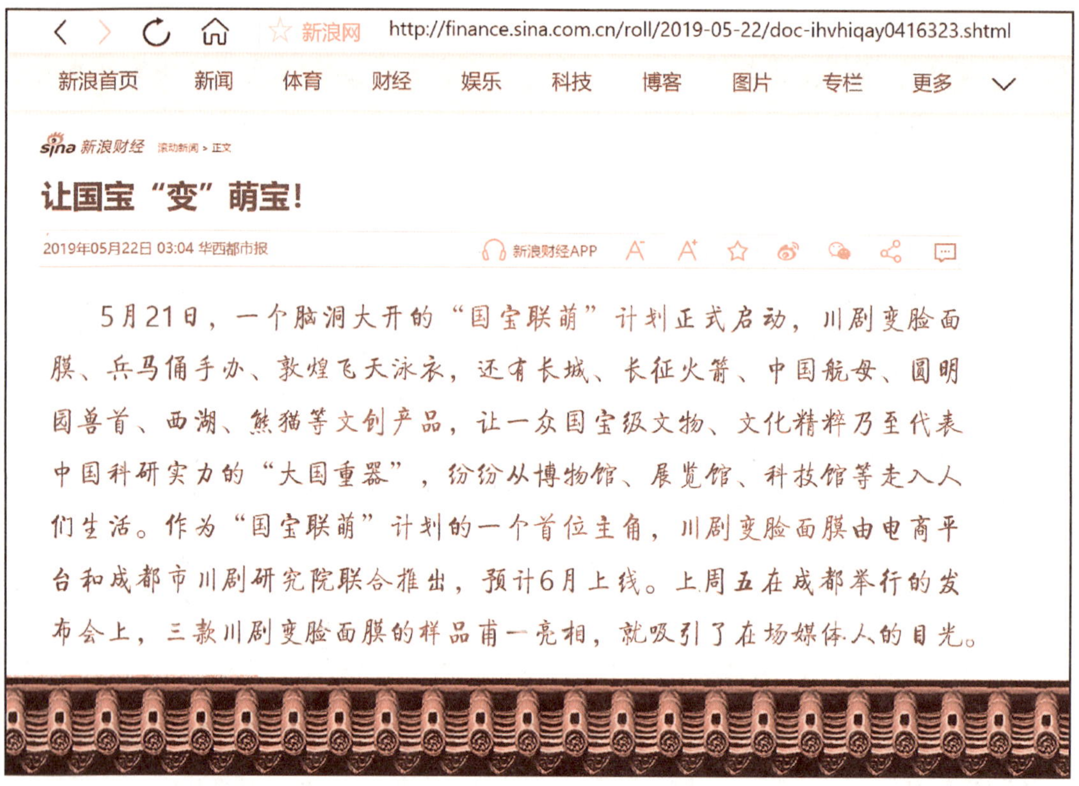

阿里巴巴发起了“国宝联萌”计划，以中国众多国宝级别的代表物品为原型，设计和推出了一系列创意文化产品（文创产品）。

首次亮相的第一组产品便是川剧变脸面膜。这个特殊设计的灵感来自三个传奇人物和他们在川剧中的脸谱形象。变脸面膜将传统元素融入新的时尚。看完这则消息后我们可以思考为什么阿里巴巴首先选择了川剧变脸元素？变脸表演在川剧表演中处于什么地位？带着这些问题，我们将了解隐藏在川剧变脸中的秘密，并回顾合译和分译的技巧。

7.4.1 例句讲解

请仔细阅读下面这篇关于变脸的文章，思考合译和分译两种技巧的综合使用。

① 川剧是中国地方戏之一，广泛流行于四川、云南、贵州省。② 变脸是川剧的最大亮点。③ 变脸可不是随便化化妆，改变一下人的妆容。④ 它是川剧中的一种特技，在很短的时间内变换多张脸谱，来揭示剧中人的内心及感情的变化，在不被观众察觉的前提下使用，达到强烈的舞台效果。表演者事前将脸谱画在一张一张的绸子上，剪好，每张脸谱上都系上细线，贴在脸上。线则系在衣服上的某个地

方，但不能让人看出来。表演时，在各种动作的掩护下，一张一张地将它们扯下来。⑤ 全程动作敏捷，不露痕迹，让人难以置信。

① 川剧是中国地方戏之一，广泛流行于四川、云南、贵州省。

第一句有两个小句，每个小句在结构和意义上都相对独立，但它们有相同的主题川剧。我们可以将后一部分作为主谓结构来翻译句子，前一部分"川剧是中国地方戏之一"可以作为同位语合并到主谓结构句中，补充说明主语。整句翻译如下：

Sichuan Opera, **one of China's regional operas**, is widely popular in the provinces of Sichuan, Yunnan, and Guizhou.

接下来的三个句子宜作为一个整体来处理的，在这个例子中你可能会看到合译和分译技巧的交替使用。为什么会这样呢？我们先通读整个部分。

② 变脸是川剧的最大亮点。③ 变脸可不是随便化化妆，改变一下人的妆容。④ 它是川剧中的一种特技，在很短的时间内变换多张脸谱，来揭示剧中人的内心及感情的变化，在不被观众察觉的前提下使用，达到强烈的舞台效果。

阅读后我们发现句子主语在推进时有变化。此外，第四句太长、太复杂，且没有连接词。我们可以对原文进行一些分析，以使翻译出来的英语句子结构更紧凑、表意更清楚。

② 变脸是川剧的最大亮点。③ 变脸可不是随便化化妆，改变一下人的妆容。④ 它（变脸）是川剧中的一种特技，（表演者）在很短的时间内变换多张脸谱，来揭示剧中人的内心及感情的变化，（变脸）在不被观众察觉的前提下使用，达到强烈的舞台效果。

这种分析有两个目的：一是展示主语的变化，二是将长句按意群分解成几个部分。经过分析前三句重新排列如下：

变脸是……亮点。变脸可不是随便化化妆……。变脸是……特技。

这些句子都谈到了一个共同的话题——什么是变脸，但这些描述在结构上有点松散。我们可以采用合译技巧将第二、第三和第四句的开头结合起来，以提高译文连贯性。现将此部分翻译如下：

As a highlight of Sichuan Opera, face changing is **not** simply a change of one's facial makeup, **but** a stunt of Sichuan Opera.

该译文紧凑连贯，首先使用了介词短语作状语进行合译，然后使用连词词组 “not ... but” 合译后两句。通过使用这种配对结构，直接以对比的方式展示了变脸的本质。此外，这里还有另一个为了简化重叠含义而进行的合并，我们将 “不是随便化化妆，改变一下人的妆容” 合译成了 “not simply a change of one's facial makeup”。我们再来看下一部分：

……在很短的时间内变换多张脸谱，来揭示剧中人的内心及感情的变化……

The performer changes several masks in seconds **to reveal the inner and emotional changes of the character in the play**.

在这一组中，两个汉语小句通过使用不定式合并成一个句子，不定式补充了主句并表示目的，这样的译文结构更紧凑。我们再来看该例子的最后一部分：

……在不被观众察觉的前提下使用，达到强烈的舞台效果。

我们可以像前一部分一样，用不定式来补充主句，表达变脸的效果。

The face changing is used without being noticed by the audience **to achieve strong stage effect**.

现在让我们看看第五句。

⑤ 全程动作敏捷，不露痕迹，让人难以置信。

第五句由三个简短小句铺排而成，其中第三句中评论性的语句 “让人难以置信” 在英语中可用一个副词 “incredibly” 简洁地表达出来。这样的评状性副词既可以修饰形容词，也可以修饰动词，可以像下面一样巧妙地整合到前面的语句中去。

The whole procedure is **incredibly** swift and flawless.

7.4.2 双语对照

川剧变脸/Face-Changing in Sichuan Opera	
川剧是中国地方戏之一，广泛流行于四川、云南、贵州省。变脸是川剧的最大亮点。变脸可不是随便化化妆，改变一下人的妆容。它是川剧中的一种特技，在很短的时间内变换多张脸谱，来揭示剧中人的内心及感情的变化，在不被观众察	Sichuan Opera, **one of China's regional operas**, is widely popular in the provinces of Sichuan, Yunnan, and Guizhou. **As** a highlight of Sichuan Opera, face changing is **not** simply a change of one's facial makeup, **but** a stunt of Sichuan Opera. The performer changes several masks in seconds **to reveal the inner and emotional changes of the character in the play**. The face changing is used without being noticed by

（续表）

川剧变脸/Face-Changing in Sichuan Opera	
觉的前提下使用，达到强烈的舞台效果。表演者事前将脸谱画在一张一张的绸子上，剪好，每张脸谱上都系上细线，贴在脸上。线则系在衣服上的某个地方，但不能让人看出来。表演时，在各种动作的掩护下，一张一张地将它们扯下来。全程动作敏捷，不露痕迹，让人难以置信。	the audience to achieve strong stage effect. Before the show, the performer has to draw facial masks on pieces of silk cloth, cut them into the right size, tie a thin thread to each mask and stick them onto his face. The threads are fastened to somewhere hidden in his costumes. When performing, the artist would pull the masks off one after another under the cover of various movements. The whole procedure is incredibly swift and flawless.

7.4.3　译技总结

如上所述，合译和分译技巧在汉译英中都比较常用，这两种技巧可使译文观点明确，层次分明，布局合理，也符合英语表达习惯。

在进行合译和分译时应遵循以下步骤：第一步，理解原文意思与作者思路；第二步，分析句间、句子内各部分关系；第三步，重新拆合词句、段落、意群。

拆/合-步骤

- 理解原文意思与作者思路
- 分析句际间、句子内各部分关系
- 重新拆合词句、段落、意群

这两种技巧不仅能单独使用，而且常同时使用，以求佳译。

7.4.4 文化表达

(1) 文化基本知识与表达

变脸是川剧中最受欢迎的元素之一。除此以外，在川剧中还有许多其他迷人的表演，如吐火——表演者从嘴里吐出一条火蛇，有时火蛇可长至一米；滚灯——蜡烛或一盏灯放在丑角的头上，而后做出一些高难度动作，如跳跃和钻板凳；水袖舞——由女性角色旦表演的特技，一边摇动长袖一边跳舞，川剧中舞水袖的方法多达40种。

川剧绝活 / Stunts in Sichuan Opera

变脸 face-changing

吐火 spitting fire

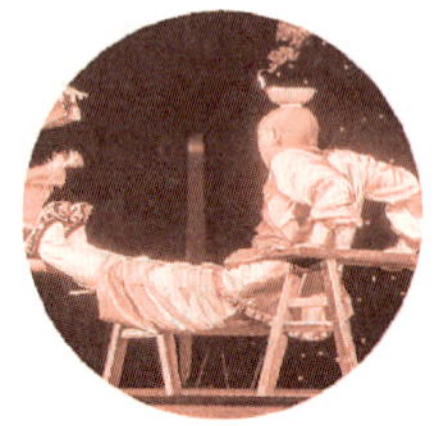
滚灯 rolling light

水袖 water -sleeve dance

川剧表演具有多样性，不仅仅是前面所提到的特技表演，更有特色丰富的唱腔。川剧是五种不同地区地方戏风格的结合，博采众长，是一种多声腔的戏剧表演。

多声腔/multi-tune

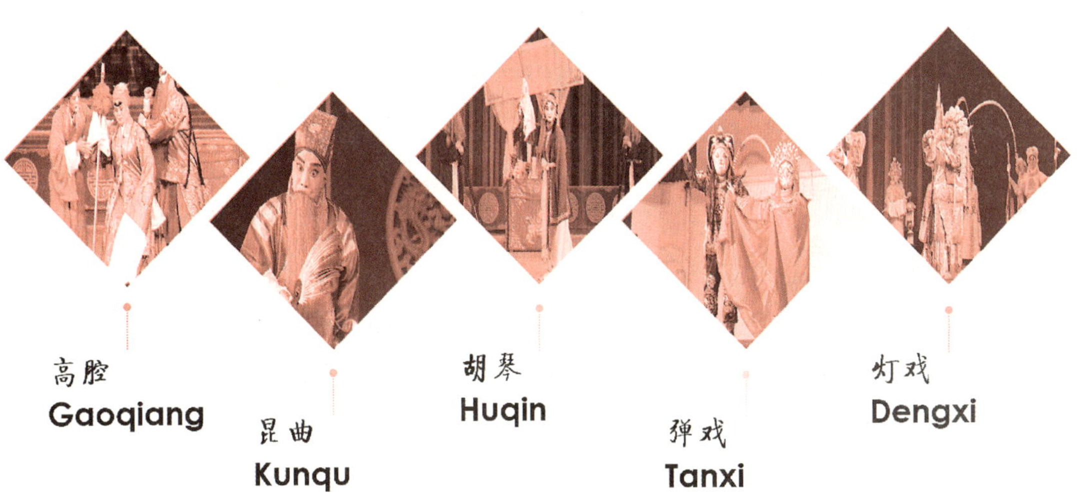

高腔来自江西戏曲，是中国戏曲四大声腔之一，唱腔高亢激越，一人唱而众人和。昆曲来自江苏，是现存最古老的中国歌剧形式之一。胡琴吸收了西皮腔和二黄的调子。弹戏源自北方，也称邦子戏。灯戏是这五种风格中唯一一个真正起源于四川的。川剧在中国戏曲流派中有着独树一帜的风格。

（2）文化知识延伸与翻译

川剧是四川文化的一大特色，早在唐代，就有了“蜀戏冠天下”的说法。川剧流行于四川省及其邻省重庆、云南、贵州等，它是融合昆曲、高腔、胡琴、弹戏和灯戏五种不同地域的声腔艺术而成。川剧剧目众多，颇受世人所爱，其名戏《白蛇传·金山寺》更是享誉国内外。川剧表演充满智慧和幽默，语言生动而活泼，具有地方生活气息。在不断地发展过程当中，川剧吸纳了众多绝技，如变脸。在中国的戏剧中，人物角色的脸谱通常是提前画好的。但是在川剧中，表演者在舞台上弹指之间就能改变脸	Sichuan Opera is a major feature of the cultures of Sichuan Province. As early as the Tang Dynasty, a proverb says that “Sichuan Opera was **unparalleled**”. Sichuan Opera is performed throughout Sichuan as well as its neighboring provinces, including Chongqing, Yunnan and Guizhou, and it took shape as a combination of five different regional **operatic** styles: *Kunqu*, *Gaoqiang*, *Huqin*, *Tanxi* and *Dengxi*. Sichuan Opera has a large number of plays and they are fairly enjoyable. A famous play is *The Tale of the White Snake: Jinshan Temple*, which enjoys great popularity **at home and abroad**. The performances of Sichuan Opera are always full of wit, humor, lively dialogues and local flavors. In its **continuous** development, the opera **incorporates** a series of **stunts** including face-changing. In Chinese operas, facial **makeup** is usually painted before performance. But in Sichuan Opera, the performer can change his or her facial makeup **in the**

（续表）

谱图案。相传变脸的由来与对抗野兽侵犯有关。以前古人为防遇到凶猛的野兽，就在自己脸上勾画出不同图案，这样做就可以吓唬野兽、保护自己。后来川剧就把这种方法搬上舞台，也就有了变脸这一门独特的艺术。	**snap of a finger** right on the stage. It is said that the origin of face changing has something to do with the resistance of wild beasts. In ancient times, in fear of coming across **ferocious** animals, people used to draw different patterns on their faces to scare animals away and keep themselves safe. Later on, such trick was applied to the stage performance of Sichuan Opera, and the unique art of face changing has thus **come into being**.

词汇

unparalleled [ʌn'pærəleld] *adj.* 无比的；无双的；空前未有的

operatic [ˌɒpə'rætɪk] *adj.* 歌剧的；歌剧风格的

at home and abroad 国内外

continuous [kən'tɪnjʊəs] *adj.* 连续的；持续的

incorporate [ɪn'kɔːpəreɪt] *v.* 吸收

stunt [stʌnt] *n.* 绝技

makeup [meɪkʌp] *n.* 化妆品；组成；补充

in the snap of a finger 一眨眼的工夫

ferocious [fə'rəʊʃəs] *adj.* 残忍的；惊人的

come into being 形成；产生

7.4.5 讨论问题

（1）川剧中的变脸技术应该被严格保护还是公开传授？

（2）你能列举一两个同时使用分拆和合并这两种翻译技巧的例子并评论其优劣吗？

7.5 单元练习

1. 单项选择。从两个备选项中选出对汉语原句翻译得较好的一个选项。

① 最吸引人的是那精彩武术和杂技表演，口吐火焰的魔鬼，或下蹲疾驰的小矮人。

A. What fascinates people most is the marvelous Kungfu and acrobatics. Players can make fire spray out of their mouths when they act as spirits, or can gallop while squatting to act as a dwarf.

B. What fascinates people most is the marvelous Kungfu and acrobatics, players can make fire spray out of their mouths when they act as spirits, or can gallop while squatting to act as a dwarf.

② 面塑俗称“捏面人”，它以调成不同颜色的糯米为主材料，用手和简单的工具塑造出各种栩栩如生的形象。

A. Dough modeling is commonly known as *nie mianren* (making dough figurines). With sticky rice flour of different colors as the main ingredient, it creates various vivid images only with hands and simple tools.

B. Dough modeling is commonly known as *nie mianren* (making dough figurines), it creates various vivid images only with hands and simple tools with sticky rice flour of different colors as the main ingredient.

③ 刺绣俗称“绣花”，在中国至少有3 000年的历史，目前传世最早的刺绣为湖南长沙战国楚墓中出土的绣品。

A. Embroidery, also known as *xiuhua* in China, has a history of at least three thousand years, the earliest embroidery that remains today is unearthed from the Chu tomb of the Warring States Period in Changsha, Hunan Province.

B. Embroidery, also known as *xiuhua* in China, has a history of at least three thousand years. The earliest embroidery that remains today is unearthed from the Chu tomb of the Warring States Period in Changsha, Hunan Province.

④ 张三禄是目前见于文字记载最早的相声艺人，主要活跃于19世纪中期。

A. The earliest cross-talk comedian known in written records is Zhang Sanlu, who performed in the mid nineteenth century.

B. The earliest cross-talk comedian known in written records is Zhang Sanlu, he performed in the mid nineteenth century.

⑤ 有人认为麻将是中国传统文化的重要组成部分，也有人认为它与赌博有关，会引发很多社会问题。

A. Some think Mahjong is an important part of traditional Chinese culture while others hold that it may lead to many social problems because it is related to gambling.

B. Some think Mahjong is an important part of traditional Chinese culture. Some others hold that it is related to gambling, may lead to many social problems.

2. 句子翻译。翻译下面的句子，注意运用本单元所学的翻译技巧。

① 中国本无狮子，中国的狮子及关于狮子的形象主要是在汉代开始从印度传入的。

____

② 京剧是中国最负盛名且影响力最大的剧种，有着200年的历史。

____

③ 每一种性格特点的人物都有一种固定的样式和颜色，例如包拯的黑额头上有一个白月牙（white crescent moon），猴王孙悟空的脸谱（mask）是猴脸的形象。

____

7.6 单元测验

1. 从两个备选项中选出对汉语原句翻译得较好的一个选项。（5×5分=25分）

① 表演动作柔和、细腻，主要表现狮子的活泼、可爱、风趣、诙谐。

A. The movements are gentle and exquisite and mainly show the lovely and funny characters of lions.

B. The movements are gentle and exquisite, mainly show the lovely, lively, funny, and humorous characters of lions.

② 中国历史上的许多辉煌成就令西方人心驰神往，其内容博大精深，其文化多姿多彩，其历史悠长久远。

A. Much of the historical splendor of China strains the imagination of Western people: its content is broad and profound, its culture is varied and colorful, its history is long.

B. Much of the historical splendor of China strains the imagination of Western people: its expanse, its cultural diversity, and the length of its history.

③ 中国戏曲起源于3 000年前的乐舞，公元900 ～ 1000年时就基本成熟了。

A. Chinese Opera originated from music and dance 3,000 years ago, 900~1000 AD was basically mature.

B. Chinese Opera originated from music-dancing 3,000 years ago and basically matured in 900~1000 AD.

④ 以前古人在遇到凶猛的野兽时，就在自己脸上勾画出不同的图案，这样做就可以吓唬野兽，保护自己。

A. In ancient times, when coming across a ferocious animal, people used to draw different patterns on their faces to scare the animal away and keep themselves safe.

B. In ancient times, when coming across a ferocious animal, people used to draw different patterns on their faces, and this way can help to scare the animal away and keep themselves safe.

⑤ 舞蹈动作既要自然,还要做好掩护,要不然就会被观众看破。那样的话,观众一生气,恐怕也要“变脸”了。

A. The dancing movements have to be natural and the action of pulling should be invisible to the audience. If the audience sees through the trick of face changing, they would probably get dissatisfied and pull a long face!

B. The dancing movements have to be natural and the action of pulling should be invisible to the audience, otherwise, the audience sees through the trick of face changing, they would probably get dissatisfied and pull a long face!

2. 翻译下面的句子,注意运用本单元所学的翻译技巧。(3×10分=30分)

① 相声(cross talk)是一种中国曲艺(Quyi)表演艺术,它起源于华北地区的民间说唱曲艺,在明朝即已盛行。

______

② 狮子是兽中之王,象征幸福和好运,所以人们通常在春节和其他节日期间表演狮子舞。

______

③ 富贵者的服装缀满精美的刺绣,穷困者的服装则简单朴素,少有装饰(ornamental)。

______

3. 将下面短文翻译成英语,注意运用本单元所学的翻译技巧,增补必要信息以帮助目的语读者理解。(45分)

秧歌是流行于中国北方地区的一种民间舞蹈形式,男女老少都可以在锣鼓(gongs)、唢呐(suonas, woodwind instrument resembling a trumpet)等乐器的伴奏下扭起生动活泼、多姿多彩的秧歌,表达自己对生活的热爱。秧歌起源于插秧耕田(transplant of rice seedlings and land cultivation)的劳动生活,又和古代祭祀(offering sacrifices to sb.)农神、祈福禳灾(averting misfortunes)有关。

______

综合测试

1. 按照提示完成句子。(5×3分=15分)

① Our Chinese ancestors constructed a very complicated theoretical framework based on *Yin-yang*, ______________ (五行) and ______________________ (12生肖).

② At 10:00 a.m. Saturday, Chinese people nationwide will ______________________ (默哀3分钟) for the deceased, while air raid sirens and horns of automobiles, trains and ships will wail in grief.

③ The image of the dragon can be seen as well in such grand celebrations as ____________ (舞龙), ______________ (赛龙舟), and so on.

④ In early Tang Dynasty, a monk named Chen Xuanzang tried to go to India, attempting to ______________ (取真经).

⑤ ______________ (京剧) is the quintessence of the Chinese culture. As a traditional art form, its __________ (服装) and __________ (脸谱) are more popular with people.

2. 从两个备选项中选出对汉语原句翻译得较好的一个选项。(10×2分=20分)

① 出生在龙年可能会像龙(的性格)。

A. A person may behave like a dragon if he is born in the Year of the Dragon.

B. Born in the Year of the Dragon may look like a dragon.

② 农历正月十五日是元宵节。

A. The Lantern Festival is on the 15th day of the first Chinese lunar month.

B. Lantern Festival is the 15th day of the first Chinese lunar month.

③ 火把节,彝族人民除虫害,庆丰收。

A. Yi people eradicate insect swarms, celebrate a good harvest for Torch Festival.

B. On the Torch Festival, the Yi people eradicate insect swarms and celebrate a good harvest.

④ 最受欢迎的请柬设计是中国字“囍”。

A. The most popular design on the invitations is the Chinese character *Xi* (double happiness).

B. The most popular design on the invitations is the Chinese character *Xi*.

⑤ 从某种程度上来说,古代中国人丧葬礼仪的规格是由死者社会地位的高低决定的。

A. To a certain extent, Chinese funeral specifications are determined by the social position of the deceased.

B. To a certain extent, Chinese funeral specifications are determined by the height of the status and position of the deceased in society.

⑥ 某些地区的生命保障系统问题重重。

A. Some region's life-support system is in serious trouble.

B. Some region's life-support system has many many problems.

⑦ 据说尼克松总统到中国访问时,在欢迎宴会上也使用了筷子。

A. It's said that President Nixon also used chopsticks at the welcoming banquet when he visited China.

B. People said that when he visited China at the welcoming banquet, President Nixon also used chopsticks.

⑧ 就餐时围桌共食是中国人的一种传统。

A. It is a tradition for Chinese people to sit around the table and share the same dishes when dining.

B. To sit around the table and share the same dishes when dining is a tradition for Chinese people.

⑨ 但随着人口的增加,很多古老的胡同已经消失,取而代之的是现代化的却没有特色的高楼大厦。

A. However, with the increase of the population, many old *Hutongs* have disappeared and replaced by modern but not characterized high-rise buildings.

B. However, with the increase of the population, many old *Hutongs* (Chinese alleys) have disappeared to make way for modern but not characterized high-rise buildings.

⑩ 庙会时老百姓从四面八方赶来，买卖物品，观看表演，品尝小吃。

A. In time of the temple fair, people come from far and wide to buy and sell goods, watch performances, and taste snacks.

B. In time of the temple fair, people come from four aspects and eight directions to buy and sell goods, watch performances, and taste snacks.

3. 翻译下面的句子，注意按照括号中的要求，有意识地运用本课程所学的翻译技巧。(5×5分=25分)

① 各家各户会根据自家的情况选择不同内容的春联(couplets)，比如商人家庭会张贴与发财有关的春联，农民家庭则选择表达丰收愿望的春联。(拆分长句并适当调整定语和状语语序)

____

② 有着2 500多年历史的大运河是世界上最古老、工程最大、里程最长的运河。(采用删减的方法，并注意调整多个定语的语序)

____

③ 中国白酒(white liquor)制作工艺复杂，原料丰富多样，是世界著名的六大蒸馏酒(distilled liquor)之一。(适当增加关联词，并下调画线部分层级)

____

④ 在这条路上运输的商品中，丝绸占很大部分，因此得名"丝绸之路"。(调整因果顺序以及地点状语顺序)

____

⑤ 婚轿(Sedan)的背后会挂上一个筛子(sieve)和一面金属镜子。(增补关于挂筛子和镜子功用的相关文化信息)

____

4. 将下面短文翻译成英语，注意运用本课程所学的翻译技巧，增补必要信息以帮助目的语读者理解。(40分)

中国的茶文化可以追溯到周朝，约有4 000年的历史。"一日三餐茶饭"成为中国人的一种日常习惯。有客人来访时，通常递上的也是一杯茶。饮茶在中国既是一种艺术也是一门学问。在中国的许多地方，沏茶的方法很复杂。中国的茶叶以独特的色、香、味、形而闻名于世。在中国各种茶叶中，最著名的是绿茶、红茶、乌龙茶（oolong tea）和花茶（scented tea）。

参考答案

第1单元

单元练习

1.

① B. The (增加冠词) Double Seventh Festival is called Chinese Valentine's Day.

② A. The (增加冠词) Double Ninth Festival is named according to the (增加冠词) theory of (增加介词) *Yin* and *Yang*.

③ A. On (增加介词) the (增加冠词) night of the (增加冠词) Lantern Festival, we (增加代词) usually eat rice dumplings and (增加连词) enjoy watching lanterns.

④ A. If (增加连词) you (增加代词) grasp the (增加冠词) order of those twelve animals, you (增加代词) can know the (增加冠词) zodiac animal of a certain year.

⑤ B. The (增加冠词) traditional food of the (增加冠词) Mid-Autumn Festival is moon cake, a round-baked cake with fillings in (增加介词) it (增加代词).

2.

① On (增加介词) the (增加冠词) Dragon Boat Festival, people (增加代词作主语) drink realgar wine and hang mugwort and calamus.

② The (增加冠词) Torch Festival is the (增加冠词) grandest festival of the (增加冠词) Yi people.

③ The (增加冠词) Laba Festival is celebrated (该词不是必须，有则更好) on (增加介词) the (增加冠词) eighth day of the (增加冠词) last Chinese lunar month.

单元测验

1.

① A. The (中国传统节日用festival表示时前面习惯加定冠词) Spring Festival is a (加不定冠词表泛指) traditional festival joyously celebrated by the (后有限定语) Hans and many of the (后有限定语) minority nationalities of China on (加介词表具体某一天) the (序数词前加定冠词) first day of the first (序数词前加定冠词) lunar month.

② B. The (中国传统节日用festival表示时前面习惯加定冠词) Lantern Festival is also marked by sports and (添加连词) other entertainments, such as the (表类别) tug-of-war, the (表类别) Dragon Dance, the (表类别) Lion Dance and (添加连词) the (表类别) Yanko Dance.

③ A. According to a (加不定冠词表泛指) Chinese folktale, Fairy Chang'e lives with (增加介词) her rabbit in (增加介词表地点) the (特指) moon palace.

④ A. In (增加介词表时间) the (中国朝代前多加定冠词) Ming Dynasty, the imperial families (增加主语) customarily began to eat the (特指) Double Ninth cake on (增加介词表时间) the (序数词前加定冠词) first day of the ninth lunar month.

⑤ B. The (后有限定语) custom of (添加介词表所属) climbing mountains during (增加介词) the (中国传统节日用festival表示时前面习惯加定冠词) Chongyang Festival is closely associated with the (特指) season.

2.

① The (后有限定成分) themes of (增加介词表所属关系) the (中国传统节日用festival表示时前面习惯加定冠词) Qingming Festival are to return home and (增加连词) miss the relatives, and (增加连词) to get close to nature.

② To clean houses before New Year Eve is a (增加不定冠词泛指类别) very old custom dating back to thousands of (增加介词) years ago.

③ Around the (中国传统节日用festival表示时前面习惯加定冠词) Chongyang Festival, chrysanthemum shows are held all around (增加介词表地点) China and people (增加名词做主语) also visit gardens to (增加介词表目的) appreciate chrysanthemums.

3.

The (增加冠词) festival reaches its (增加形容词性物主代词) climax on the (增加介词、冠词) Lunar New Year's Eve. All people living away go back home for (增加介词表目的) reunion no matter how far they (增加代词做主语) are. All the (增加冠词) family

members get together to (增加介词表目的) have their (增加形容词性物主代词) yearly sumptuous dinner. Among (增加介词) the (增加冠词) dishes, a (增加冠词) fish course should be served. However, the (增加冠词) fish must not be eaten up, as some people would emphasize, for the sake of "*niannian youyu*" (having a surplus every year)(增补文化信息).

第2单元

单元练习

1.

① A. The Chinese word for wine is *jiu*, a homonym of the Chinese (增补上下文隐含信息) word for "long", symbolizing longevity.

② B. Even numbers belong to *Yin* (the feminine and negative principle) (增补文化语义), while odd numbers belong to *Yang* (the masculine and positive principle) (增补文化语义).

③ A. Tomb-Sweeping Day is the day for Chinese people to sweep the tombs of their deceased families (增补隐含语义).

④ B. "Double Ninth" is identical in sound to "forever" in Chinese (增补隐含语义).

⑤ B. When pronounced together, it sounds like "*zao sheng gui zi* (having a lovely baby soon) (增补文化语义)".

2.

① Life is given by one's (增补代词) parents and extended through one's (增补代词) children.

② During the Spring Festival, the character fu (福), which signifies happiness (增补文化语义), is pasted upside down (*dao*, a homonym for "coming" in Chinese) (增补文化语义) on the door to express a wish for happiness.

③ Tomb-Sweeping Day is close to the Cold Food Festival, a Chinese traditional festival to memorize the deceased (增补文化语义).

单元测验

1.

① A. *Cuju*, a kick-ball game (增补文化语义), was popular to play on Tomb-Sweeping Day in ancient China.

② B. The traditional funeral custom of Manchu is that no haircut shall be had until a hundred days later after the funeral (增补文化语义).

③ A. Tomb-Sweeping Day is not only (增补关联词) a traditional Chinese (增补背景信息) festival, but also (增补关联词) the most important festival of sacrifice in China (增补上下文隐含信息).

④ A. The (增补定冠词) Han people and some ethnic minorities mostly sweep tombs on Tomb Sweeping Day.

⑤ B. Traditional Chinese weddings are an (增补不定冠词) important part of Chinese culture.

2.

① I envy the happy life of (增加隐含语义) mandarin ducks in pairs but not a lonely (增加隐含语义) immortal life.

② Red represents happiness and auspiciousness in China, which is the reason why (增加关联成分和上下文隐含逻辑语义) beautiful Chinese women are referred to as Red Faces.

③ "Backing Home" refers to a (增加不定冠词) woman's first visit to her (增加形容词性物主代词) parental home after marriage.

3.

In ancient times, the (增补冠词) Chinese word (增补隐含语义) for marriage means dusk, which is considered as the auspicious time of the day (增补文化语义). Hence, the (增补冠词) ritual of couples' getting together was called "rituals of dusk". People (增补主语) always fill their weddings with red things to (增加介词表目的) express blessings and respects, for they regard the color red as the symbol of happiness, success, and good luck. A marriage is not only a combination of the couple but also the symbol of the unity of two families. Inviting relatives and friends to the wedding symbolizes the relationships and the formality between people. The sound of musical instruments in the wedding usually is loud enough to (增加介词表目的) make nature know and to (增加介词表目的) demonstrate the importance of the marriage.

第3单元

单元练习

1.

① A. "蜿蜒" 和 "流动" 没必要都翻译，这里只译 "蜿蜒/meandering" 即可，"流动/

flowing”之意已经包含其中，删除后可使译文更简洁。

② B. 删减范畴词“长度/length”和“意义上的/in the sense of”。

③ A. 删减“颜色/color”，以使译文简洁。

④ A. 删减范畴词“精神”，“傲然”与“不屈”意思接近，只译“不屈/unyielding”即可。

⑤ B. 删减“发生/happening”，以避免译文重复。

2.

① Orchids symbolize integrity and nobility in Chinese culture. (删减范畴词“品格”)

② The area preserves a wealth of rare plants and animals. (删减范畴词“资源”)

③ Without perseverance, you are sure to fail. (删减范畴词“精神”)

单元测验

1.

① A. “光辉灿烂”属于意思重复的两个词语叠加而成的一个四字成语，翻译时为使译文更加简洁，符合英文表达习惯，只需用“splendid”来表达其意思，删减重复。

② A. “它们的形象”中，“形象”属于范畴词，在翻译过程中，为使译文更加简洁，可以省略。

③ B. 翻译四字成语“千丝万缕”时，删减重复。

④ A. “品质”属于范畴词，为使英语行文更流畅，翻译时可以省略。

⑤ A. 删减范畴词“地位/position”，译文更简洁。

2.

① Chinese dragons are fictive animals in legends. (删减范畴词“形象”。)

② Hebei is located in the central area of North China, facing Bohai in the east, Taihang in the west, and Yan Mountain in the north. (为了避免重复，“临”“倚”“偎”三个意思相近的字，用一个单词“face”译出。)

③ The country has an extremely complicated and diverse climate, including various temperature zones as well as manifold wet and dry areas. (“多种多样”和“各式各样”都由两个意思相近或相同的词语组合而成的四字词语，为避免重复，翻译的时候分别只需翻译其中一个，所以分别翻译为“various”和“manifold”。)

3.

The giant panda finds bamboos at different altitudes (删减范畴词“高度”). In the area of 1,600~3,600 meters above sea level, the giant panda finds fresh and delicious (原文“脆嫩清香”语义繁复，适当删减) bamboo shoots and branches in different seasons (删减重

复:“春夏秋冬”“季节交替”). The eating habits of the giant panda are very amusing. He walks in a noble manner, looking around (删减重复:“东瞧瞧,西嗅嗅”) for just the right bamboo. Having found it, he adjusts himself to the most comfortable sitting position, bends over the bamboo stem with his “hands”, bites the bamboo into two sections and munches on them from both hands, like a kid eating a sugar cane.

第4单元

单元练习

1.

① A. The cheongsam is a female dress with (动词“具有”转为介词) distinctive Chinese features.

② B. Hunan cuisine is characteristic (名词转形容词) of thick and pungent flavor.

③ A. That well-known novelist is a great lover (动词“酷爱”转为名词) of Sichuan cuisine.

④ A. Silk is in (动词“时髦了”转副词) and synthetic fibers are out (动词“过时”转副词,整句简洁明了). B选项整句译文略显臃肿,且为逗号粘连句。

⑤ B. Chilies are an absolute necessity (形容词“必需的”转为名词,其他常用表达如“... is a must”) in Sichuan cuisine. A选项中absolute应变为absolutely,即修饰形容词需变成副词。

2.

① The cooking show is still on (动词“进行”转为介词“on”). 其他翻译方法,如The cooking show is still going on 也可。

② It is believed that (主动转被动) China had tea-shrubs as early as five thousand years ago.

③ *Qipao*, as (动词“是”转化为介词“as”) an exquisite Chinese dress, originates from China's Manchu Nationality.

单元测验

1.

① A. 形容词词组“文化历史悠久的”转为介词词组“with a time-honored civilization”, B选项结构稍显繁复。

② B. 否定转肯定,语言地道,语意更强。

③ B. 汉语偏正结构“王室女性穿的”转为介词词组“for the royal women”,表达清楚简洁。

④ A. 否定转肯定,表达简明到位。而B选项机械仿译原文中的两个否定结构,表达烦冗。

⑤ A. 动词“考虑”转为名词“consideration”并加“full”,构成习惯用语“take full consideration of ...”,辞达意明;译文B中“fully”与动词“consider”割裂开来,不甚理想。

2.

① Her new dish is a great success (动词转为名词).

② Can you give an accurate (副词转为形容词) translation (动词转为名词) of the names of these tea tools?

③ He is a great liar (动词转为名词).

3.

Chinese Moutai originated in the Han Dynasty which was over 2,000 years from (动词“距今”转为介词) now. Moutai is famous (动词“扬名”转为形容词) for the features like being clear and transparent in color (形容词“清”“透明”转为名词化的动名词短语), being smooth, fresh and cool in taste (形容词“柔绵”“清冽甘爽”转为名词化的动名词短语) and its long-lasting fragrance. Now, Moutai is called (主动转为被动) the national liquor in China.

第5单元

单元练习

1.

① B. The artificial landscape in the Summer Palace is harmoniously combined with (具体转抽象、主动转为被动:“融为一体”) natural hills and peaceful lakes.

② A. The Great Wall is a cultural relic and a unique (“独一无二”的翻译:具体转为抽象) natural landscape.

③ B. Although the problem of the design for the structure of the bridge has been overcome (句型转换:主动转为被动), we are still confronted with (主动转为被动) many difficulties concerning its actual construction.

④ B. Finally, after innumerable (具体转为抽象) difficulties had been overcome (句型转换：主动转为被动), the Hong Kong-Zhuhai-Macao Bridge was fully opened (句型转换：主动转为被动) on July 7, 2017.

⑤ A. Most of the buildings in the Forbidden City were built (句型转换：主动转为被动) with wood, roofed (句型转换：主动转为被动) with yellow glazed tiles and built (句型转换：主动转为被动) on blue-and-white stone foundations, looking solemn and brilliant (具体转为抽象).

2.

① The Great Wall is a must (具体转抽象：必不可少的参观游览项目) for most foreign visitors to Beijing.

② The Hong Kong-Zhuhai-Macao Bridge stretches 55 km across (动词“横跨”转介词) the Lingding channel near (动词“位于”转介词) the estuary of the Pearl River.

③ When the immersed tunnel was finally perfectly placed (具体转抽象+主被动转换) in its designated position, some of the workers were so tired that they slumped to the ground (具体转抽象：一屁股) and slept right away where they lay (具体转为抽象：七倒八歪).

单元测验

1.

① A. Chinese has a multiplicity (形容词转为名词) of complicated (作谓语的形容词转为前置形容词) rivers and landforms, and the ancients took local conditions into account and used local resources to ensure a perfect addition to Nature (具体转为抽象).

② A. From west to east, the curve of Great Hall of the People is like the letter “W” (形象转换：将“山”字形译为英文中更易理解的字母“W”).

③ A. A winding (词类转换：动词转为形容词，避免一句中出现双谓语) corridor links every hall of the Lingering Garden.

④ B. The Summer Palace, a royal garden of the Qing Dynasty (谓语转同位语), was constructed (句型转换：主动转为被动) in 1765.

⑤ A. The natural stone walls can only be dimly seen (句型转换：主动转为被动) as if the mysterious ancient times have appeared again.

2.

① Square-shaped (形象转换：“口”字型译为方型“square-shaped”，使译文更清晰明了)

in flat surface, Great Hall of the People boasts a courtyard in the center where flowers and trees are planted.

② Sanxingdui Museum cannot only be seen as a continuation (词类转换：动词转为名词) of the supernatural powers of the Sichuan people in the past, but also reflects today's aesthetic taste.

③ Stretching (具体转为抽象) 400 km in Hubei Province, Mt. Wudang boasts the grandest religious architectural complex in the world.

3.

Construction (具体转为抽象：开凿；动词转名词) of the Buddha began in 713 AD. The construction was led by a Chinese monk named Haitong with the hope of taming turbulent waters (具体转为抽象："减杀水势"，也可用control一词) and rescuing all creatures (具体转为抽象："普度众生"). After his death (具体转为抽象："圆寂"；动词转为名词), however, the construction was unexpectedly suspended (主动转为被动). Many years later, two Jiedushis (regional military governors) in Sichuan Province resumed the construction which was eventually completed (主动转为被动) in 803 AD. Altogether, the construction lasted for 90 years.

第6单元

单元练习

1.

① A. The Tang poetry, a precious cultural heritage of China (调整层级：汉语小句 ↘ 英文同位语；调整语序：后移"中国的"), occupied a significant place in the field of Chinese literature and poetry (调整语序：后移"在中国文学和诗歌中").

② B. As a traditional custom during the Spring Festival (调整层级：汉语小句 ↘ 英文介词词组，同时合并成一个英文句子), pasting couplets is also an important way for the Chinese people to celebrate the Spring Festival (调整语序：后移"中国人欢度新年春节的"). A选项照译汉语句式造成英文有语病，两独立小句在英文中不能仅用逗号连接，还应有关联词。

③ A. With (调整层级：小句 ↘ 介词词组) the tragic love story of Jia Baoyu and Lin Daiyu (调整语序：后移"贾宝玉和林黛玉的") as the main theme, the novel describes the decline of four feudal noble families (调整语序：后移"封建官僚四大家族的"). B译

文为逗号粘连句；同时太长的前置定语变为后置修饰语较符合英文习惯。

④ B. The story tells about the monk named Hsuan Tsang who successfully arrived at the "Western Regions" to bring back the Buddhist sutras (调整层级：原文中"到达西天"和"取回真经"是并列关系，译成英文时后一个降级为动词不定式作状语) after many trials and much suffering (调整层级：汉语时间状语从句 ↘ 英文介词短语after；调整语序：后移). 该译文在经历调整语序和层级后，层次清晰、主次分明、结构紧凑。A选项译文机械照搬汉语流水句式，句式松散而无连接词。

⑤ A. In the 120-chapter novel (调整层级：完整小句 ↘ 介词短语), the first 80 chapters were written by Cao Xueqin and the left 40 by Gao E. B选项机械照译汉语句式，英文中三个独立句子无关联词连接，成为逗号粘连句（语病）。

2.

① The Spring Festival couplet is a unique Chinese (按照英文习惯调整定语位置：后移) literary form with a long history (调整层级：汉语小句 ↘ 英文介词短语；合并句子).

② The subjects of Tang poetry were rather extensive, ranging from natural phenomena and political dynamics to social customs and personal feelings (调整语言层级：小句 ↘ 非谓语动词词组，且合并成第一小句的状语), and embracing almost every aspect of people's lives (调整语言层级：小句 ↘ 非谓语动词词组，且合并成第一小句的状语).

③ The text of couplets is concise and delicate, which (调整层级：汉语独立小句 ↘ 英文定语从句，合并句子) symbolizes the Chinese great expectation for the future (调整语序：后移) and conveys people's good wishes of the new year (调整语序：后移).

单元测验

1.

① A. 将状语"在中国古代封建社会"位置后置，更符合英文行文习惯。

② A. 将短语"身上乏倦"下移为词"tired"(调整层级：短语 ↘ 词)。

③ B. 将分句"我还做梦呢"下移为副词"unknowingly"(调整层级：分句 ↘ 词)。

④ A. 将分句"译成了几十种文字"下移为分词短语"Published in scores of languages"；动词"青睐"转为名词"a preferred reading"。

⑤ B. 将分句"怕吃官司"下移为介词短语"for fear of being jailed"(调整层级：分句 ↘ 介词短语)。

2.

① Written in the 18th century (调整层级：汉语完整小句 ↘ 英文分词状语), *A Dream of*

Red Mansions is a famous (按照英文排列多个形容词习惯调整语序：前移famous) Chinese classical novel.

② The essences of Chinese military security thoughts (调整定语位置：定语后置) were captured (主被动转化) in *The Art of War*, an ancient military masterpiece renowned in China and the world at large (调整定语位置：定语后置).

③ Mencius maintained the idea that human nature is essentially good. (调整定语位置：定语从句变名词性从句并后置)

3.

The Four Great Classical Novels of China (形容词转介词，后移) refer to the four greatest and most influential novels written in the Ming and Qing Dynasties (调整语序：后移). Nowadays, the four novels have already been adapted into movies or TV series, favored by lots of audiences (调整层级：汉语独立小句 ↘ 英文分词作后置修饰语). Being high in artistic standard (调整层级：汉语独立小句 ↘ 英文分词作状语), the Four Great Classical Novels are precious heritages of Chinese nation (调整定语语序：后移) and pioneering works in the history of Chinese literature (调整状语语序：后移).

第7单元

单元练习

1.

① A. 原文3个排比成分都有修饰语，使得整句较长，宜采取分译。B译文机械照译整个汉语长句句式，分句间没有添加必要的关联词，译文不合语法。

② A. 该译文适当地进行了分译，清晰地表达了原文意思。B译文机械照译整个汉语长句句式，分句间没有添加必要的关联词，译文不合语法，同时第二个分句中两个with短语的连用使得结构繁复、语意不清。

③ B. 前两个小句为同一个主语"刺绣"，后一个小句主语为"最早的刺绣"。采用分译能够体现主语之间的变化，使得结构更清晰、句式正确。A译文两分句中间无关联词，为典型的逗号粘连句，不合英文语法。

④ A. 增加关联词合译松散分句，可避免句子短小而琐碎。B译文小句间无关联词，是典型的逗号粘连句。

⑤ A. 两处增加关联词，合译松散分句。B译文完全机械照译汉语行文，对比关系不够明确，尤其是第二句中的两个分句为逗号粘连句，不合英文语法。

2.

① Originally there was no lion at all in China. The lions in China and their images were imported from India in the Han dynasty. (原句中的第二小句具有较多修饰和限定成分，宜分译；如若合译得较好，无语法错误，也可得全分。)

② Beijing Opera is the most popular and influential opera in China with a history of almost 200 years. (主语一致的两汉语短句宜合译，这样句子结构紧凑，如若翻译成 Beijing Opera is the most popular and influential opera in China and has a history of almost 200 years亦可以得较高分值，但如果没有用像and一样的关联词，形成逗号粘连句，只能得低档分。)

③ Each person of a certain character has a fixed pattern and color. For example, there is a white crescent moon on Bao Zheng's black forehead and Monkey King Sun WuKong's mask is an image of a monkey face. (分译，含有比方的长句宜分译。)

单元测验

1.

① A. 适当合译或者删减意思相近词组。译文B中两小句仅用逗号连接，形成逗号粘连句；同时后半部分机械照译原文每个单词，译文显得纷繁复杂。

② B. 原文为具有总分关系的四个小句。该选项通过调整层级，将原文的后三个小句降级为词组，整体合并到原文总说句上，同时对原文由同义词组构成的四字词组进行了一定程度的合并或删减。译文A机械照译整个汉语句式和由同义词组构成的四字词组，显得繁复别扭，且后两个小句间缺少连词连接。

③ B. 增加关联词 "and"，合译两个简短句子，使行文紧凑。A译文中 "乐舞" 译为 "music and dance" 不准确，且两小句间无关联词，不符合英文语法。

④ A. 增加 "to"，用不定式形式将原文第三小句合译到前一小句中去，可使译文紧凑流畅，层次分明。相反，B译文照搬原文并列关系，仅仅增加了 "and" 连接原文第二、三小句，整个译文显得松散、不简洁。

⑤ A. 原句比较长，宜在 "要不然" 前断句分译。

2.

① Cross talk is one of Chinese *Quyi* performing arts. (拆分) It originated from the folk vocal art and has enjoyed a popularity since the Ming Dynasty. (原文为三个相对独立的小句组成的一个汉语长句，且没有使用关联词进行显性链接；翻译时宜进行适当拆分。)

② As the lion, king of animals (小句降级转化为同位语成分，合并到第二小句中),

symbolizes happiness and fortune, people usually have lion dancing during the Spring Festival and other festivals and holidays.（原句由三个小句组成，第一、二小句和第三小句构成因果关系。这里可以考虑像参考译文一样，将第一、二小句进行部分合并，与第三句整体上形成更明确的因果关系。）

③ There are more decorations in the costumes of nobles, while (增加连词合并松散小句) those of the poor tend to be simple and less ornamental (原文松散并列的第二、三小句浓缩合并为复合谓语).（原文为三个小句，第一句和第二、三小句用逗号隔开，形成对比关系，而第二、三小句为松散并列关系。可像推荐译文一样适当地进行合并，这样句间关系清楚，层次分明。）

3.

Yangge is a form of folk dance popular in Northern China. (整句较长且分句主语不同，采用分译) Males and females of different ages are able to perform the lively and colorful *Yangge* with accompaniment of musical instruments such as *gongs* and *suonas* (woodwind instrument resembling a trumpet) (后　移). (分　译) By doing this, they are expressing their enthusiasm for life. Originating from land cultivation and transplant of rice seedlings (小句降级为分词词组), *Yangge* is also related to the ancient practice of offering sacrifices to the god of agriculture in hope of (增减连接成分，合并短语) ushering in good fortunes and averting misfortunes.

综合测试

1.

① Our Chinese ancestors constructed a very complicated theoretical framework based on *yin-yang*, the five elements and the 12 zodiac animals.

② At 10:00 a.m. Saturday, Chinese people nationwide will observe three-minute silence to mourn for the deceased, while air raid sirens and horns of automobiles, trains and ships will wail in grief.

③ The image of the dragon can be seen as well in such grand celebrations as dragon dances, dragon boat races, and so on.

④ In early Tang Dynasty a monk named Chen Xuanzang tried to go to India, attempting to acquire true sutras.

⑤ Beijing Opera is the quintessence of the Chinese culture. As a traditional art form, its costumes and facial masks are more popular with people.

2.

① A. A person (增补冠词、代名词) may behave like a (增补冠词) dragon if (增补关联词) he (增补代名词) is born in the (增补冠词) Year of the Dragon.

② A. 增补冠词&介词，调整语序。

③ B. 增补介词、冠词、连词。

④ A. 增补文化语义；增补冠词。

⑤ A. 删减范畴词"高低"；增加冠词。

⑥ A. 删减重复"重重"，换用英语习惯表达in serious trouble。

⑦ A. It's said (主被动转换) that President Nixon also used chopsticks at the welcoming banquet when he visited China (调整语序).

⑧ A. 用it作形式主语，调整语序，使句子结构更平衡，调整"就餐时"的语序。译文B机械照搬原有语序，译文显得头重脚轻。

⑨ B. However, with the increase of the population, many old *Hutongs* (Chinese alleys) (增补文化语义) have disappeared (降级合并) to make way for modern but not characterized high-rise buildings. A选项中replaced没用被动语态。

⑩ A. In time of the temple fair, people come from far and wide (具体转抽象) to buy and sell goods, watch performances and taste snacks.

3.

① Each and every household would choose Spring Festival couplets with different content (形容词词组转介词词组，调整语序：后移) according to their own circumstances (调整语序：后移). (切分长句) For instance, merchant families would paste couplets related to making a fortune (调整语序：后移), while farmer families would choose couplets expressing the desire for a good harvest (调整语序：后移). (原句稍长，整体上宜分译)

② With a history of more than 2,500 years, it (代词，避免和后面的canal一词重复) is the longest, the largest, and the most ancient (调整语序：形状修饰语在前时间修饰语在后，删减"工程"和"里程") canal in the world.

③ Chinese white liquor has a complicated production process and (增加关联词，合并松散的并列分句) can be made from various raw materials, making it one of the six world-famous distilled liquors (调整层级：并列小句降级为分词状语).

④ The Silk Road got its name because (调整：果前因后) silk comprised a large proportion

of commodities transported along this road (调整：后置).

⑤ At the back of the sedan hang a sieve and metallic mirror that are believed to protect the bride from evil (增补文化语义).

4.

With a history of 4,000 years (转化词类、降低层级、前置、合并), tea culture in China (形转介、后置) can be traced back (主动转被动) to the (增加冠词，下省) Zhou Dynasty. It is a daily habit for the Chinese (形容词转介词、后置) to have meals and drink tea three times a day (调整主语位置). When (增加连词、并句) guests come, it is often a cup of tea that the host (增加主语) serves (调整语序). Tea-drinking is both an art and learning in China (后置). In its (增加代词避免重复) many places, the way of making tea is very complicated. Chinese tea leaves are famous throughout the world for its unique color, fragrance, taste and appearance (后置). Among their (增加代词避免重复) various kinds, the most famous are green tea, black tea, oolong tea and scented tea.

参考文献

[1] Baker, Mona. *Routledge Encyclopedia of Translation Studies*[M]. Shanghai: Shanghai Foreign Language Education Press, 2004.

[2] Shuttleworth, Mark &. Cowie Moira. *Dictionary of Translation Studies*[M]. Shanghai: Shanghai Foreign Language Education Press, 2004.

[3] 常峻.生肖[M].上海：上海辞书出版社,2004.

[4] 陈宏薇.汉英翻译基础[M].上海：上海外语教育出版社,2011.

[5] 陈棵可，许希明.汉语主语省略句及其英译的对比研究[J].现代语文(语言研究),2013(8).

[6] 创想外语.用英语介绍中国(双语阅读)[M].北京：中国水利水电出版社,2019.

[7] 范仲英.实用翻译教程[M].北京：外语教学与研究出版社,1994.

[8] 方梦之.译学辞典[M].上海：上海外语教育出版社,2004.

[9] 冯友兰，赵复三.中国哲学简史(英汉对照)[M].北京：外语教学与研究出版社,2016.

[10] 寒布.故宫——北京的世界文化遗产[M].北京：北京美术摄影出版社,2004.

[11] 何疏思.港珠澳大桥通车！“超级工程”背后都有哪些故事？[N].21世纪英文报.2018-10-25.

[12] 黄兴亚，孙永林，周青.走进中国文化(英汉对照)[M].昆明：云南大学出版社,2015.

[13] 黄晔明.英语四级翻译200篇[M].广州：世界图书出版广东有限公司,2017.

[14] 李红帆.北京游[M].北京：中国发展出版社,2008.

[15] 李西宁，王健.喜马拉雅山探险[M].济南：山东科学技术出版社,2001.

[16] 刘谦功.中国文化欣赏读本[M].北京：北京语言大学出版社，2014.
[17] 刘泽权.《红楼梦》中英文语料库的创建及应用研究[M].北京：光明日报出版社，2010.
[18] 龙毛忠.华东理工大学出版社[M].上海：华东理工大学出版社，2016.
[19] 庞进.中国龙文化[M].重庆：重庆出版社，2007.
[20] 孙晓朝，杜鹃.每天读点中国文化·民俗风情(英语阅读系列)[M].大连：大连理工大学出版社，2010.
[21] 王志茹，陆小丽.英语畅谈中国文化[M].北京：外语教学与研究出版社，2017.
[22] 周济.中国人的文化(中英对照)[M].上海：上海文化出版社，2009.
[23] 朱华.四川导游：汉英对照[M].北京：中国旅游出版社，2007.
[24] 朱永春.中国建筑精华[M].北京：中国建筑工业出版社，2000.
[25] http://www.chinadaily.com.cn/
[26] https://www.ted.com/